Gemini Betrayal

Rachelle Jarred

Gemini Betrayal
Copyright and Disclaimer

The information and images contained in this book, including cover art, are protected under all Federal and International Copyright Laws and Treaties. Therefore, any use or reprint of the material in the book, either paperback or electronic, is prohibited. Users may not transmit or reproduce the material in any way shape or form – mechanically or electronically such as recording, photocopying, or information storage and retrieval system – without getting prior written permission from the publisher/author.

All attempts have been made to verify the information contained in this book, Gemini Betrayal, but the author and publisher do not bear any responsibility for errors or omissions. Any perceived negative connotation of any individual, group, or company is purely unintentional. Furthermore, this book is intended as entertainment only and as such, any and all responsibility for actions taken in reading this book lies with the reader alone and not with the author or publisher. This book is not intended as medical, legal, or business advice and the reader alone holds sole responsibility for any consequences of any actions taken after reading this book. Additionally, it is the reader's responsibility alone and not the author's or publisher's to ensure that all applicable laws and regulations for the business practice are adhered to.

A Word From The Author

I would like to thank God for blessing me with the gift of writing. I would also like to thank my significant other for being here, and for supporting my dreams. I also dedicate this book to my children; thank you for making me proud to be your mother. To my mother for being there, my dad who is looking down on me from heaven, my friends, and my family: I thank you all for your continuous love and support.

Lastly, I want to thank my new guardian angels, my niece, Jasmine, and my baby sister, Shyra; who lost their lives at a young age. They were gone too soon but I know God had another job for them and now they will live through me and our family. Continue to rest in paradise.

To my readers:

I would like to thank you all for continuing to read my novels and following me on my journey. Also, thank you for making my first novel, Nymphopervtress: The Desiree Logan Story #3, and my second novel, No Trespassing #1, known and loved enough to be featured on Amazon's Top Best-Selling List. I may have taken a break but I'm back now to heat up the streets with my latest novels. Stay tuned!!!!

Contents

Prologue

This shit was crazy. I was getting arrested because of some shit my twin had done. She was only five minutes older than me and you would swear that she was five years older the way she carried things.

We were both in the game and had been since our mother had gotten killed two years ago on our 21st birthday. It was so fucked up how shit had gone down. Those fools that were from a rival gang were sitting outside our house waiting for an opportunity to take us out. But those niggas had gotten theirs. We rode out that night and found the marks that took our backbone. We drove out to Maryland and dumped them at Cedar Hill Cemetery.

We were the twins that people knew not to fuck with. Those niggas had gotten lucky but they weren't lucky enough. It didn't even matter that they were some little young bucks trying to be gangsters. We had no mercy on them as we let our bullets reign down on their souls.

I, myself, was the more cool, calm, and collected thug. My sister on the other hand was the hot head between the two of us. And that's why now I was sitting next to her in the back of the damn paddy wagon. We were looking like fucking twiddle dee and fucking twiddle dumb. This was the life I lived and breathed every day of my life.

Chapter One

It was a normal day for us. The squad was out on the block and making their paper like a regular taxpayer working their nine-to-five. Only thing, we didn't have to wait two weeks for a check that we can make in a day. That was the best part of this job. The bad part about this occupation was the fact that you never knew when 12 was gonna jump out on ya. Even worse, we had to stay on our toes so we wouldn't end up on a t-shirt.

My name is Antonio Desmond Hall and I have a twin whose name was Antonia Dana Hall. We were like the new aged Bonnie and Clyde. We were twenty-three but we have been hustlers since the tender age of seven. Our mother, Marie Hall, was the wife of a hustler. Our father, Big Tone, was the head of the organization and ran multiple territories across the East Coast. He had product coming in from Jamaica, Cuba, the Caribbean, even Afghanistan. He showed us how to cut it, weigh it, price, and everything in between.

My mind was strictly focused on school but my sister she craved this lifestyle. I was born into the game, no matter whether I wanted a part in it or not. It was either 'get down or lay down.' Our father drilled that in our heads every single day of our lives. Now he was doing a twenty year bid for drug and gun extortion.

"What's up, sis?" I said walking up to Antonia.

"What's up, bruh? You hanging today?"

"Fo' sho. You know how I go."

"True that. Aye, so check this out. Word on the street is that the little pussies that's been trying to sell on our block got a shipment coming in."

"Word? When?"

"Tonight. They getting the drop at Goodwin Park. The connect's guys are gonna drop the package under the slide and then the cats gonna go scoop it up. All it takes is for one person to get to it before they do."

"Yeah but who is gonna do that?"

"Me, nigga. You going with me, too."

"How we gonna get to the slide unnoticed?"

"Well, the thing is this. Ol' boy named Chuck gonna be the driver and the pick-up boy. All we need to do is distract him while you go in and get the package."

"And how do you suppose that we distract him?"

"Leana."

"Leana? I thought she wasn't down with you no more?"

"She ain't but money talks. I offered to pay her a pretty penny for her work," Antonia said smiling.

"How pretty is this penny?"

"A gee."

I just shook my head. My sister was crazy giving a G to that broad. Not only did she go behind my sister back and was sleeping around but this bitch was sleeping with the enemy. When that nigga cut her off for the next hoe, she came running back. My dumbass sister welcomed her back with open arms. She did whatever for that girl and she got played in the end. Me, on the other hand, I didn't trust her. Never did and I never would. We finished up our rounds on our corners. Antonia hopped in her all white Dodge Charger and headed to her house on Langston. I hopped in my all black Dodge Charger and followed behind.

We arrived at her split level family home in record time. We had a meeting there in twenty minutes for tonight's hit. We went in the house and chatted for a few minutes.

"So who riding out with us tonight, Tia?" I asked her as we sat in the kitchen. I opened up a beer and took a swig.

"Well it's gonna be you and me, of course. Then we got Leana as the distraction, Cam as the lookout, and Sienna as the shooter."

"You bringing Sienna along too?"

"Hell yeah. It's just a precaution. And you know she a good shot. She loves being a sniper," Antonia said laughing.

"Yeah that's true," I said. Sienna was a good shot and there was no doubt about that. We first met Sienna when some guys were trying to rob her. We were headed to her rescue when she pulled out a nine and let it bark. She shot one in the leg, one in the arm, and the other in the side. The rest of the guys had hauled ass. She been on our team as our female hitman ever since. I flashed back to the present day when I heard a knock at the door.

"It's Sienna and Leana," Antonia said looking through the peephole.

"What's up, twins?" Leana said upon entering the house.

"Shit, nothing much, boo," Antonia stated.

"Waiting on this nigga Cam now," I replied gruffly. I still didn't feel comfortable with her here but since my sister said it was cool, I guess it was cool.

"Oh, no need. He was pulling up right behind us. He out there on his celly," Sienna said.

"Cool, cool," I said loading my gun.

"What is that for?" my sister asked me. "Sienna is the only one that should be strapped."

"That's right," Sienna agreed checking her bullets in her Uzi. "I'm ready for war."

"Yeah, and I will be too," I said putting my gun on safety and putting it down in my pants.

The door flew open and Sienna and I drew our weapons. It was just Cam's slow ass. "What the fuck y'all trynna blast me for, fam?"

"Nobody fucking with your dumbass, Cam?" Antonia replied rolling her eyes. I don't know what it was but she always had an attitude towards Cam. I asked her about it in the past and she told me to mind my fucking business.

"Are you ready, my nigga?" I asked Cam.

"I'm always ready, son," he replied. We went over the plan two more times before finalizing everything. We all dressed in our black attire before heading out to our all black Ford Explorer. We specifically got this truck for transporting our supply and weapons but tonight, it was gonna be an accessory to a robbery. We drove towards Goodwin Park and dropped Sienna and Cam off so they can go to their spots unnoticed. We parked in a driveway down the block and jogged back up to the park.

At 12 midnight, we saw an all-black Chevy Caprice with North Carolina tags pull up. They stopped by the playground and left moments later. The plan was going well so far. Five minutes later, we spotted another all black vehicle park in front of the park. The passenger from the Caprice had already been out and dropped the package under the slide.

"Go ahead, Leana," I ordered. She adjusted her short dress and headed towards the car. The passenger had already gotten out and was heading towards the package. I could see her leaning into the driver window and putting her charm on the driver. I radioed in on my walkie-talkie and told Cam and Sienna to get into their positions and be ready. From where I was, I could see Antonia heading towards the package as well as the guy. "Everybody move in."

Leana pulled her little pistol out from under her dress and pointed it at the driver. "Got him," she said into her walkie-talkie.

"Good girl. Antonia where you at?" No response. "Antonia come in." *What the hell was she doing?* I ran to where she was and I saw that she had her hands full. She had her gun pointed at the delivery boy and he had his boys with their guns placed on her.

"These motherfuckers trying to shoot me, twin."

"That bitch gonna die if she don't drop that bag," one of the gunmen said through clenched teeth.

"Not a chance. I guarantee you bitch ass niggas gonna drop before this bag does," Antonia said with cockiness.

"Look nobody gon' shoot nobody out this motherfucker," I said moving my gun back and forth between the three guys. I saw Cam come out of the shadows with two guns drawn as well.

"It looks like we got a party going on, guys," he said laughing.

"Yeah something like that," the delivery boy said.

"Look we gon' take y'all product whether y'all want us to or not," I said standing closer to the delivery guy.

Gemini Betrayal

"You ain't taking that product up off us, Holmes," the other gunman replied. "You're gonna have to kill us first."

"Your choice," I said. I shot my gun in the air and I let it pop. Two more pops rang out and two bodies hit the ground. I looked on top of the building and saw Sienna sitting there with her gun pointed. When I looked down, the two gunmen were laying there lifeless. *Damn she good!!* I said to myself. Now only the delivery boy and driver remained.

"Now, what you gotta say, tough guy?" Antonia said antagonizing the man.

"Look we don't have time for this shit, Tia. Pop his ass and let's go. I hear sirens. She did as I said and shot him right in the heart. We all ran out the park and headed towards the truck. Leana saw us and shot the driver in the temple before following in tow.

We sat in the truck without making a move. We saw a swarm of police fly to the scene of the crime. When they all went into the park and became distracted, we nicely backed out of the driveway and headed to our stash house. Another one for the team.

Gemini Betrayal

Chapter Two

We got to our stash spot on Mercy Ave and headed inside.

"Them niggas was not fucking with us," Antonia said all loud and obnoxiously.

"Yo, kill that noise, sis. You don't wanna wake up the neighbors."

"Man fuck them neighbors. They can get it, too. Fuck you mean?" she said walking up to me.

I hated when she acted like this. It sickened me sometimes that we actually shared DNA. We were total opposites. She was always acting like a dude and talking reckless. I guess she knew she could because everybody was scared to come near her. I didn't pay her ass no mind.

Cam came between us. "Y'all both need to chill. Damn, Tia. What the fuck is your problem?"

"Nothing my problem and this ain't your fucking business. This is between me and my twin."

"No you wrong," he said. "We a family and whatever this beef you two got going on is affecting all of us. We can't be turning our backs on each other."

"Fuck all that noise you talking. My bro know what's up," she said heading for the door. When the door closed, we listened. Her car started up and she drove off. Typical Antonia.

Gemini Betrayal

"What the hell was that about, Tony?" Leana asked with a concerned look on her face.

"I don't even know, Lea. You know my sister. She is the true definition of a Gemini."

"You got that right," Sienna said in agreement. "You better watch your back around her, Antonio."

"What you mean, SiSi? That's my sister."

"Yeah she is but that don't mean shit in the streets."

"She's right, dawg," Cam said.

"Fuck all that. Let's get this product packaged and ready for tomorrow's sales." We put on our gloves and got to work. Honestly, they all may have been on to something. My sister was acting more crazier lately. As long as it didn't affect the business sales, I could really care less about her acting like a spoiled brat. There was work that needed to be done.

Chapter Three

Iwoke up to the smell of money. Whenever I woke up to that, I automatically knew it was gonna be a rewarding day. I checked the time and it was only 8 a.m. I didn't have to hit the block until noon so I decided to go hit up the gym. I took a quick shower, threw on my sweats and a tank top. I looked in my closet and all I had were Jordans and Stacy Adams lining my shelves. I spotted a pair of New Balance on my closet floor. *"I really need to buy workout sneakers"* I thought to myself. I decided to wear those; not like I had much of a choice.

I grabbed my duffel and jogged down the stairs, snatched my keys off the key hook and locked the door. I decided to drive my Lexus to the gym. It was an older model but it was still sitting pretty on 22s. I had to ride nice even if I didn't look nice after a workout. I threw my bag on the passenger seat and drove away.

As I rode through my hood, I saw some of the base heads that worshipped our product. They showed me love by not going anywhere else for their fix and I showed it back by looking out when they came up short. I peeped as I drove outta habit. I saw my corner boys hustling hard, a few broads with skin tight shorts on, and then there were the law-abiding citizens. They made me sick sometimes but, hey, if they didn't bother me, I didn't bother them.

Once I got to the gym, I headed straight to the boxing room. Thought I would hit the bag a little before I ran on the treadmill or ran some laps. It was only a couple of guys in here which was good. I found an empty spot off to the side and took it.

I was throwing combos like it was a second nature to me. In actuality, it kind of was. I fought to stay free every day when I was out on the block. I fought my entire life just so I can wake up to another day. I was in my zone when I heard somebody call my name. I turned only to see an old friend.

"Oh shit. What's up fool?" I said dapping up my homie Reggie. He and I went to middle school together. He had gotten locked up for ten years, for beating some dude to death for hitting his sister. I saw the entire altercation and I think the dude was actually done for by the time he threw the fourth blow.

"What's up, son?"

"Nothing much. Just been cooling."

"Yeah and working."

"Yeah you know. How long you been out?"

"I been out for a week or so now, bro. A nigga hurting though, fam," he said holding his head down.

"I feel you. What you looking to do?"

"Man, shit, anything. You got any openings in your organization? You know I'm good with my hands."

"Yeah I remember," I said chuckling. "Check this. You know where I be. Come holla at me around two and I should have some work for you."

"Cool, cool. Good looking out, Tony," he said dapping me up. He walked away and I started back, abusing the bag. I went for ten more minutes before going to treadmill.

It was even more deserted up here. "Damn, everybody must be at work," I said aloud. I hopped up on the treadmill and turned on my iPod. I was running on the treadmill as I listened to Juicy J. I noticed a

Gemini Betrayal

fine brown skinned cutie come in and get on the treadmill three rows ahead of me.

I watched as she paced from slow to fast. I never took my eyes off her. I couldn't if I wanted to. She had long black hair, nice curves, probably DD breasts, and that ass. Oh, my lord, that ass. I could sit a cup on top of that thing. It was nice and plump like a Georgia peach. Then she had the nerve to be teasing a brother with those tight ass spandex pants on. No way was I leaving here without that girl's digits. I turned off my treadmill and walked her way.

"Excuse me, miss, but I didn't catch your name."

"I didn't throw it at you for you to know either," she snapped back. *Well damn!!* I thought to myself. This chick obviously didn't know who I was.

"I'm Antonio. And you are?"

"I'm obviously not gonna finish my workout in peace," she said cutting her machine off. She got down and introduced herself. "My name is Christian, but all my friends call me Chris."

"So can I be your friend?" I asked with a smile.

"Sure you can but you have to earn my friendship."

"How do I go about doing that?"

"Well for starters, you can ask me out on a date" she said, stepping close to me. She was so close I could smell her cucumber melon body wash mixed with sweat.

"Okay. Well, Christian, would you like to go out with me tomorrow night to dinner and a movie?"

"Nope, I can't," she said cheerfully. She grabbed her bag and walked away.

"So when?"

She turned around quickly. "Just kidding. I would love to go out. What's your number?"

"2023972256," I replied. She dialed my number and my phone rang. "Got it."

"You better." She turned back and walked away. I stood there with my eyes glued to her ass; watching it bounce up and down in those pants. I had to get up in that tomorrow. No ifs, ands, or buts about it.

✳✳✳✳✳

I had gone home, showered and was now out on the block. It was hot and everybody was out getting their medicine from us. They done cashed those first of the month checks and started losing their minds. We damn sure wasn't complaining none. We were making money hand over fist. It was bumping on the block.

I got a call from my sister. What the hell did she want now?

"Yeah, sis?"

"Yo, Tony, where you at, son?"

"Over here on Market and Vermont. Why what's up?"

"Nothing, nothing. Just checking in with you. I'm over here on Piedmont and Savannah."

"Cool. How's your sales?"

"Man, I'm over here rolling in dough."

"That's good. We need to go out and celebrate."

"Yeah we do. We can go tomorrow."

"No can do. I got a date."

"A date? Lil' bro going out on a date? That's what's up. What's her name?"

"Christian."

"Cute name. How she look?"

"Great."

"How her ass look?"

"Bye, Tia," I said hanging up on her. She always acted like she was a dude instead of a chick. Sometimes I think she enjoyed females more than I did. I don't recall ever even seeing my sister with a dude now that I think about it; except when we were in school.

It was 2 o' clock on the dot when I had seen Reggie walking up to me.

"What's up, partner?" he said dapping me up.

"Partner? Man where the hell they have you at?" I asked laughing.

"They had me all over, son. Shit. I'm just glad to be back home, you feel me?"

"Yeah I do. So look I need you to be my left hand man. Starting tomorrow, you gonna start out with this little package and I'm gon' see how you do with that. If you good, then you gonna have a spot on the team. But if you don't, or you try to cross us," I said looking him dead in his eyes, "we will kill you. No questions asked."

"Understood, Boss." He got his package and went on his way. I hope I wasn't wrong about him. That's all I would need from Antonia if something goes wrong.

*****

Today was a great day. Me and my twin decided to just kick back later on that night. It was nice for us to just be on some chill shit, rather than at each other's throats like always.

"So I'm curious, sis. Why do you like woman so much?"

"I'm not sure really," she said sipping her Jack Daniels. "It's just a fascination I have with the female body."

"I guess I understand. So you telling me we could actually get along and talk about females all the time?"

"Yep. Females and funds," she said laughing.

"I'll drink to that." We clanked our glasses together and took the rest of our drinks to the head.

We were laughing and cooling like the good old days. Her phone rang and she looked at the caller id. She hesitated then sat it back down. "Who was that?" I asked curiously.

"Nobody. But, look, I'm gonna catch up with you tomorrow, lil bro," she said standing up.

"What the hell? What's going on, Tia?"

"Nothing, Tony. I'm just really tired all of a sudden," she proclaimed as she pushed me out the door.

"Okay, well, see ya," I said retreating down the stairs. "Good night, sis."

"Night, bro" she said slamming the door. That was odd. Whoever it was that called her must have been real important. I wasn't gonna think about it though. I just got in my car and drove home thinking about Christian.

*****

"Do you think he expects anything?" he asked Antonia.

"No, Boo. We're good. Trust me."

"But what if he gets a suspicion about us? You know how your brother is."

"Cam if you don't chill out! Sheesh. All we have to do is keep on going back and forth like normal and he will never know," she said continuing to kiss him.

Antonia and Cam have been keeping their relationship a secret for the past three months. If Antonio had ever gotten wind of it, he would be pissed. Not that he had anything against Cam, but he know how his sister was when it came to men. She would lead them on then drop them without any notice and move onto the next. Not even giving a damn how she hurt them. She lived by her motto: "money over niggas. And they only good for two things: to eat me and fuck me." Surprisingly, it wasn't like that with Cam though. She actually did care for him but he stayed on his toes when it came to her.

She pulled Cam's shirt from over his head, exposing over thirty prison tattoos and a toned six-pack. She loved the way his body looked. At six-foot-two and 210 pounds of pure goodness, he laid beneath her 140-pound frame atop her California king bed. She kissed all over his chest before unbuckling his pants. He helped her out so he could hurry and get inside her. "You got the condom, Cam?"

"Yeah I do, but why we still gotta use these damn things, Tia? They get on my damn nerves, boo."

"How about this? You either put it on and fuck your girl or you can fuck some hoe without one. And if you do, don't come back this way because I don't want nothing you catch."

Gemini Betrayal

"Why you always gotta act like that?" he asked putting the condom on.

"Because it works every time," she said laughing. She kissed his lips and laid on her back.

"Oh it's funny, huh?"

"Mmhmm."

"Let's see if you be laughing when I get up in your guts," he said. He rubbed on her clit a little before entering. She gasped deeply as he put every inch in her vagina all at once. He sexed her so good until the wee hours of the morning. Once they both had reached their climax, they fell asleep, panting.

Chapter Four

It was a bright morning, but something was off. For some reason, it just seemed like today was gonna be a bad day. I checked my phone like I did every morning. I had two missed calls, three messages and one video message. The two calls were from this chick named Destiny I knew from growing up. Now I hooked up with her whenever I flew out to Cali since she moved out there about five years ago. The video message was also from her. She was playing with her freshly shaved pussy and sticking a dildo in and out of her. My morning wood got harder. The video ended and I started it back over. I watched it at least three times so I could get my nut off. I sent her a 'good morning' text and told her I would be coming out to spend this weekend with her.

I got up and headed to the bathroom. I washed my face and brushed my teeth before heading downstairs in my boxers, went into the kitchen and made me a bowl of cereal. I didn't really want this shit but I couldn't complain. What I really wanted was to come downstairs to a home cooked breakfast that was being prepared by a big booty beauty wearing my shirt as a nightshirt. The only female that had ever done that was Destiny. She wanted us to settle down and become an item but I wasn't ready. There was also this girl named Janae that cooked for me all the time though. I sat and reminisced about her.

I met Janae at a club where she worked as a stripper. She was the total package. Big ass. Big titties. She cooked, she cleaned, and she was a bookworm. The only thing that was wrong with her was the fact that she was too fucking smart. That bitch stole all my money out of my safe when I was away for a weekend. I had over five hundred thousand saved up for a rainy day and that bitch took every dime. I

Gemini Betrayal

never understood why. I gave that hoe endless money. I bought her whatever she wanted. I gave her the motherfucking world! And she turned her back on me. I vowed to kill that bitch if we ever crossed paths again. The same thing was on Antonia's agenda. But fuck all that. It was time for me to get back on my grind. I quickly finished my breakfast and jogged back up to my room. I hopped in the shower for twenty minutes then got out to find something fly yet low key to wear today.

As I was searching my closet for something to wear, my phone buzzed. I walked over to it and noticed that Tasha had texted me back.

Destiny : good morning baby

Me: what's up shorty?

Destiny : just thinking about you. I been thinking about you all nite long

Me: I know. I got the video you sent LOL

Destiny : LOL did you like it?

Me: of course. I can't wait to see you this weekend boo

Destiny : likewise

Me: well I'm getting ready to hit the block baby girl

Destiny : ok be careful. I love you Tony

Me: okay

I don't understand why she always said that she loved me. I mean I had love for her but I wouldn't say that I loved her. Maybe it was just a female thing. I decided on wearing some black Levi's and a white v-neck t- shirt with my white 5s. They were fresh out the box. Destiny had gotten them for me when they came out and I never wore them until today. I had to be careful not to scuff them or anything because I planned on wearing them this weekend when I took her out.

I picked up my burner cell phone and called my sister. "What's up, Tia?"

"Nothing much, bro. I'm in the house."

"In the house? What the hell you doing in the house and there's money to be made?"

"I'm just gonna chill today. I'm having female problems right now," Antonia replied.

"Gross. The fuck? I don't wanna hear that shit, son."

"Well don't ask. Imma holla at you later, Tony."

"One." I hung up.

Antonia put her burner cell phone back down on the night stand and turned back over to Cam. He was laying in the bed with nothing but socks on. "Good morning, baby," she said kissing his lips.

"Hey, baby. Who were you on the phone with?"

"That was my brother."

"Oh. Well what he say?"

"Just about why I was in the hou-"

Cam's burner cell started ringing. It was Antonio.

"What's up, fool?" he said as soon as he answered.

"Where you at, Cam?"

"I'm in the crib chilling."

"Oh yeah? So why the fuck you ain't bring your ass outside?"

"What you mean?"

"I've been blowing my horn and banging on your door for ten fucking minutes. We gotta go pick up this package from the Ricans before noon, nigga."

"Oh, I didn't mean I'm at my crib. I'm at a lil' breezy spot," he said quickly lying.

"Well, what's the address? Imma come scoop you so we can hurry up."

"I, uh, I can't give you the address, bro."

"Why not?"

"Cautious reasons, fam. Imma be there in ten minutes. Wait for me."

"Aight."

Cam hung up and he and Tia quickly gathered their scattered clothes. They both quickly showered and got dressed. Tia put on some black cargo pants and a tank top with some shell toed Adidas while Cam replayed his outfit from the day before. They ran down to Tia's car and hopped in. Tia only lived about ten or fifteen minutes from where Cam lived. Upon arriving close to his house, they shared one last kiss before Cam got out and jogged around the corner. Tia just sat in the car hoping to go unnoticed. Cam came up onto Antonio's car and tapped the window.

"What's up, bro?"

"Nothing, nigga. What the fuck took you so damn long?" Antonio barked.

"Nothing. I'm about to run in the crib and change right quick."

"Your ass got two minutes."

Cam ran into the house and called Antonia back.

"Hey, baby, you can go ahead and leave."

"Aight, boo. Imma see you on the strip later on."

He quickly changed into his thug attire and grabbed his gun before running back outside. Once he was in the car, they drove off.

"So who house were you at, Cam?"

"Damn, son, you nosey as fuck," he said laughing. He was actually stalling to make up lies to cover his ass.

"Well, you know me. I gotta make sure I ain't skeet up in nobody you fucking. You know how these thots be."

"True shit. But you ain't been up in her."

"I hear you. It's only one way to find out. We gonna go out and I want you to bring her."

"She be working two jobs, bro."

"Damn, I need me a shorty like that."

"You got one. Destiny."

"Man, Destiny? She special but I don't know about that man."

"Well I do and you got her nose wide the fuck open and she loves your crazy ass. I don't know why but she does," Cam said laughing.

"Fuck you, dawg."

✳✳✳✳✳

They arrived at the connect house moments later. They were frisked by the guards and led up the steps to the office of Big Johnny Vega. He was the most known drug distributor in the United States and the Islands. Nobody fucked with him. He was untouchable but people tried. And those that tried ended up in a box if they were lucky. If they caught Vega and his boys on a bad day, they would end up shark bait.

"Tony, my boy. How are you my friend?" Johnny asked in his heavy Puerto Rican accent.

"I've been good, papa. What you got for me today?"

"100."

"100?! Why so much, Johnny?"

"Well, you and your team have been good to me over the years. So I wanted to give you some extra to work with. Besides my last corner boy and his squad tried to skip town with my product and my money. And you know what happened to them right?"

"Shark bait?"

"Not this time. Let's just say they are gonna go good with my spaghetti dinner."

What the fuck!? This nigga was eating people?

"I'm really gonna enjoy that meat and sauce tonight," he said laughing. His goons joined in with the laughter. Cam and I just laughed nervously. What kind of sick person ate people? I didn't wanna know nor did I wanna end up as a helping on their plates neither. We gave him the money for the product we wanted and he gave us ours as well as the extra weight. Cam and I loaded the product in the trunk of my car and headed to our warehouse.

The entire way home we just rapped about the early days of our hustling years. We were only twelve when my father put us on. He taught us everything before he got sent up the river. Everything that I learned, I had taught to my sister. She, in turn, took to the streets like they were her family. She ate, breathed, and slept the streets. God forbid if she ever got caught up, she going down for real.

$$*****$$

We arrived at Tia's house an hour and a half later. We walked in and I found my sister bending some chick over the kitchen counter.

"What's up, fellas?" she asked as she slammed the dildo inside the girl. The girl moaned and continued to get her pleasure as if we weren't even there. That was fine with me even though it was a little uncomfortable watching this.I was definitely going to get on her case about that.

"Nothing much," I said walking over to her. I stood next to her and observed the beauty she had bent over. She had a tattoo of a naked girl with two guns drawn on her back. The tattoo was sexy, no doubt. "We just finished up with Jefe. He gave us extra."

"That's what's up. You know we going to get this shit out and be done before this week out so don't fret," she said as she grabbed the girl's breasts and continued to hump her.

"Yeah, I know, Tia. I'm gon' let you finish handling business. Just hit me up when you get a chance," I said heading out the kitchen.

"I'm already done, big bro. You wanna turn?" she asked as she pulled out the chick and turned away from us as she removed her dildo.

"Naw, I'm straight."

"Come on, daddy. Come play with, Ms. Kitty," the girl said walking over to me.

"Naw I'm good shorty. My man might wanna have a go though."

Gemini Betrayal

"How bout I take on both of you," she responded flicking her tongue across my ear.

"I don't think you can handle that, little lady."

"I don't think she can neither," Cam said walking into the kitchen. He was adjusting his penis through his jeans and eyeballing the girl.

"I like a good challenge," she said grabbing both of our hands. She led us to the spare room at the end of the hall. As soon as we closed the door, she pulled at our clothes. She got my pants opened and dropped to her knees in front of me. She licked and slurped my dick to life. It felt so good having her warmth on my penis. I wanted to explode but I wasn't going to. If her head game good, I couldn't wait to see what that pussy was like.

Cam stood alongside of me stroking his dick. The chick grabbed his and started massaging it. She took my dick out her mouth and replaced it with his. She did the same to him that she did to me. He had his head thrown back in ecstasy. I knew that shit felt bomb to him. We always said that if a bitch didn't give a good blow job then that bitch had to get gone. I pulled her up away from him and walked her over to the bed. I lifted her dress over her waist and bent her over the bed. I pulled a condom out my pocket and put it on my erect penis. Without warning, I slammed my dick inside of her still wet vagina.

I put all nine and half inches up inside of her. She had to be a hoe. I could barely feel her walls around my dick as I fucked her. I saw Cam come over to the bed. He had taken his pants off and laid down on his back in front of the girl. She instantly started sucking my homeboy off again. I grabbed the back of her head and moved it up and down. I continued to bang her back out but I wanted that ass. I pulled out and put my dick in her ass. It went in with such ease. Go figure. I fucked her for a few moments and pulled out after noticing Cam trying to lie underneath her. She climbed on top of him and rode him like he was a black stallion. I took the opportunity to get back inside her ass.

This bitch was the real MVP. She was taking both of us at the same damn time just like she said she would. She moaned loudly and it was getting my dick harder by the second. I smacked her ass and left a hand print on her light skin. I grabbed her waist tight and pulled her close to me before nutting right between her cheeks. I hopped off the bed and removed the condom before straightening up my clothes. I watched as Cam finished her off moments later. They got off the bed and straightened themselves as well.

"Thanks for the good time, fellas. Especially you, Tony," she said, handing me a piece of paper after pulling her dress back down. "Call me sometime. Maybe we can have a one on one session."

"No problem," I said taking the paper out her hand. I might call her on a night I really need some action but other than that I had no need for her.

We all walked out the room together and noticed Tia sitting in the living room, eating buffalo wings and pizza. "About time y'all finished. Goddamn," she said with her mouth stuffed.

"Damn, were we really that long, sis?"

"Long enough for me to go out and get food. Y'all niggas eat up."

"Bon Appetite" Cam said, reaching in the box. Tia quickly smacked his hand away.

"Yo, what gives, T?"

"Nigga, if you don't take your narrow ass in there and wash your funky ass hands," she said, looking like a mother scolding her child. He quickly retreated back to the kitchen to wash his hands. I had shit to do.

"Yo, sis, I'm out" I said dapping her up.

"Where you heading to, bro?"

"Just going to go home and relax. I'm on my chill shit the rest of the day."

"You okay?" she asked, eyeballing me suspiciously.

"I'm straight, Tia."

"Aight, son. Peace out. Love you."

"Love you, too." I walked out the house and yelled back at Cam as he was coming back to the living room.

"What was that about?" Cam asked as soon as Tony closed the door.

"I don't know, Cam. He said he going home to relax."

"Oh, true. So what we gon' do tonight?"

"First, we gonna eat. Then you can eat me and so on and so forth."

"I like the sound of that, mami" Cam said walking over to her and placing his arms around her waist.

"I bet you do" Tia said grabbing his ass.

"Yo, Ma, damn this pizza. I want you now." He scooped her up into his arms and carried her up to the room. He went to work as soon as they entered the room.

It was nonstop kissing, hugging, and biting. They went at each other like some damn pure bred pit bulls. By the time they were finished, Tia's breasts were covered in his love marks. He, on the other hand, was covered in scratches from his neck down to his lower back. They laid up in bed, next to each other and said nothing.

"I think I'm in love Cam" Tia whispered, into his chest.

"That's nice to know" he said, patting her on the back as if she were an infant.

That's nice to know? Is that all he could say back? What a damn slap in the face.

Chapter Five

Today is a new day and is hopefully gonna be a successful day in the hood. Tia and I had opened shop early today to get our product out first thing. It was the first weekend of the month and everybody and their mama was out flossing with that welfare check. We didn't give a damn who it was, money talked. When all them folks money ended up being gone from being spent on their drug habit, we would look out and run them a tab. So whenever the first hit, we hit it big as well.

Tasha had walked up to me to get her fix. Tony knew her from back in the day when they were teens. Back in her prime, she was a bad little chick. She had curly hair, big brown eyes, and had a nice petite body. She wanted to be with Tony so bad that she did whatever he asked of her. If he told her to sneak out, she would; just to spend time with him and get her needs taken care of. She ended up having a child but lost him to her mom when crack took over her life. Now, as she stood before him, Antonio was shocked to think that the girl that was once his potential girlfriend was now buying and running tabs just to get a fix.

"Hey, Tony? Whats up with you, boo?"

"Nothing much, Tash. How you feeling today?"

"I'm gonna be feeling real good when you give me my fix," she said laughing. He just shook his head in dismay. She handed him a twenty and he handed her a small vial. "Thanks, Tony. Hey you wanna hangout tonight? I can cook for you."

He thought about it for a second but declined. "No, sweetie, I'm good on that. Maybe we can hangout some other time. I like my lady to be all dolled up when she's on my arm."

"I'll be sure to keep that in mind," she said smirking before walking away. She was off to the crack house where she lived with other fiends and slept with the guys just so she could get some of their medicine once hers ran out.

Antonio was disappointed to say the least. She was a really smart girl. She had aspirations of becoming an attorney that put people like him away. He still had high hopes for her even if she didn't have any for herself.

He checked his phone and saw that it was already after five. *"Damn!! time flew by"* he thought to himself. He stepped off the corner for a minute and went to his car. It was his turn to watch out for the jump out boys and to count his cash. This was out of habit and it came natural for him to do this. Whenever somebody was looking for him, they always knew that at 5, he was in his car to get some peace of mind before he closed shop.

He reached his car and got in. He observed the strip and saw his employees getting their grind on. He loved to see his family working together with no problems. It kept him at ease and the enemies at bay, knowing that he and his crew couldn't be touched. He looked around for a few more minutes then locked his car doors. It was time to count his cash for the day.

He pulled out his wads of cash from his front pockets and started counting. He counted out twelve hundred. "Damn. Not bad for a few hours. Selling all these products really pays off," he said aloud.

"You damn right it pays off" somebody said, from the backseat. He had a gun pressed to the back of Antonio's head. "Give me your money" the guy said.

"You must not know who I am bruh" Tony said with a straight face. He didn't flinch or nothing as the guy pressed the gun harder into his skull.

"I don't give a fuck who you are, nigga. I want the money. I want them vials you got left as well because I know you got some."

"Look, man, I ain't got shit. So you needs to bounce, my nigga" Tony said reaching alongside the driver seat. He took the safety off and was getting ready to blow this nigga head off.

"You got to the count of three to give me that cash. 1…2…"

Pop. Pop. Pop.

Tony ducked in the seat as the shots rang out. It was blood splattered all over his car from the dude in the backseat. Somebody had shot him. But who? He turned to look behind him. It was Tasha. In her hand, she held a small .34 caliber revolver. It was probably her father's old gun and he gave it to her for protection.

Antonio got out the car. "Thanks for saving my ass" he said to Tasha.

"No problem" she said nonchalantly. "I still care about your ass even though you been carrying me."

"It's not even like that, Tash."

"That's what your mouth say, Tony. I gotta go" she said, turning around on her heels.

"How about that date tonight, Tasha?"

She stopped in her tracks. She turned around gleaming. "I thought you wanted your girl to look good when you take her out. If you haven't noticed, my attire has been worn for the last few months."

"It's cool. Let me make a phone call. Stay right here" he said, as he stepped off to call Antonia.

"What's up, little bro?"

"Nothing much. Tasha just saved my ass."

"Tasha? Basehead Tasha?"

"Yeah and don't call her that."

"Man, look, I call them like I see them."

"Anyway, she saved my life and I need you to do me a favor."

"Saved your life? How did she do that, Tony?"

"Look, some lil bitch ass nigga thought I was sweet for it and tried to get me for my cash and product. She shot him through my back window. I need you to get Cam and Rocky to come and burn my car and get me a rental ASAP."

"Anything else, master?" she asked sarcastically.

"Yeah. Come scoop Tasha and get her ready for our date tonight."

"Date? Motherfucker you ain't going on no date with her."

"Like I said come get her. I need to catch a ride from Slim so I gotta go." He hung up the phone and walked back over to Tasha. "My sister is coming to scoop you and get you ready for tonight."

"But I don't have any money, Antonio."

"Don't worry about that, shorty. I got you."

"I like the sound of that" she said, with a smile.

"I'm glad you do. Make sure she takes you to get a nice dress. I'm taking you out somewhere special."

"Where are you taking me?"

He noticed Antonia pulling up to them. "You can't know now" he said laughing. "Guess you have to wait and see." Tony handed his sister his credit card and told her to have him a nice rental car by seven.

"Fuck all that rental car shit, Tony. You can use the Camaro tonight."

"The Camaro? You don't let nobody drive that car. What gives?"

"Shit, she saved your life" Antonia said, looking towards Tasha. "She must be a special one. She didn't have to do that but I'm glad she did. She alright with me as long as she don't try to cross us."

"I'm good, Tia. Thanks."

With that, they peeled from the scene and headed towards the mall. Moments later, Slim pulled up and Tony jumped in. "Take me to the mall, cuz. I gotta get fresh for tonight."

"Meeting with the connect?"

"Naw. I got a date."

"A date? Nigga I don't even remember the last time I heard those words come out your mouth" he said, laughing heartily.

"Just drive, dawg."

Off to the mall they went to get ready for the evening's festivities.

✶✶✶✶✶

Tasha was finishing up her final touches for the night. Antonia was a big help and Tasha really appreciated it. Tasha was looking over herself in the mirror and couldn't remember the last time she looked so beautiful. She had to shower for over thirty minutes to get all the dirt and grime from her skin. Antonia graciously helped her because she could tell this date meant a lot to her.

"I wanna really thank you for everything, Antonia" Tasha said, glowing and strutting in the three way mirror. She had chosen a short dark green mini dress and some Liboutin red bottoms with spikes. Her accessories were silver and she had a single silver hair pin to adorn her long curly hair. She looked amazing.

"No biggie, Tash. My brother used to talk about you all the time."

"He did?"

"Yeah. When we used to get out of school or after he seen you, he would always come home and talk about how special you were and how he wanted to be with you forever."

"Really, Tia?"

"Yep."

"I never thought that he would ever say anything like that."

"It was because of your drug habit that made him skeptical of you."

"What do you mean?"

"He thought that you would steal from him."

"I would never do that, Tia. I love your brother."

"You love him?"

"I always have."

"Does he know that?"

"No and he won't."

"Why not?"

"I'm not ready for him to know. So can we keep this between us, please?"

"Sure, no problem."

"Thanks" she said, hugging Antonia tightly.

She tensed up at first but eased her shoulders down and hugged her back. *"I guess she isn't all that bad. All she needs is a girlfriend. And hey, I could use a bestie"* Antonia thought to herself.

$$\star\star\star\star\star$$

The restaurant they went to was lovely. He had taken her to a nice little place called Le Cienga. It was a French spot that played jazz music all night. He wanted to show Tasha a great evening. He had reservations prepared for their candlelight dinner.

"This place is amazing" Tasha replied, looking around the exquisite atmosphere. "You must bring all the girls here, huh?" she asked.

He chuckled a little before answering. "Nah, baby girl. This is my first time here actually."

"You don't say"

"Yep, it is. I'm excited as much as you are believe me."

Gemini Betrayal

"I wanna make a toast" Tasha said, picking up her glass of champagne.

"A toast? A toast for what exactly?"

"A toast to us. Being friends again and possibly more"

"Again? I don't recall us ever stopping" Antonio said, sipping from his glass.

"That's good to know. Maybe we can just work on possibly being more" Tasha replied, taking another sip.

"We will see" he said, looking at her.

Their food arrived and they tore it up. They had a great conversation and were so into each other. Before they knew it, it was almost midnight.

"Oh shit, it's late, Tony" Tasha said, laughing from the buzz that she had gotten from the champagne.

"Yeah, it is. Time sure flies when you're having fun"

"You're actually having fun with me, Antonio?" Tasha asked, with bright eyes.

"Yeah I am. It reminds me of the old days. But, other than that, is there some place you would like me to take you?"

"Tony, come on now. You and I both know I stay in drug spots. Any one you drop me off at will do" she said sadly.

"Why are you like this, Tasha?"

"Well, to tell you the truth its because of a guy"

"A guy?"

"Yeah. This guy I used to date was a pimp and I was unaware of it until he had a party one night. He wanted me to have a threesome with him and a girl so I did. He told me to sniff a little coke to ease my mind so I did. Well, that one girl turned into two girls. That eventually turned into guys I knew and then random guys. The coke numbed me so much I had gotten used to it and it had become a second nature to me. It was like breathing"

"I see. You ever thought about quitting? You know getting yourself together?"

"Of course I have, but then real life set in and I run back to it. I need help, Tony" she said, tearing up.

"Do you need help or are you just saying you need help?"

"I need help, Antonio"

"Let's go" he said, grabbing her hand. They walked out to the car and got in.

"Where are we going?"

"I'm taking you home" he replied, starting the car.

"Okay"

She nestled back into her seat and quickly dozed off.

When she awakened, they were pulling up into Tony's driveway.

"What are we doing here?"

"I said I was taking you home"

"Oh ok. So you want some booty, huh?" she asked laughing.

"Hey I'm a man, but we don't have to do anything. We can just chill. I was really enjoying your company and I'm not ready for you to leave yet"

"That's fine with me. We can go talk"

Tony led her into the house and gave her a quick tour. They headed back to the kitchen to drink some tea before relaxing in the living room.

"You have a nice place, Antonio"

"Thanks. I try to keep it clean for when I have a beautiful woman coming over"

"That must be everyday, right?"

"Not at all. This is actually the first date I have been on since I don't know when"

"You've gotta be kidding me, right? As fine as you are and you can't get a date? Something must be wrong" she said, laughing and rubbing his thigh.

His penis jumped a little in his pants. "Nah it ain't that, Ma. I be busy and nobody catches my attention really"

"And I did?"

"You have always had my attention" he said, gently rubbing the side of her face.

"Don't do this, Tony"

"Don't do what?"

"Try to make me feel beautiful just so I can give you some pussy"

"I didn't even ask you for sex, Tasha. I like you for you"

"I wish I could say the same thing about you"

"You don't like me?" he asked smiling.

"I love you" she blurted out.

He just sat there stunned. "You love me?"

"Yes, Tony and I always have"

"Come here" He took her into his arms and kissed her deeply. He began rubbing on her body and they both were starting to get hot.

"You never have to worry about me leaving you, Tasha"

"You promise?"

"I promise"

She stood up in front of him and unzipped her dress. Dropping to the floor, it exposed her still flawless skin. She had a couple of track marks but they were hardly noticeable. She was sporting a lace baby blue bra and thong set "I wanna give myself to you"

"And I will gladly accept it" he replied. He reached into his wallet and took out a condom. He unzipped his pants and stroked his penis.

"Let me help you with that" Tasha said, walking over to him. She kneeled down in front of him and took his penis into her small hand. She gently massaged it until she gave it life. She put her mouth on it and went to work. It only took a few moments before it had become rock hard like she wanted it to be. She took the condom from him and placed it on his penis. She got on top and rode him like there was no tomorrow.

They had sex until the wee hours of the morning. They couldn't even move from the couch; not that they really wanted to. Tasha was laying on top of Antonio in his arms.

Gemini Betrayal

"You never have to worry about anything anymore, Tasha" he said, stroking her hair. "You can stay here as long as you want.

He fell asleep after that.

Chapter Six

"Happy birthday to you. Happy birthday to you. Happy birthday Tony and Tia. Happy birthday to you" everyone present in the room sang. Antonio had tuned out everything and looked around smiling at everyone that had come out to celebrate him and his sister's birthday. There was always love when his friends and family were near.

"Hurry and and blow out the candles" he heard their mother say. He and his sister leaned over and blew out the candles and heard gunshots instead of an applause. Glass shattered from the window and everyone ducked down. They managed to get up and they ran outside locked and loaded as more shots rang out. Tia managed to hit a tire and the driver lost control of the car. Me, my sister, and the whole squad ran down to the car. The guys were getting ready to make a run for it but we shot them all down. We headed back to the house only to realize our mother had been shot and was lying face down in a pool of blood.

We had the guys clean up the mess on the streets and everything before we called the police. When they arrived they asked a bunch of questions that we didn't answer. We didn't know them clowns. We don't know why they shot our mother. No it was not a drug-related incident. After all their questions came to an end, they told us they would call if they heard anything. We knew they weren't because it was already gonna be taken care of.

I awakened from my sleep only to find Tasha coming upstairs with two plates in each hand and a bottle of syrup in her arms. "Good morning" she sang as she sat down with the plates in her hand.

"What is this?" I asked, sitting up in the bed.

"Well, a lot of people like to call it breakfast" she said, laughing. She had made some eggs, pancakes and bacon.

"Real funny, Tash. You can cook right?" I asked laughing.

"Eat up and you tell me" She ain't have to tell me twice. I poured syrup over my pancakes and dug in. It was so good I finished it in under five minutes. Now that's what I'm talking about. A beautiful woman that can cook. I wonder what else she could do. I guess only time would tell.

"Breakfast was good, Tasha. I'm glad you ain't kill me" I said laughing.

"Keep it up, Antonio"

"I'm just joking. I'm getting ready to hit the block. You can chill here if you want but I don't want you out there messing around with no crack or none of that shit"

"You have my word, baby"

"Aight, cool" I headed for the shower and she took the plates downstairs. When I came out the shower, my clothes were already prepared for the day. "Are you kidding me?"

"What's wrong?" she asked puzzled.

"I didn't expect you to lay my clothes out for me. That's what's up. Thank you"

"No, problem. But I have a better way you can thank me" she said, coming around to me. I noticed all she had on was some lace boy shorts and a tank-top that I'm sure she got out of the spare room where Tia often slept in.

"What did you have in mind?" I asked. She snatched my towel off and threw it on the floor. She got down on her knees and blessed a brother. I was enjoying the hell out of her mouth. I gripped her head between my hands and began to thrust in and out of her mouth. My whole dick was going inside her mouth. I felt throat and all. Not one time did she gag. She pulled my hands away from her head and got up. She walked back to the side of the bed she was on and removed her underwear. She got up on the bed and kneeled down into a doggy style position. I quickly went around to her and grabbed a condom out the drawer. I examined her ass as I got ready to go in. I massaged her ass cheeks then inserted myself into her. She moaned loudly at the first deep thrust.

I started out with long hard strokes. Somehow my pace quickened fast and I started pumping rapidly and deeper until we both climaxed. I washed my penis off before getting dressed and she laid down saying she would take a shower in a lil bit.

I got dressed and grabbed my phone and gun. When I looked back over, she was drifting off to sleep. "I guess I was good" I said, cockily to myself. I left her a few bills on the table and left. There was money to be made.

As soon as Tasha heard the door slam, she jumped up and ran to the window. She watched as Tony got in his car and sped off. As soon as the car was out of her eye, she ran to get her purse to find her special friend. She dug around until she felt a small baggie in the corner of the handbag. She pulled it out along with a small compact mirror and razor. She cut up the coke a little before rolling up a dollar bill and sniffing the lines. When she was done, she showered and laid back in the bed; as she plotted on where she was gonna start snooping at first in the big house.

$$***** $$

"Man, it's slow as fuck out here today" Cam said to Rocky.

"You ain't never lied, Bro" he said. They were standing on Michigan Ave trying to sell their product and pick up some of the college girls. Neither were working in their favor. Just when Cam was getting ready to step off for a moment, a fly little shorty walked his way. He didn't even let her pass he just pulled her back by the hand.

"Yo, yo, yo, why you walking past me, ma?"

"Do I know you?" she asked puzzled.

"Naw, but I'm giving the opportunity now to get to know ya boy"

"I think I'll pass" she said, walking away.

He didn't even go after her. He left it at that and directed his attention back to Rocky.

"She just cold played you, dude" Rocky said, doubling over in laughter.

"Fuck all that noise you talking, Rock. That hoe gonna wish she talked to me"

"Man fuck her. What about Tia?"

"Man, shhh. What the fuck? You trying to get me killed?"

"Are you kidding me? Tony still don't know you fucking his sister? I don't know why y'all just wont tell him. It ain't like he actually gonna give a fuck. You his right hand and that's his sister"

"You think that shit mean anything to him? He would kill me" Cam said, looking around to make sure Antonio wasn't in ear shot of their conversation.

"I think y'all both over exaggerating. Just tell him"

"There's something else though"

"What? You sleeping with their cousin, too?" Rocky asked, laughing.

Gemini Betrayal

"Naw, man. Antonia told me she loved me"

"Whoa, man, what? Tia actually said that to somebody? Let alone your black ass? What did you say?"

"I told her cool"

"Cool? What the fuck does that even mean?"

"It means I'm a thug and I wasn't saying that shit back. I got love for her but I don't love her. At least I don't think so"

"I don't know son. Maybe you should think about it. You probably do and just don't know it"

"Naw, I don't think so my nigga"

"Aight, man, if you say so. But look I'm 'bout to head to the Southside and hit the streets on that side. Hit me up if you wanna hangout tonight. It's Sunday but we could play some cards or something"

"Aight, cool. I think I'm about to jet, too, on the real. I'm gonna go find Tone and let him know we about to bounce"

"Aight" They dapped each other up and Rocky got in his Impala and sped off. Cam looked around for a second for any potential customers before stepping off himself.

He found Tony standing on 18th street and headed his way. "What's up, son?"

"Shit, shit. Just working the block. You know how I go"

"True, true. I think I'm done for the day so I'm gonna just head home. You know, if that's cool with you, Boss"

"It's cool, Cam. I think I'm going head in, too. Tasha at the house waiting for me"

Gemini Betrayal

"Damn, you left that basehead in your house all day, bro?"

"Yeah, what's wrong with that? And stop calling her that"

"Man, look. I call them like I see them. And that bitch is a straight basehead. It's cool if you're a little sweet on her though" he said, laughing.

"Anyway, yeah, she there. She said she wanted help so I'm gonna help her"

"Well, you just be careful. Call me if you need me, Tone"

"Peace"

They did their special handshake that they have been doing since they were young kids before parting ways. As Antonio walked towards his new Malibu, he took a quick trip down memory lane.

He and Cam met on the playground when they were ten. They lived in the same complex but never really paid attention to one another. Some guys were messing with Antonia and Antonio fought the biggest one who seemed to be the leader of the pack. Out of nowhere, one of the asshole kids that was with the pack, picked up a branch and hit Tony on the back of the leg. He fell to the ground and saw Antonia running towards him with a pipe she found in the alley. One of the guys that they knew by the name Chino tripped her and she hit the ground. He tried to kick her but it got intervened when Cam picked up the pipe and hit him in the back of the head.

The three of them together took on the seven bullies and ran them out. From that day on, they had been thick as thieves. Antonio loved Cam like a brother and would die for him. The same went for Cam. Antonio got into his car and headed home thinking about all the mischief he and his best friend had ever caused.

Of course, everyone says they will be friends until the end. Hopefully their end won't be so sudden.

Gemini Betrayal

✳✳✳✳✳

Knock. Knock.

Tasha damn near jumped out her golden brown skin when she heard the banging on the front door. Thinking it was one of Antonio's crew members or maybe, even his sister, she hurried down the stairs.

Knock. Knock. Knock.

"What the fuck?" Tasha yelled, as she snatched the door open.

"Um, who are you?"

"I'm Tasha. Who the fuck are you?"

"I'm Destiny."

"Well congratulations. What do you want?"

"I would like to know where my boyfriend is. Or better yet, maybe you can tell me why you're wearing that in his house?" Destiny replied, looking Tasha up and down. All Tasha had on was a cami and some Pink boy shorts that made her ass plump and perkier than usual.

"Well, this is what my man likes"

"Bitch, please. You must be here with somebody else"

"No, not all. I'm waiting for Tony to get back home so we can have a repeat of last night"

"Last night?"

"Yeah, last night. We had mind-blowing sex and it was great" Tasha could see Destiny getting hot so she kept going. "He ate my pussy and I sucked his dick. I deep-throated that thing like it was nothing. He came all in my mouth and I swallowed every drop of his cum. He didn't even whisper your name, Deborah"

"Hoe, my name is Destiny" she replied, stepping a little more into the house and closing the door behind her.

"Oh, ho, ho. So now I'm a hoe because I'm taking care of my man's needs?"

"Bitch he's mine" Destiny replied, as she swung at Tasha. She connected with her chin as she threw a left hook.

Tasha retaliated quickly by throwing a right of her own. She hit Destiny with a combo before letting her drop to the floor. She got on top of her and threw blow after blow. Destiny managed to grab her hands and push her up off of her and ended up on top of her. She grabbed Tasha by the throat and slammed her head several times on the floor. Tasha grabbed at Destiny's blouse and managed to pop the buttons off and exposed perfect breasts.

Destiny pulled at Tasha's shirt and pulled it off and threw it across the room. Tasha pushed her off top of her and kicked her across the room. She stood up and charged at Destiny but she was ready. She picked up the cordless phone off the table and slapped Tasha with it. Tasha lip started bleeding and that infuriated her.

She picked up the fire poker from by the fireplace and hit Destiny with it. She hit her in the head, the chest, her back, everywhere.

"You had enough yet, bitch?" Tasha yelled at Destiny.

"Fuck you."

"Suit yourself"

Tasha threw the stick down and went to choke Destiny. Destiny wasn't giving up without a fight that was for sure. She choked Tasha but her grip was entirely stronger. They didn't even notice Antonio come in until the front door slammed shut.

"What the fuck is going on?" he yelled and they froze.

Chapter Seven

"Who the fuck is this bitch, Antonio?" Destiny snapped.

"No, who the fuck are you, bitch?" Tasha shot back as she pushed Destiny.

Destiny was coming back towards her just when Antonio grabbed her by the arm. "Chill the fuck out, Destiny"

She snatched her arm from his grasp and looked at him. Pure pain and hurt was written all over her beautiful face. "I asked you who she was, Antonio"

He looked at her defeated. "She's an old friend. That's all"

"That's all, huh?" she asked looking back and forth between the two. "So why is she in your house and half dressed?"

"I don't know why, baby. I don't even know how she got in here"

"Oh, you don't, Tony?" Tasha said, rolling her eyes at him. "Well, let me refresh your memory. We went out last night on a date then you brought me back here. We fucked all night then went to sleep. I made you breakfast in bed this morning and we fucked again this morning before you left out. Anything else you would like to know, honey?" she asked Destiny sarcastically.

"Nope, nothing at all. Antonio, you're a fucking pig and I'm leaving" Destiny said, as she headed toward the door.

"Baby, don't go" he said, grabbing her hand.

"Don't fucking baby me you fucking bastard" she said, pummeling him with her fists. He blocked the blows but some actually connected. "I don't ever wanna fucking talk to you again. I fucking hate your black ass" She stopped hitting him and picked up her bag and walked out the door. Antonio called after her but she ignored him. She got in her car and drove away with tears falling from her hazel eyes. She never looked back.

Antonio came back in the house and walked past Tasha.

"What you looking sad for, Tony?"

"Because I just lost my girlfriend"

"Well no need to be sad, love. You still got me and I ain't going nowhere"

"Yeah, you are"

"And where the hell am I going?"

"You about to bring your ass over here and suck daddy off until I tell you to stop"

"That's cool with me. I know you stressed and I'd be glad to please you"

She knelt down in front of him as he sat back on the sofa. She slobbed and bobbed on his penis until he passed out on the chair. She used that as an escape.

She quickly got dressed and ran around the house picking up valuable shit. She collected one of his Rolex watches, a diamond cut pinky ring, and a platinum chain. She crept back downstairs and he was still asleep. She went through his pockets and took his money out of his pocket. She counted the money and it totaled one thousand dollars. She cheesed so hard that you'd think her cheeks were about to burst. She left out the house and gently closed the door.

She didn't leave a note or anything. She had to get back to the Southside quick. It was time to get her fix.

$$*****$$

"Is this shit real?" Nikko asked Tasha as he examined the pinky ring. Nikko was her coke man. He always hooked her up and that's why she has been a loyal customer to him for the past four years.

"Hell yeah, it is. Now come on, how much smoke can I get?"

"Shit!! at least a half ounce for six hundred."

"Six hundred? That's a shitty ass fucking deal"

"Bitch, please. This is the highest quality and the rarest in this area. I get my shit from the Colombians out in Miami"

"Naw fuck that. I think I'd be better off selling the damn thing. At least I will get more money for it" she replied, reaching for the pinky ring. Nikko pulled back keeping the precious jewel out of her reach. "What are you doing? Give me my shit, Nikko"

"Naw I think I'm gonna hold on to it. I think it looks kinda nice" he said, slipping it on his finger.

"You got me fucked up if you think you keeping my shit"

"It ain't even yours, bitch. So fall back" he replied, as he turned on his heels and began to walk away. Tasha pulled her gun out of her purse real quick.

"Give me my shit back before I shoot your ass, Nikko" she said, cocking her pistol.

She heard him chuckling. "What you gonna do with that?" he asked, with his back still facing her.

"I'm gonna blow your ass away if you don't give me that damn ring back" She moved in closer.

"You've got to be joking" he said, continuing to laugh. "If you can get it off my hand you can have it back."

"You not gonna try nothing are you?"

"No, I'm not" he said genuinely. "If you bad enough to take it from me, then go right ahead"

She slowly walked over to him and pressed the gun to the back of his head. She pulled on his pinky until the ring slid off. "Give me everything you got in your pockets" she said, as she backed up a little to put some space between them.

"I ain't giving your basehead ass nothing, bitch. You must think I'm a motherfucking chump"

"You are and I'm the bitch with the gun so let's go"

Nikko stood there for a second before he started emptying his pockets. He pulled out five hundred in cash and about six little baggies with coke in it.

"Throw me the drugs" she said, with the gun still pointed at him. He tossed the bags over to her and she picked them up. She quickly ran over to a table and dumped two of them on the table in a line. Her gaze was still fixed on Nikko and she snorted the two lines. She could feel the drugs instantly kicking in and it felt great. "Now give me the cash" He did as he was told and threw the money over her way. It slipped through her hands and she knelt down to get it. Nikko used this opportunity to catch her off guard.

He ran full speed towards her and tackled her to the floor. "Get the fuck off of me" she yelled. He punched her several times before he grabbed her around the neck.

"You must have thought I was just about to let you take my shit and roll out. Is that what the fuck you thought, bitch?"

"Nikko, you're hurting me" she said, hitting him and trying to grasp some air.

"I don't give a fuck, you fucking junkie hoe" he said, tightening his grip more around her neck. Her hard punches soon became soft taps. He looked into her eyes and watched as the life slipped away from her body. He gripped her neck a little longer before he snapped it. He sat on top of her and smiled down. He had not one bit of remorse for killing Tasha. He was sick.

He picked up her lifeless body, dragged her over to the bed and threw her on a mattress. He pulled off her clothes and removed his as well. He positioned himself behind her and rammed his dick in her vagina. He had always wanted to fuck Tasha but she always told him "over my dead body" So now he was fucking her dead body.

Tasha never liked Nikko and he knew it. He was a loser when they were in high school and now he was a drug dealer. He thought money would change her mind but it didn't. He was still suffering from bad acne that made her wanna throw up. Well now, he didn't have to worry about that because she was gone.

He fucked her until he couldn't anymore. He sexed her corpse from every which way. "*Might as well since she willingly doing it*" he thought. He finished and stood over her. He grabbed his dick and released his urine all over her. "Now you can rest on you filthy hoe" he said. He quickly got dressed and grabbed the ring and the money she had stashed in her bra before he left the crack house.

He went outside and there was no life to be found. He did see two crackheads but they were so high that they didn't even notice him. "*Oh well*" he thought to himself. He got in his Chevy Impala and headed home. He pushed Tasha in the back of his mind and smiled at his achievement as he drove to his home on Saratoga.

*****

Antonio had awaken to a dark house. No lights were on. No music. Just a dead eerie silence surrounded him. He reached for his phone to call Tasha when he noticed she wasn't lying next to him.

"You have reached the voicemail box for" he heard the recording say. He quickly hung up the phone. He dialed it again thinking he dialed the wrong number. The same thing happened. He didn't know what was going on. He got up and headed upstairs. Finding out that she wasn't, he headed back to the living room and paced back and forth trying to figure out where she could be. He called his sister. "Maybe she went to kick it with her" he said, aloud to himself.

"What's up, twin?" Antonia said, after picking up on the second ring.

"Shit, sis. Ay, have you heard from Tasha?"

"No I thought she was with you. Why the hell would she be with me?"

"I thought she might have come to you after what happened earlier"

"Wait, what? What the fuck happened earlier?"

"Destiny showed up at my house and they got to wrecking. Destiny left and Tasha stayed. Well, at least I thought she did. I just woke up and she's gone"

"Well, could you blame her? You gave that girl high hopes and shitted on her. And Destiny, too. I liked her. You need to fix shit with Destiny, bro"

"What about Tasha?"

"No offense, I know you like her but she a basehead. Nothing more and nothing less. Let that crack hoe go, man"

He hung up on his sister. He had to find Tasha. He slipped on his Jordans and grabbed his keys. He had to go look for her and apologize.

He jumped in his car and sped off in search of Tasha.

He reached his destination twenty minutes later. He looked around at all the buildings and frankly he didn't know where to start. He remembered seeing her in one particular building so he started there first.

He walked down to the building and noticed Nikko standing on the corner. Nikko didn't like him because Antonio was slowly but surely stealing all of his customers. He vowed that one of these days, he was going to have it out with Nikko but today was not the day to be fucked with. He walked up to him and tried to be as cordial as possible.

"Hey, Nikko, what's up, man?"

"Don't you fucking what's up me, Antonio. You got some nerve coming around here after you took all my damn customers"

"I don't understand what your beef is, bro. We both making money"

"I ain't your fucking bro, dawg. Get that shit straight now"

"Anyway. Have you seen Tasha? I really need to speak with her"

"Yeah, I seen her fine ass" he said walking over to Antonio. He noticed the pinky ring that adorned Nikko's hand. He knew it was his but he wasn't sure how the fuck he got it.

"That's a fine piece of jewelry you got there, Nikko"

"Thanks. I got it from Tasha"

"Tasha huh? It looks vaguely familiar"

"I bet you would say that. Look Tasha ain't here so you can get the stepping, my nigga"

"Naw, naw, naw bruh. I think she is here and you know exactly where she is" he said pulling his nine from his hip.

"Really, dawg? You gonna really shoot me over a bitch?"

"Naw because you stole my shit. Give me my damn ring, cuz." Nikko took the ring off and handed it to him. "Now take me to Tasha"

"You don't want to see her in the condition she is in right now"

"I've seen plenty of people strung out and high off this shit. This ain't gonna be no different. I don't even know how you even lured her down here to get that shit. She said she was quitting"

"And you fucking believed her?" Nikko said laughing. "I thought you were much smarter than that, college boy"

"Just get moving" I said, pressing the gun to his temple.

"Whatever you say"

He walked up the steps into the house leading Antonio to where he had left Tasha's body. Antonio looked around disgusted at what he saw. Everybody was either slumped over drooling or prepping their veins to shoot up. *"And I do this shit to my people for money"* he thought to himself. They stepped over one guy that looked like he had overdosed. He was just lying in the middle of the hall lifeless. They reached the room and walked in.

Antonio walked further into the room covering his nose from the stench of urine. His eyes fell upon Tasha. He walked over and tried to wake her. "Wake up, Tasha" he said, shaking her. He shoved her a little harder and she still laid there. He picked her up and her head fell back. It was just swinging back and forth. He noticed she didn't have a pulse. She was dead.

He dropped her body and turned back toward Nikko with his gun pointed. "What the fuck did you do?"

"I ain't do shit. She was like that when I found her earlier"

"So you just left her there, huh? Why didn't you call the cops?"

"Why in the hell would I have them pigs up in my spot? They would've taken me in for questioning"

"Well now, I'm asking the questions. And I'm gonna ask you one last time" Antonio said putting a bullet in the chamber. "What the fuck did you do?"

"Aight, man, fuck. That bitch tried to fucking rob me. And frankly I don't know why you give a fuck. She robbed your ass, too"

A shot rang out and Nikko dropped to the floor. Antonio had put a hot one right in his left thigh.

"Aahhh, fuck" he screamed. He tried to get up but Antonio shot him in the right thigh. His body dropped to the floor entirely. Antonio went and stood over top of him. "Don't kill me, man. Fuck. Please don't kill me"

Antonio just blankly stared at him. He raised his gun to his head. "I bet Tasha begged for you not to kill her, too, but you did. Fuck you" he pulled the trigger and Nikko's head dropped. His breathing became faint and fair.

Antonio heard sirens in the distance. He hurried and checked Nikko's pockets. He pulled out all the cash and ran out the house. The sirens were getting closer. He jumped in his whip and sped off. As he turned the corner, he heard the police cars screech to the scene.

He dipped around every corner like somebody was chasing him. He hit three abandoned cars and almost a pedestrian. He picked up his phone and called Destiny.

"What the fuck do you want, nigga? Didn't I tell your ass I was-"

Antonio cut her off. "Yeah, Baby, you did tell me that. Can I come and see you, please? I want to apologize."

"You can do that over the phone"

"Please, Destiny"

She thought about it for a second. "I'm at the Country Inn over in Capitol Heights"

"I'm on my way" he said, hanging up. He had finally slowed his car down. He drove the posted speed limit of 35 the rest of the way to the hotel. He got there and called Destiny. "What room are you in?"

"212"

I walked over to the desk and told the receptionist I was visiting someone in room 212. She called up to the room and Destiny told her it was okay for me to come up. "You can catch the elevator up to the second floor. Your sister said you can come up"

I looked at her strangely and chuckled. "That's not my sister, miss"

"That's too bad" she said, as she turned and sashayed away. I couldn't help but stare at her round ass. She was cute. He walked away from the desk and headed toward the elevators.

I rode the elevator to Destiny's floor and got off. I walked down to her room and the door was already open. I assumed it was okay so I walked in. I found her laying on the bed wearing only a bra and panty set. I closed and locked the door behind him. "What's the occasion?" I asked licking my lips.

"Nigga please. I wore this for you but you already had some goodies before I got here" she snapped.

"I'm really sorry about that, Destiny"

"You're sorry for what exactly? Because you got caught or because I had to see that? Maybe it's because you forgot about me. Which was it?"

"Everything," he said climbing up on the bed next to her. "I really am sorry, Baby"

"Whatever, Antonio"

"Let me make it up to you"

"How?"

"First, I can give you this" I reached in my pocket and pulled out a thousand dollars. I handed it to her.

"What the hell is this for?"

"For you to go shopping or whatever"

"I don't want your fucking money, Tony" she said, throwing the money at my face.

"Well, what do you want?"

"I just want you. Is that so hard? I want you to love me as much as I love you. I want you to be honest and keep shit a hundred with me"

"I can do that" I said, dryly.

"No, motherfucker. I want you to mean it"

Gemini Betrayal

"I will do that for you, baby. And nothing like this will ever happen again" I said, kissing her on the neck. She started to melt like butter. She snuggled under me and started to kiss me.

Their lips were locked and their bodies were entwined with one another. He removed her bra and sucked on her nipples. She moaned loudly and grabbed his hair. She threw her leg across his and held him there. They continued to kiss and she began to strip him out of his ensemble. He removed her panties and went face first into her vagina.

"I'm so sorry, baby" he repeated over and over as he gently kissed her sweet center. "I will never hurt you again"

"Shut up and take care of me, daddy"

He got up on his hands and prepared to enter her. He stopped and grabbed a condom out of his pants pocket. She halted him.

"We don't need that anymore"

"Are you sure?" he asked. She opened her legs and welcomed him. "I take that as a yes"

He entered her pleasure place and made sweet love to her. They sexed until 3 a.m. "I love you, Antonio"

"I love you too, Destiny" he replied. She smiled to herself with her back towards him. She snuggled underneath him and they spooned the rest of the night.

"I actually told her I loved her and I think I actually meant it" he said to himself. And he drifted off to sleep.

Chapter Eight

The next few days were gloomy. Tony wasn't out there with his team. He had too much on his mind. Destiny had gone back home yesterday so he had all day to sit around his house and clear his mind. He heard a knock at the door. He walked over and looked out the peephole. It was Cam and Antonia. "What y'all want?" he said with an attitude as he opened the door.

"Well, damn, what a welcome" Antonia said, to her twin brother.

"What's up, dawg? Ain't nobody heard from you in a couple days. Everything trill?"

"Naw not at all" he said sitting on the couch.

"Well, what's up then?" Cam prodded.

"Have y'all ever thought about the damage we do?"

"What damage?" Antonia asked with her eyebrows scrunched up.

"Selling crack to our people"

"No I don't. All I'm worried about is my money" his sister responded. He just shook his head and looked to Cam.

"I'm in the same boat with Tia bruh. Fuck them baseheads, man. We can't help what they are. We can only keep them happy."

"True shit" Tia agreed.

"I think I'm out the game"

"What the fuck you mean?" Tia said, standing up.

"I'm done. That shit is the reason why Tasha dead now."

"Hold the fuck up. What? When did she get killed?"

"The day I was looking for her. And that bitch ass nigga Nikko killed her" I said, as I scooted back on the chair and threw my head back.

"That's fucked up" Cam said, shaking his head. "So what we gonna do now?"

"What you mean?" I asked. "It's a family business so it's going to Tia"

"You think it's that easy to get out, huh, little bro? What you think Big Tony gonna say?"

"Man, fuck what he gotta say" I said, yelling a few octaves. *I couldn't stand our father. All I wanted to do was go to college and make something out of myself. I came home after graduating college and inherited Big Tone's empire. I never wanted it. I just wanted to be a regular taxpayer. My mind was made up.*

"Okay, Tony" Tia said. "Calm down. I will take over"

"Thank you"

"If you ever change your mind, you can have your seat back"

"Thanks but no thanks. My mind is set"

"Okay. Well we have something to talk to you about"

"What is it?"

"Well" she started. She walked over and sat next to me on the sofa. "Cam and I have been dating for the past few months"

"That's all?" I said, laughing.

"What's so funny, bruh?" Cam asked confused.

"Man, look, I'm happy y'all finally told me"

"You mean you knew?"

"Fuck yeah. I don't give a damn who my sister dates. Just don't fuck her over" I said, with all seriousness on my face. I stood up and walked over to Cam. "I know you will take care of her"

"True shit" he said, dapping up his best friend.

"Now if you love birds will excuse me, I want to be alone and I will see y'all tomorrow at the church"

"Church?" they said in unison.

"Yeah, for Tasha's funeral"

"Yeah we will be there" Antonia said, dapping up her brother. She kissed him on the cheek.

"What was that for?"

"Just because I love you bro. I just want you to remember that"

"Love you too, sis" I said, standing up and hugging her. We haven't hugged each other so tightly since our mom had gotten killed.

"We out" Antonia said, as she broke our hug.

"Holla" I responded as I headed up the stairs.

"Holla" Cam yelled back. He and Tia left out the house and she locked the front door with her key.

She hoped her brother would be okay through this entire ordeal with Tasha. She hadn't seen him this down since they lost their mom. He had Destiny and he knew he always had her and Cam by his side even if nobody else was.

Antonio couldn't wait for them to leave. He laughed to himself at the thought of them thinking that their relationship was a secret. He looked at the time and saw that it was 7 p.m. It was early but he was tired. He hopped in a quick shower. He let the steamy hot water wash all his pain away. Well at least a couple pieces of it.

He got out and threw on a pair of boxers. He texted Destiny and told her that he loved her and that he was going to bed because he was tired. She texted back 'I love you more and sweet dreams'

"I don't know what I would do without her" I said aloud. I had cut off all the lights and went to bed. I had a long and dreary day ahead of me tomorrow.

✲✲✲✲✲

The next day finally came. Tony laid down on the bed looking up at the ceiling. He hadn't get much sleep last night. Whenever he tried to sleep, he saw the image of Tasha laying there on that dirty mattress lifeless. Neck all broken and bruised in a puddle of piss. Was it his fault that she had gone back to the crack house? He thought so, whether anyone else said it or not. He looked at the clock. 8 a.m. He had an hour before he had to leave out. He got up, showered and picked out his outfit for the day. He chose his all black Armani suit and a platinum cross and his platinum pinky ring. He was dressed to kill.

By the time he finished getting dressed, it was 8:45 a.m. He decided to head to the church.

He rode through the streets of his neighborhood listening to music by 2pac. He played the greatest hits album the entire way

Gemini Betrayal

towards the church. He arrived at the church and it looked like a block party outside. There were so many people standing about that he noticed. Her mom, her brothers, cousins, and people from the neighborhood. He parked his car, took a deep breath, then headed towards the crowd.

He was approached first by her little brother, Twan. He and Antonia had known Twan for years. He was one of those good boys that turned into a hood nigga. Antonio always admired him and vice versa.

"What's up blood?" Twan said, giving Tony some dap.

"What's up, fam?" I replied.

"Shit just chillin'. Chillin'. How you been?"

"Good. Just been working like shit"

"Yeah, I hear that"

"Sorry about what happened to Tasha, Twan"

"Yeah, me too. I swear I'm gonna find out who did this bitch nigga shit to my folks and handle they ass."

"It's taken care of, blood"

"What you mean?"

"I handled it already" I said, in a much lower tone.

"Cool, thanks fam"

"No problem"

"Aye, but look, check it. I'm looking to be put on with your crew. You got me?"

"I think we can find a place for you"

"Good looking out"

"It's all good. But I'm gonna see you inside" I said, as I saw one of Nikko's homeboys approaching. He wanted to stay out of sight.

I walked into the church and ran into Tasha's mother. "Hey, how're you doing Mrs. Owens?"

"Oh, Antonio" she said, hugging me tightly. "I'm so glad that you came"

"Of course"

"It means a lot to me. How's your sister and father?"

"They're good. My sister and everybody else should be here shortly"

"We're already here" Antonia said walking up behind her brother with Cam and the rest of the gang with her.

"Hello Antonia" Mrs. Owens said sternly. You could feel the tension in the room. Mrs. Owens always had a problem with Antonia for some reason.

"Hey, I'm sorry about what happened to Tasha"

"I bet you are. You and your thugs just be good today" she said. She gave me another hug and a kiss on the cheek before heading into the sanctuary.

"What the fuck was that about?" Antonia asked her brother.

"I don't know Twin" I said, laughing. "That lady has never liked you. Maybe it's because y'all tried to break in her house when y'all were teenagers"

"Bullshit," she replied laughing. "Damn that old lady can hold a grudge"

"You know it" he replied. They heard music starting and they got quiet. "Time to head in" he said and the crew followed closely in tow.

They all lined up and made their way up to the casket. When it was Antonio's turn, he hesitated and stood there. His sister and Cam both placed reassuring hands on his shoulder and he went. He looked down at Tasha's lifeless body and thought she looked beautiful. Compared to how she looked the last time, she looked so much more at peace. He leaned down and kissed her. He whispered softly into her ear, "I will always love you, baby girl." He kissed her again and placed a single white rose inside her casket.

It took over an hour before every person in attendance could view the body. After the very last person left the casket, it was going on 11 a.m. They closed the coffin and her mother went hysterical. Everyone tried to console her but it worked to no avail. Her younger daughter had to take her into the hall until she got herself under control. We all focused our attention back on the pastor who was ready to give his sermon.

"Let us bow our heads in prayer for this beautiful young woman" he began.

✳✳✳✳✳

We all rode in unison behind the hearse to the cemetery. There were so many cars we blocked an entire roadway. I know those that were visiting their loved ones were pissed, but so the fuck what? It was much love here for Tasha. We walked over to her burial site and awaited the late arrivals. Once every late black person arrived, the pastor continued.

I don't know what it is, but it seem like when pastors preach, they never stop talking. They break into a sweat and preach harder. On this occasion, I didn't mind. I was here for Tasha and I was gonna be here until they opened the gates to heaven for her spirit. The pastor told us all to bow our heads as he said another prayer before putting her in the ground.

We bowed our heads but my instincts started kicking in. I looked up and saw a black car with tinted windows creeping up the hill. They were going too slow for my liking. I tapped my sister and she looked in the same direction. She nodded and reached behind her back to grab a hold of her piece. She tapped Cam and he did the same. All around the crowd, our goons were getting prepared, even Twan had his piece. We were being as inconspicuous as possible.

The car drove closer to us and we saw the windows slowly come down. As soon as it got close enough, the passengers of the vehicle opened fire. Everyone was ducking and trying to take cover from the array of stray bullets. Tasha's mom became hysterical and dropped to her knees by her daughter's casket as it hit the ground. Antonia and Cam grabbed Mrs. Owens and took her to safety as the rest of us continued the shoot out. It was Twan's bullet that hit the back tire and blew it off the car. It screeched to a halt and its occupants jumped out. We all went after them on foot and let our bullets rain down on them. We caught every last one of them. Shot their legs up and all.

Antonia shot one in the back of the head while Cam shot one of the niggas multiple times in the back. The last dude belonged to me and Twan. He was crawling thinking he was about to get away. Not a chance. We caught up to him and flipped him over on his back.

"Aaghhh" he yelled in agony.

"Shut the fuck up" I said. I stepped on the nigga left leg as Twan stepped on the right.

"Who the fuck sent you?" Twan asked enraged.

"Fuck you, Nigga" he spat at Twan.

Twan cocked his gun and shot him in the shoulder. The dude screamed out in pain. I could hear sirens in the distance. They were definitely headed our way. I didn't ask questions I just shot the nigga square in the head. I watched his blood ooze out onto the cemetery grass. I recognized him. I didn't have time to tell Twan. We just got in the cars with everybody else and got the fuck out of dodge.

By the time the police had arrived, nobody from Tasha's funeral was in sight. No face, no case.

Gemini Betrayal

Chapter Nine

Later that night, I called Tasha's mom and apologized. She assured me it was perfectly fine and that she knew I was looking out for the fam. I told her she was absolutely right. We shared a couple laughs and shed a few tears before hanging up after a forty-five minute conversation. It was always nice talking to her. Made me wish I still had my own mother to talk to.

Antonia and the crew came over dressed in their war attire. I called Twan over as well so he could meet everybody before we headed out. He arrived right on time.

"What's up, Twan" I said, as I let him in the house.

"Hey what's up, Tony" he replied, dapping me up.

"Hey Antonia, you remember Twan right?" I said, as I led Twan over to the rest of the crew.

"Yeah I do" she said, as she stood. "Good looking out today" she replied, dapping him up and pulling him into an embrace.

"No problem. Gotta protect the fam" he said. He eyed Tia up and down. He always had a thing for her. And everyone in the room saw it. Cam noticed what was going on and intervened.

"What's up, Bruh?" he asked pushing Antonia to the side and grabbing Twan's hand. "I'm Cam, Tia's man"

"Congratulations I guess," Twan said. Everyone around the room chuckled at how jealous Cam was acting. Everybody except Cam anyway.

"Now that everybody is acquainted, it's time to get down to business" I began. "Sis, I know I put you in charge, but I got this run. We doing this for Tasha"

"Lead away, little brother"

Antonio went on to tell everybody his plan. He informed the crew that it was the twins Dennis and Drew that sent their goons to shoot up the burial site today.

✲✲✲✲✲

Antonio and Antonia knew the Johnson twins from their teen years. Their first encounter with them was when Dennis had bumped Antonia in middle school. She hit the locker pretty hard. This infuriated her and she went after him. She chased him down the hall until they came to a dead end and a group of kids had barricaded them in.

"Fight, fight, fight, fight" they chanted. Antonio and Drew saw the commotion going on and headed down there as well, neither expecting to see their other half.

Antonio pushed through the crowd just in time to see his twin two piece Dennis. He stumbled back a little, came back and tackled her. Antonia saw her brother but did not ask for any assistance; she never did. Dennis had her on the ground and managed to punch her a couple times. She managed to get from under him and landed another right hook. Drew saw this and jumped in.

He ran up behind Tia and grabbed her by her arms. Dennis regained his balance and went over to Antonia. He landed blow after blow to her face and midsection. Finally, Antonio jumped to his sister's aid. He grabbed the fire extinguisher from the wall and bust Drew over the head with it. He hit the floor with a thud.

He and his twin went on to jump Dennis while his brother laid on the tile floor unconscious. Before you knew it, people from northeast where the Johnson twins

Gemini Betrayal

lived jumped in as well as people from southeast where the Hall twins resided. It was the biggest brawl ever in the history of school fights.

Eventually, somebody notified the principal and the police officers at the school because they all came running down the hall. They were on their walkie-talkies calling for backup. The crowd of students dispersed so they wouldn't risk suspension.

A can of tear gas is what almost stopped the fight but it didn't work. They continued their royal rumble blind and all. Next thing you knew, everyone involved were being handcuffed and taken off to juvie.

We got off with self-defense charges and were able to go home while our enemies both got sentenced to two years in a detention center for assault.

✳✳✳✳✳

"I should've known it was them bitch ass niggas" Tia said, standing and punching her hand with her fists.

"Baby calm down" Cam said to her.

"Fuck that! I'm not calming down shit. Them niggas gotta die. Tonight" she said, with fire in her eyes.

"Everybody calm down!" I yelled over them. "Now look, we all need to go in there with a clear head and one thing on our mind" I said, getting quiet and looking around at the crew.

"What's that?"

"Blood"

Everybody nodded their heads in unison. They all got their weapons together. Sienna and Leana were already at the spot awaiting our arrival. We piled into our Yukon and the Suburban and headed for war.

We got to the Johnson's household within twenty minutes. They still lived home with their parents in their basement. We could see them through the basement windows. We hit Sienna and Leana on their walkie-talkies. They were ready and so were we.

They sashayed over to the house in their little skirts and tight tops. Their roles were strippers. We saw Drew leaving downstairs to head upstairs to the front door. Cam, Tia, Twan, and I made our move towards the basement door. Where we were, we could hear Leana and Sienna at the door.

"Are you sure this isn't the right house?" Leana asked.

"Yeah I'm sure" Drew replied. "But since y'all lovely ladies already here, y'all might as well stay and dance for me and my homies"

"Nah ah, fuck that" Sienna said in her ghetto voice. "We here to make money, Nigga. Let's go, Jazzy"

"Naw wait" he said, grabbing Sienna's hand. "I got money" he said, pulling out a wad of cash.

"Well you should've said that at first. Shit" Leana said, leading the way in the house.

Roughly about ten minutes later, we heard music starting to play but we still hadn't received the signal from the girls yet. We peeped through the window and saw Leana and Sienna going into the bathroom with their bags.

The plan was for them to tell the guys they had to change and then throw us a signal. Moments later, we heard the walkie-talkie chime twice and we moved in.

We headed to the side of the house and down the steps. We kicked in the basement door with guns drawn. They were taken back but they were ready as well. "What the fuck is going on here?" Dennis yelled as he pointed his gun at me.

Gemini Betrayal

"What!! You didn't think we was gonna find out that you and your crew shot at us today?" Antonia said.

"Man fuck y'all and that bitch Tasha. That bitch robbed my brother and thought shit was sweet. We got to her too late but we still had to get her ass back so we did what we had to do."

"What you say, Nigga?" I said, through clenched teeth and cocking my gun.

Dennis just stood there with a smirk on his face trying to intimidate Tony. Just then Sienna and Leana came from the bathroom with their guns drawn as well.

They pressed their guns to the back of the twins' heads along with their friends. They collected the guns and put them in their bags. They went across the room to where their crew was, never losing eye contact.

"Any last words before you bitches die?" Tia said, cocking her gun. Twan and Cam cocked theirs too.

"Fuck you" Drew said.

Twan just laughed. "No, Nigga. Fuck you" he said, and opened fire. The whole gang shot up their enemies in the basement. No one stopped until they heard their guns clicking and begging for more ammo. Only then did they all run from the basement and to the vehicles. When their parents got home, they would be welcomed by the pungent smell of their good for nothing ass sons.

$$*****$$

"Where have you been all day?" Destiny said, as soon as Tony walked into the house.

"Come on, Destiny, man. I don't feel like this shit tonight"

"Feel like what? I wanna know where the fuck you been and I wanna know now"

"Can you just leave it alone, please?" he asked.

She looked him over quietly. Nope. She wasn't letting it ride. "You was with that bitch Tasha wasn't you?"

"What?"

"You fucking heard me"

"Man you tripping. You don't even know what you're talking about"

She ran behind him as he headed towards the bedroom punching him in the back and yelling. "You are such a fucking liar. I hate you. You're a piece of shit, Antonio Hall. I don't know why I keep coming back to you. You want that bitch? Go be with that bitch then"

Antonio had had enough. He swiftly turned on his heels and grabbed Destiny by her throat and slammed her against the wall in the hallway. He got so close to her face that their noses were touching. "Chill the fuck out" he said. "If you must know, yeah I was with Tasha. I went to bury her today"

"What?" she said, through tears.

"Now, leave me the fuck alone" he said, letting her go.

"Baby, I'm so sorry. Is there anything I can do?" she asked sincerely, as she gasped for air.

"Yeah, there is. Leave your keys to my house and my car and get the fuck out. And never come back"

"What? I wont leave"

"Either leave or I will have my sister come remove you."

"Well, you better do that because I'm not going no motherfucking where."

"Suit yourself" Antonio called his sister and she informed him she was on her way with Sienna and Leana. He hung up the phone and went to grab a beer and sit on the sofa.

Ten minutes later, Destiny was still there and the squad had arrived. They banged on the door and as soon as Antonio opened the door, they bum rushed Destiny. Tia went after her first and they threw blows at one another. Sienna jumped in the mix and then Leana. Antonio just sat there looking at them jump Destiny.

"Don't beat her up too bad, Sis. I did love her"

"Fuck that, hoe" she yelled, stomping on Destiny's head. After torturing her for all of ten minutes, they kicked and dragged her from the house across the lawn to the sidewalk. Tia gave her big brother a hug and told him she would hit him up tomorrow.

They walked past Destiny's limp body on the sidewalk. Tia spat on her and told her to stay away from her brother.

Destiny laid there until they drove off. She got up and took that walk of shame three blocks to her house. She vowed that she would get revenge on all they asses. She just had to wait for the right opportunity to take them out.

$$*****$$

A few days had gone by and the streets were quiet. Dennis and Drew's parents came home to the blood bath in their basement and went ballistic. They had SWAT, DEA, FBI, and DCPD all over their house looking for clues. Luckily for us, we never left any evidence.

Gemini Betrayal

I heard a knock at my door. I decided not to answer it. Whoever it was would've known to call before they came. I was still laying in my bed when I heard my door come crashing in and several footsteps coming up the stairs. I wasn't sure if it was somebody coming to rob me or not. I'm glad I never left any drugs, money or guns laying around my house in the open. Maybe it was the police. Shit. They would try their best to fry my ass.

"What the fuck is going on?" I yelled at them. Police officers filled my bedroom. They had their guns drawn as they forced me to my knees. They cuffed me and the lieutenant came into my room and got in my face.

"We know you had something to do with the shit that went down at the Johnson's house"

"Man, I don't know what the fuck you're talking about" I said, struggling to loosen the cuffs on my wrists.

"Bullshit, Antonio. I know you and your gang of misfits killed those boys and I'm gonna prove it"

"Fuck you Gaines"

The last thing I saw before I blacked out was Gaines' closed fist coming towards my face.

✳✳✳✳✳

I'm unsure of how long I was knocked out for but when I woke up, I was in one of the few interrogation rooms at fifth district police station. My vision was blurry and the bright lights were burning my fucking eyes. I couldn't even stretch my arms how I wanted because one hand was cuffed to the table.

It took me a moment to adjust my eyes to the light in the room but when they did, I saw Gaines sitting across from me with his partner.

"Morning Sunshine" he said to me and they both started giggling like something was funny. I just stared back at them with a mean mug on my face.

"You hear the man talking to you, Boy?" Gaines' partner Deputy Wilson replied.

"Boy? I got your fucking 'boy' you punk ass hick" I yelled across the table.

"What did you say to me?"

"I ain't stutter motherfucker. You heard what the fuck I said, cracker"

He came to my side of the table and hit me with a left hook. I stood up and swung back at Wilson with my free hand. I landed a right hook to his face. Then here come Gaines' ass. He held my arm behind my back while Wilson repeatedly hit me in the face and in the midsection. After a few minutes, they let me drop back down into the seat.

"Now that we got you under control, how about you tell us what you know"

"I don't know shit" I said, spitting blood from my mouth onto the floor. I leaned back in my chair and started laughing.

"What the fuck is so funny, Hall?" Gaines yelled at me.

"You two motherfuckers are what's funny, Gaines."

"That's Lieutenant Gaines to you motherfucker"

Gemini Betrayal

"Whatever, man. Look, can I leave? You have nothing to charge me with."

"Oh yeah, smart ass? How about assaulting an officer?"

"Petty ass charge. I'll be out in six months at the most" I said, cockily.

He looked at me with fiery ass. "What would you say if I told you your sister already sold you out. She already told us you were the one that killed those Johnson boys. Now what you gotta say?"

"Do I need to call my lawyer? I already told you I didn't have nothing to do with it. So can I go?"

"I fucking hate you you son of a bitch. One of these days I'm gonna catch your ass and you'll be buried under my fucking jail. Release him, Wilson" Gaines said, as he stormed out the interrogation room.

All I could do was laugh as I was set free and headed out the room.

"We're gonna bring down you, your sister and your entire crew one of these days. Just watch" Wilson warned me.

I turned and looked back at him. "Not a chance you fat fuck. Me and my crew ain't messy. But good luck with that" I winked at him and left. I collected my things from the desk and headed out the precinct. The first person I called was my sister.

Gemini Betrayal

Chapter Ten

I had called Tia's ass so many fucking times in the past hour. She hadn't answered me not one time. *What the fuck is she doing?* I thought to myself. I drove by her house and her car was there. I shook my head as I parked behind her charger and went up to the door. Something didn't seem right when I hit the porch. The door looked as though it had been kicked in.

I ran back to my car and grabbed my gun. I pushed the door the rest of the way open and eased inside. I walked around the downstairs level and saw all the damage. Her apartment had been ransacked. I wonder if it was the feds. Maybe a hit? I wasn't sure. I had to find my sister. I crept up the stairs towards the bedrooms and it looked worse than the downstairs. The cops had definitely been here.

I walked into her room and I heard somebody rummaging in the closet. I stopped walking because I didn't want them to hear me. Whoever it was was surely looking for something. I cocked my gun and aimed right at the person. Seconds later, they emerged from the closet and I fired. *Pow!*

"Yo, man, what the fuck" my sister said.

"Tia, what the fuck are you doing? And why the fuck you haven't been answering your damn phone?"

"Chill, dad" she said with a chuckle. "Remember I am an adult now and this is my house last time I checked" she said, sarcastically. She was carrying two big duffel bags out of her closet. "I was in here cleaning out my safe and I left my phone in the truck. I gotta find a new stash spot"

"What the hell you mean chill? I almost blew your fucking head off"

"But you didn't. Besides I would've killed your black ass"

"How? You ain't even got your gun on you"

"I always got my gun, sweetheart" she replied, pulling her gun from under her shirt.

"Anyway, the cops raided your shit didn't they?"

"Yep. You?"

"Yeah, this morning. That shit was crazy. Gaines got me good" I told her, showing her my slightly swollen eye.

"His ass got me too, bro" she said, pulling her shirt up and showing her back where she was hit with the night stick.

I shook my head. My sister looked pissed the fuck off. I couldn't blame her because I was too. "So where you gonna stash your stash?"

"Not sure. I was thinking at Cam's place. I'm gonna crash there until I find a new spot. I'm gonna put this house up for sale after the people come repair the doors and stuff"

"Cool, cool. I'm gonna just go ahead and straighten up my crib since I know you're okay"

"I'm always gonna be okay" my sister said.

I smiled at her and headed out the room. I turned back around and told my sister I loved her. She told me the same and I left. I was glad she was okay. Her stubborn ass would have killed me as she had me worried like that. Oh well.

I lit a cigarette and headed home. I got to my house and saw my house was fucked up just like my sister's. I wondered if anybody else got hit this morning. I sent a mass text to everybody and told them we were gonna have a meeting tomorrow at my sister spot. I waited for replies as I cleaned my house.

It took me two hours to get my house straight and back in order. I went and checked my secret spots where I kept my money and drugs. They were untouched so I was good. Those pigs still ain't have shit on me. I checked the time and it was going on 6:30 p.m. I decided I would kill some time and go to the grocery store and the liquor store.

I drove down the parkway bumping Kevin Gates as I headed to the grocery store. I pulled in the shopping center and saw all the cars. I knew I was gonna be there longer than I wanted to be. I just sucked it up and grabbed a cart and headed inside.

I strolled through the aisles picking up the necessary and unnecessary shit. I walked into the canned goods aisle and scanned the shelves.

You know how you can feel somebody staring a damn hole in your fucking head? I felt like this right now. I didn't wanna make it obvious but I did wanna make it known. I quickly turned my head to the left and saw a woman. She turned her head away as soon as I turned mine. I didn't think nothing of it. She walked off and I went back to what I was doing.

Moments later, I went to another aisle and there she was again. What the fuck is this about? I brushed it off thinking I was just being paranoid. I was skimming through cereal boxes and noticed her heading towards me out the corner of my eye. Of course, I didn't let on that I knew.

"Excuse me" she said, easing in between me and the cereal. She stood on her tippy toes and grabbed a box off the top shelf. I looked her over and was impressed. She had a nice plump ass in some

Gemini Betrayal

too damn tight jeggings, a pair of adidas, and a belly shirt that showed off a heart tattoo and a belly ring.

"I didn't catch your name" I said, when she started to walk away.

She turned back around. "Excuse me?"

"I said I didn't catch your name" I repeated, walking a little towards her.

"That's because I didn't throw it" she said, with a smirk.

"Oh!! you're feisty. I love my women feisty."

"Your women? Oh!! I'm your woman now?"

"Well, I mean, you can be" I said, smiling. She laughed a little and smiled back.

"I don't date guys whose name I don't know"

"It's Antonio. And you are?"

"Tameka. But my friends call me Meka"

"So can I be your friend?"

"That all depends. Are you single?"

"I surely am"

"Well sure then"

"Where's your phone?" I asked.

She handed me her iPhone 8 plus and I put my number in it. I dialed my number and saved my name in her phone.

"Glad you have an iPhone, miss" I said.

"And why is that?"

"So you can FaceTime daddy when you get home"

"Daddy, huh?"

"You damn right. Make sure you call me tonight"

"If I don't?"

"If you don't, I'm gonna blow your phone up until you answer"

She laughed and promised she would call me later. We both walked away barely keeping our eyes off one another. I ran through the rest of the grocery store then made my way to the line. The cashier rang up all my stuff and I was surprised I had gotten so much. That shit came up to a little over $200!

"You forgot my stuff, boo"

I turned and saw Meka. I smiled. "Ring her shit up too bro" I said to the cashier. After he finished ringing up all of her items, I pulled out my wad of cash and paid the cashier. I saw her eyes damn near pop outta her fucking head. I chuckled inside. We loaded our carts with the bags and headed to the parking lot.

I put my groceries in the car then I helped her put hers in her car. I opened her car door for her and she kissed me on the cheek. I instantly got a bulge in my pants. She saw it and smiled. She sat down in her car and pulled me closer to her. She kissed my dick through my pants and I was stuck. I stood there for a few minutes as I watched her drive away. I got in my car and sped home. I had to hurry and get home and bust this damn nut!

✳✳✳✳✳

Gemini Betrayal

I got my nut off and I was feeling good. I was just chilling now, watching the highlights on ESPN. I was checking the messages on my phone and saw that everybody had confirmed for the meeting tomorrow. I sat my phone down and continued to watch tv. Not too long after I finished the highlights, my cell phone rang and I picked it up. It was a FaceTime call. Once I accepted it, Meka's pretty face blessed my screen.

"What's up, beautiful?" I said to her licking my lips.

"Oh, nothing much. I'm just getting out the shower" she said, moving the phone back so I can see she had on nothing but a purple towel. My eyes bucked and my penis shot up through my jeans. I licked my lips as I looked back at her.

"Oh I see. Maybe I can come help you lotion up that beautiful chocolate skin. What you say?"

"I say no"

"No?"

"Yeah, no. I would rather you just enjoy the show"

"What show?"

I heard an R. Kelly song turn on in the background and she sat her phone down. I watched as she danced out of her towel and stretch her body showing off her curves, breasts, and ass. She looked great. I sat there just lusting at the site of her as she grabbed a bottle of baby oil and massaged it into her skin.

She looked back at me with seductive eyes. "Keep watching"

"I am"

She got off camera for a second and came back carrying a box. She positioned herself on her bed and opened the box. She pulled out a big black dildo and started sucking it. My mouth dropped open as she started slobbing and spitting all over it. I lost it when she started deep throating her toy.

"Goddamn, girl. You got skills" I said, rubbing my dick.

"I'm just practicing. I haven't sucked a real one in such a long time" she said, starting to lick the tip and exposing her pierced tongue.

"Well, maybe I can be your practice dummy. You know if, um, you you need me to. I don't mind" I said, sounding like a babbling idiot. She laughed and ended the call. *What the fuck?* Before I had a chance to call her back, a text came through:

Meka: 16745 Old Terrace Lane Bowie, Md be here ASAP I am super horny.

I jumped up and got my shit and hurried to her house. Once I arrived, I noticed her car and knew I was in the right place. I parked in the driveway and headed to the front door. I rung the bell and she opened the door.

She stood there wearing nothing but some red high heels. I walked inside and closed the door, following closely behind her. She led me to a room at the end of the upstairs hall. I assumed it was her bedroom but boy was I wrong. She opened the door to a room that had nothing but a la-z-boy recliner, a stripper pole, a pool table, a big flat screen and wireless speakers on the wall. She grabbed me by the hand and pulled me into the room and locked the door. She sat me down in the chair and turned the music on.

I watched as she gyrated and climbed up and down the pole. She danced on my lap and woke up my dick again. She unzipped my pants and pulled my dick through the hole in my pants. She licked the tip until it stood at attention then went to work; just like she did her toy.

Gemini Betrayal

"Oh shit" I said, watching her go up and down on my dick. I was so caught up in the sound of the music and her slurping that I didn't hear the footsteps in the hall.

It sounded like a damn stampede in the hall and they were quickly making their way towards us. Suddenly, the door came crashing in and the lights came on. She pulled her head up from my lap and terror graced her face.

"What the fuck is going on in here, Meka?" a big Godzilla looking motherfucker yelled at her.

"Nothing, Baby. Nothing at all. I was just playing around" she said, standing up.

"Playing around? Bitch you got me fucked up" he said, charging towards her. He grabbed a fistful of her hair and slammed her face into the wall repeatedly. I zipped up my fly and jumped up. "What you think you doing, player?" he asked me as he dropped her to the floor.

I looked down at her helplessly and saw her face was swollen and covered in blood.

"Aye look, fam, I ain't got shit to do with this" I said, standing my ground.

"Oh well!! that's where you're wrong, my nigga" he said, stepping closer to me but I stood right there like he was the same size as me.

"I don't know what the fuck going on but like I said, I ain't got shit to do with this. If this your bitch, then you need to put a leash on that hoe"

Before I knew it, I was on the floor. This bitch ass nigga really fucking hit me! I was about to get up when three more niggas came in and jumped on me. I was getting punched and kicked in the head, the ribs, my face, my back; everywhere.

I'm not sure how long they were kicking my ass because I was going in and out of consciousness. I heard yelling in the distance and footsteps on the stairs. I was being carried down the stairs by the three niggas and thrown outside into the yard. I got up spitting blood out as I staggered towards my car.

I got in and started the car up. I didn't even know where the hell I was going but I just knew I had to get away from here. I drove a couple miles down the road still in and out of consciousness. I was struggling to keep my eyes on the road and head to my sister house at least. Before I got to her street, I had blacked out.

Chapter Eleven

I opened my eyes and my vision was blurry. I could hear sirens and yelling all around me. What was that smell? Is that smoke? What the fuck was going on? I heard glass shattering and felt someone pulling on my clothes. But why? They were tugging and the seat belt was getting tighter with each pull. Then it fell from my body and I could tell I was being pulled out of my car.

The sound of sirens became louder and voices became more audible.

"What the fuck happened to my brother?" I heard my sister yelling.

"Ma'am, I'm gonna need for you to get back please" I heard a man say.

"Fuck that! Where are you taking him?" I heard another man say. It sounded like Cam.

"He's going to Southern Maryland. You can meet us there" he replied. I heard doors slam and that was that. I felt something get put on my face and arm simultaneously. I guess I was in an ambulance.

I felt speed bumps and potholes under me and that shit made my back hurt. Twenty minutes later, the ambulance came to a halt and I was rushed inside. They took me through the ER entrance and before I knew it, I was gone again. The number 23 was the last thing I saw before blacking out.

*****

I woke up not realizing I was still in the hospital until I heard the steady beeping of the monitors. I adjusted my eyes to my surroundings and I saw flowers on the table by the window in my room. I wanted to get up to see who they were from but I couldn't. My body was so stiff and felt heavy.

I was about to buzz the nurse to bring me some water but the door to my room flew open and in comes my crew. Loud and obnoxious as ever.

"What's up, dead man" my sister said laughing. She dapped me up and it hurt a little because my arm had a cast on it.

"Dead man? Sis, you see I'm still here" I said, laughing.

"You're not dead yet, my nigga. You drove your fucking car into my damn truck bro. My shit all fucked up man"

"Sorry, Tia"

"You will be 'cause I'm suing your black ass for destruction of property and pain and suffering" she said. We all burst out in laughter. "But naw, for real Tony, I'm glad you're still here. What the hell happened?"

"This bitch I met yesterday invited me over. Her man came home and his boys jumped me and he fucked the girl up."

"So who is this bitch?" Leana asked.

"And who are these niggas 'cause a bitch ready Boss" Sienna chimed in.

I smiled at them because these two were always ready to fuck some shit up. Antonia was good at picking them for our team.

Gemini Betrayal

"The address in my phone y'all" I said, pointing over by the flowers where my stuff was. My sister walked over and pulled it out of my bag.

"Who sent these flowers, Antonio?"

"Didn't one of y'all?"

"Nigga please. Me in a flower shop?" she said, sarcastically. "Cam, did you send them?"

He, too, shook his head no. So did Twan, Sienna, Leana, and Rocko. My sister went to retrieve the card and read it aloud:

"I hope you enjoy the flowers because I'm gonna make sure these be put on your grave soon"

What the fuck? Who the fuck sent that bullshit?

"On the real, Tony, where the fuck is that address? It's probably that bitch ass nigga that sent these" my sister said. She unlocked my phone once I gave her the password. She found the texts from Meka and found the address. She quickly put everybody in a group text and sent it. Everybody phones went off simultaneously.

She walked over to me and looked me in the eyes. She kissed me on my forehead and told me with no emotion, "We got this" She turned and walked out the room and left everybody else.

They all stared at me and one another. I called Cam and Sienna over to me and told them to make sure they kept an eye on my sister until I got out the hospital. They agreed that they would and left. I was left alone. Just me and my thoughts.

I was silently wondering to myself who in the world sent those flowers. It could have been Meka. But I don't know. Nobody knew I was here; unless they were watching me. This shit was madness. I couldn't just lay my black ass in this hospital. Whoever sent those flowers was probably coming back for me.

Gemini Betrayal

I pulled the iv from my arm and disconnected everything else. My entire body was sore as hell. My arm had this cast which means it was either broken or fractured. I didn't really give a flying fuck right now. I was just worried about getting the hell outta this damn hospital.

As I was making my way over to my clothes, the nurse came in. "Uh, uh, uh, Mr. Hall. You need to get back in bed" she said, walking over to me.

"Naw, I'm good. I feel great. I'm just gonna check myself out and head home"

"I'm afraid that's not possible. You suffered a minor concussion and a fractured arm and bruises. They want to keep you overnight for observation"

"Look lady, I have to get out of here"

"I don't think so"

I reached into my bag and pulled a wad of cash from my pants and handed it to her. "Please" She hesitated before taking the money from my hands. She closed the door to my room and helped me get dressed. I thanked her and slipped out, moments after she left.

I refused to sit here like a sitting duck and wait to die. They had me fucked up.

***** *****

I caught an Uber from the hospital all the way to my house. That ride was long as hell but at least my driver was cute. She talked a hole in my head and had me laughing. Really took my mind off the pain and stuff. I got her number as we pulled up at my house and told her I would be calling her.

I walked into my house and sat down on the couch. I couldn't even make it up the stairs to my bedroom. My entire body was aching. I texted my sister and told her I needed her to pick up my meds from the pharmacy and she texted back with an "okay"

I sat for a few moments wondering how the fuck I was gonna get payback myself. My squad said they were gonna handle it but I wanted a piece of the asses myself. I texted her back:

Me: aye yo Tia keep dat nigga alive. bring him 2 me

Tia: will do bro

I struggled to get up and head to the kitchen. I remembered I had some oxy in the kitchen drawer that I took from this chick I used to fuck around with. Once I finally reached the kitchen, which seemed like forever, I pulled the pill bottle from the drawer. I opened it up and took three pills with no water. I sat at the table until I regained some strength. And wouldn't you know it, the goddamn doorbell rang! I don't know who it could have been. My sister had a key so it couldn't be her.

I limped to the front door. Whoever it was continuously rung the damn bell and it was pissing me the fuck off. I grabbed my gun for safety and kept going. As soon as I was inches from the door, the ringing stopped. It was sunny out so I could still see somebody standing there.

"Who is it?" I said as I looked through the peephole.

"It's me," a female voice said. It was Destiny. *What the fuck did this bitch want?*

I opened the door and stood in the doorway. "What the fuck you want, Destiny?"

"Oh my God. What happened to you, Tony?" she asked, sounding concerned.

"I was in a car accident. Now what do you want?" I asked again, leaning against the door frame with my busted arm. That shit hurt like fuck so it wasn't too long before I stood back up.

"I just want to talk. Can I come in?" she asked, trying to get past me.

"Naw, you good right where you are. I don't like trash in my house."

"Trash? How could you say that to me Antonio? I loved you. I still do"

"You don't love shit, bitch"

"I do fucking love you. I want you back"

"And why the hell would I take you back? You caused a scene at my house, my sister and them had to fuck you up and you disrespected my fri-"

"Fuck that bitch Tasha, Antonio. That bitch wasn't your friend. You was fucking that hoe behind my back. I was back home in Cali and you over here fucking her. I'm glad that bitch dead"

I started laughing at her as I watched how red she turned and her chest heaving. This shit was fucking hilarious. I looked at her teary eyes. I wasn't sure if she was crying because she was heartbroken or pissed off. Frankly, I didn't give a rat's ass. "Look, Destiny, I don't know what you came here to accomplish but I think you should go"

"I'm not going nowhere goddamnit. Not until we work this shit out"

"You really think I'm gonna take you back after this now? You gotta be outta your fucking mind"

I saw over top of Destiny's head that a red car pulled up. The windows were pitch black. She was yelling but I didn't hear shit she was

Gemini Betrayal

saying. I saw the front and back passenger windows slowly roll down and guns show. I quickly pulled Destiny inside with my right hand as the first shot rang out.

We dove onto the ground and I dropped my gun. She saw it and picked it up and started shooting back. The car screeched off and she slammed the door and came to my aid. She helped me get onto the sofa and checked to make sure I didn't get shot or anything. I just stared at her.

"What?" she asked, as she caught me looking at her.

"Nothing. Now, I remember why I fell in love with you"

She smiled and kissed me softly on my lips. Instead of retreating, I offered my lips back. We were so caught up with each other I didn't know my sister came in until she slammed the door back.

"Well, well, well. What the fuck do we have here?" she asked, looking back and forth between Destiny and me.

"We made up, Tia" I said.

"That's fucking great" she said, throwing my pills at me. She walked over to Destiny and grabbed her by her hair. "Bitch, I'm keeping my eye on you. I still don't fucking like your dirty ass"

Destiny knew not to reply because she knew my sister was trigger happy. She just nodded her head in agreement.

"Yo Tony, we still on it. I'm picking you up around midnight. Cool?"

"Cool."

"Baby, where you going at midnight?"

"Bitch, if you don't sit there and shut the fuck up. Damn. Mind your business" my sister intervened. "Peace out Bro" she said, leaving out the door. "Nosey ass bitch" I heard her mumble as she was closing the door.

I just laughed on the inside at how much my sister hated Destiny and she made sure she knew. I looked back at Destiny. "Guess it's me and you again" I said.

She smiled with joy as she kissed me again. She cut on ESPN for me and informed me she was going to make dinner. She disappeared into the kitchen and I was left alone with my thoughts.

I hope I'm not going to regret this later.

Chapter Twelve

"Alright, everybody know what to do right?" Tia asked the crew. Everybody nodded their heads in unison.

They were outside Meka's house ready to run up in there and kill everything in sight. Cam went up to the door and picked the lock. Once he heard the lock pop, he gently eased the door open and everybody else followed in tow.

It was dark and quiet in the house. Sienna turned on the laser on her gun as she scanned the living room. Once they checked all the rooms downstairs, they all headed upstairs. The upstairs was cleared too.

"Well this was a waste of time" Twan said.

"We gonna get they ass next time" Tia said.

"We might not have to wait for a next time" Cam said, as he peeped out the window by the door. Meka, her boyfriend Jason, and his brother, Marlon, were pulling up in the driveway.

The crew tiptoed and spread out downstairs so they would be unseen. They heard the door open and close. It was showtime.

As soon as Tia caught one shadow close by her when the lights flickered on, she hit the first person over the head with the butt of her gun. It just so happened to be Marlon. He dropped to the floor with a loud thud.

"Yo, what the fuck is going on?" Jason bellowed. But Sienna came up behind him and hit him across the face with her rifle. Not hard enough to knock him on his ass but he was leaking blood. Sienna backed up a few steps but kept her weapon aimed at his head. He wiped the blood from his mouth and charged towards her.

Twan clotheslined him and he hit the floor. Four guns were pointed at him. Tia looked and noticed that Meka was just standing there unmoved by what was going on.

"Bitch get over here" Tia said, using her gun to motion Meka towards her. As Meka got closer to Tia, she noticed the bruises that were horribly covered with makeup. She looked down at Jason. "So, you like putting your fucking hands on women, huh?"

"Fuck you, bitch" he said, spitting blood out at Tia. They all threw their heads back in laughter and Tia kicked him multiple times in the head.

"See, I was gonna let my brother have all the fun with you but I think I want a piece of your ass too" she replied. "Twan? You and Cam get this bitch nigga up and tie his ass to a chair" She looked back at Meka. "Her ass, too"

They followed the orders given and waited for more. Tia stepped in front of Meka.

"So, you thought shit was gonna be all sweet after your punk ass boyfriend and his boys jumped my brother?"

"Your brother? Are you talking about Antonio?"

"Duh, bitch" Tia yelled. "Damn you're dumb. Sorry, I gotta kill you baby girl because you are pretty as hell" she said, cocking her gun.

"So are you" Meka replied, looking up at Tia. Tia hesitated for a second. "Can I have one request please?"

"I guess" Tia replied.

"I have never kissed a girl. Before you kill me, do you think you can?"

She looked at her confusingly but obliged. Tia tongue kissed Meka right in front of everybody. Cam was getting pissed. Everybody in the room could tell when they looked at him.

"Thank you" Meka said. She closed her eyes and told Tia she was ready to die. Tia hesitated again before putting the gun to Meka's head. Just as she was about to pull the trigger, blood splattered all over her clothes. She looked behind Meka and saw that Cam did the job.

"Cam, what the fuck?" she yelled.

"Fuck that, Tia. Don't Cam me. We came here to do a fucking job and you in here trying to fuck a bitch"

"You need to calm the fuck down, nigga"

"No, you need to keep your fucking head in the game. Stop worrying about other shit"

"Well, maybe I need to stop worrying about your ass too, then. How about that?"

"Oh fucking well!! I'm just trynna do my job, get paid, and go the fuck home"

"Fuck you, Cam" She moved over to where Jason was. Without saying anything, she shot Jason in both knees.

"Ahhh fuck" he screamed. Blood was staining his jeans and saliva was staining his t-shirt.

Tia looked at Cam. "Clean this shit up, nigga. No fingerprints, no casings, no nothing. This shit better be motherfucking spotless. Sienna? I want you and Twan to wrap this nigga legs in plastic and duct tape his hands and mouth. Put him in the trunk of their car. I will take it from there"

"Okay" they said in agreement.

"Any questions?" Nobody responded, so she took that as a 'no.'

She headed out the door and heard Cam call her a bitch. She didn't even feed into his bullshit. She was already pissed off. He was doing nothing but adding fuel to the fire. Little did he know she wanted to snap his fucking neck like a twig.

She walked to Jason's car and put on her gloves. She opened the door and got in the driver's seat. She saw Twan and Sienna quickly carrying the body towards her. She popped the trunk so they could easily just toss him in there. Once the trunk was closed, she backed out the driveway and headed towards her brother's house.

She dialed Tony's number and he answered on the third ring.

"Yo" he said when he answered.

"Ready to ride out?"

"Yeah"

"Be there in ten"

Click.

She turned on the radio to ease her mind a little.

Meanwhile, at Antonio's house, he was being assisted by Destiny to get dressed in his all black attire.

"So, you're not gonna tell me where you're going, huh?"

"I'm going to work, Destiny" he said, sounding exasperated.

"What kind of work, Antonio?"

Gemini Betrayal

"The less you know the better" he said, checking his watch. His sister would be there soon. He grabbed his gun and headed down the stairs. Destiny was right on his heels as he headed towards the door.

"I don't like this, Tony" she said, folding her arms across her chest.

"Oh well. If you don't like it, you can leave right out that door and don't come back" he said, nicely. And just as nicely, she shut her mouth, went and sat her ass on the couch. Tony came over and kissed her forehead before leaving out the door. Good timing, too, because his sister was pulling up out front.

"Where that fool at, Sis?" he asked, once he got in the car and closed the passenger door.

"In the trunk. Where we taking him?"

Antonio thought for a second. "Take him to the beach"

"The closest beach is Ocean City"

"So, what's your fucking point?" he asked sharply.

"Calm your ass down, Bro. I know you a little fucking mad behind this shit but don't take it out on me. You better watch your fucking mouth" Tia snapped.

"You better watch your fucking mouth" I shot back. He picked up the phone and called Cam. Told him to be out Ocean City because they were gonna need some gas and a ride back down the road. He turned the radio up after finishing his call and no more words transpired between the twins.

✳✳✳✳✳

They arrived at the beach within an hour and a half. Cam was parked a block away. The plan was to torch the car and haul ass.

Tia parked the car and killed the headlights. They quickly and quietly exited the vehicle, making their way to the trunk. They both simultaneously pulled Jason out the trunk. Antonio cut the duct tape from his legs and told him not to move. Once he grabbed his aluminum bat out the trunk, they escorted Jason onto the beach.

"Move, motherfucker" Tia yelled at Jason. She was mad at both Cam and Tony right now and Jason was gonna feel her wrath. They led him to the water's edge.

"You got any last words?" Tony asked in his deep voice.

"Please, please, please don't kill me, man. I didn't mean to do that to you" Jason begged, as he turned around to face them.

"Oh really? Just like you ain't mean to shoot at me earlier?"

"What?" both Jason and Tia said at the same time.

"Yeah this nigga came by and did a drive by on my house earlier when Destiny came by"

"That wasn't me man. I swear"

"Shut the fuck up" Tia said and shot him in the shoulder.

"Fuck all that" Antonio said to his sister. Let's just get this shit over with" He put duct tape over Jason's mouth and stepped a few inches away. He gripped his bat as tight as he could and swung. It cracked Jason right in his ribs. Then his legs. Then his back. Tony couldn't stop. He was like a maniac.

Tia ran up on Jason and shot him multiple times. As they were fleeing the scene, they saw Cam finishing up pouring the gasoline all over Jason's car. Once he noticed them, he threw a match and the car instantly went up in flames. They all ran to the other vehicle and sped

Gemini Betrayal

away from the crime scene. They hit the highway quicker than they had planned. Once they were far away enough, they all erupted in laughter.

"That shit was cool" Cam said aloud.

"Yeah it was, bruh" Tony agreed.

Tia didn't say anything. She was still beefing with them. They ignored her and just kept their conversation going.

Within a couple hours, they were close to home.

Whoop. Whoop.

"Oh shit!! it's the police" Cam said to the others.

"Everybody stay calm" I said. I pulled over to the side of the road and the cop car pulled up behind me.

"Stay calm? Niggas, it's weapons in this bitch" Tia said, in a low voice through clenched teeth.

"Just shut the fuck up. Damn"

Antonio looked out the side mirror and saw that it was Lieutenant Gaines walking towards them. "Fuck. That's Gaines"

Nobody said nothing. They just shook their heads in silence.

Gaines tapped on the window with his flashlight. The window rolled down and he flashed the light inside. "Well, well, well. If it ain't my two favorite people. The Hall twins"

"If it ain't our least favorite Barney Fife looking ass cop, Gaines" Tia said.

"Watch your mouth, Antonia" he said sternly.

"Oh what you gonna do? Flash your light at me?"

"I'm warning you, Bitch"

"Oooh, like that hurts me. Your mama's a bitch if I'm a bitch"

"What can we do for you, Gaines?" Tony interjected. He was getting irritated with their back and forth.

"Well, for starters, your license and registration, asshole." Antonio reached into the glove box and retrieved his information. He handed it over to Gaines who in turn snatched it and walked back towards his squad car.

"What the fuck are we gonna do with the guns?" Cam asked, being all paranoid.

"It's a secret compartment in the floor. Put them in there. All three will fit"

Cam did as he was told and relaxed a little bit. Antonio looked over at his sister.

"Take that shirt off Tia"

"Oh damn I forgot. Here, Cam, put this in there, too"

Ten minutes later, Gaines came back to the car. "I need to check your vehicle"

"You have no reason to" Antonio said calmly.

"I do what the fuck I want. Now get the fuck out the car and get on the ground" he yelled. All three of them got out and laid flat on the ground. They heard Gaines calling for back up as he searched the car.

Moments later, two more squad cars pulled up and they all started searching. And guess what they find? The motherfucking guns and bloody t-shirt.

"I knew y'all asses were up to no good" Gaines said to them. "Stand up!" They all slowly hopped to their feet and stood there. "All three of you bastards are going down. And the others are too"

"You ain't got shit on us" Tia said, with a smirk.

"Oh yeah? How about your fingerprints on these guns?"

"And? Our guns are registered"

"Bullshit"

"True shit"

"I fucking hate you. You fucking black bitch"

"Fuck you, cracker" Tia said and spit at Gaines.

And that was all she wrote.

All the officers jumped on them and beat they ass. All you saw were fists and nightsticks and feet kicking towards the crew. They were beat on by the police for all of ten minutes before they were all cuffed, thrown in the backseat of a cop car, and courted off to jail.

✳✳✳✳✳

"So, are you gonna fucking tell me what I wanna know, Cameron?" Gaines asked, in a calm tone.

Cam looked at him. "Didn't I tell you to call me, Cam? Nobody calls me no fucking Cameron"

"I don't give a fuck what people call your punk ass. You better tell me who those guns belong to or your ass is going down"

He lit a cigarette and inhaled the smoke. He blew a cloud of smoke in Gaines' face.

Gaines didn't like that shit at all. He grabbed the back of Cam's neck and slammed his face against the steel table. His grip got tighter as he tried to get the truth out of Cam. After several minutes, he let him up.

Cam gasped for air and continued to smoke his cigarette.

"You might as well tell me Cam and let me help you"

"How the fuck can you help me?"

"I don't want your black ass. I want Antonio and his sister; the fucking ringleaders of the organization. Give them to me and the rest of you all walk. Trust me, I know all the members of y'all crew all the way down to the corner thugs. Help me and I will help you.

Cam pondered for a few minutes and took a couple puffs off his cigarette again. He looked at Gaines and said with a straight face, "Fuck you"

"I wish you hadn't done that. I thought you were smarter than that. But I guess not"

"Nope. I'm just another dumb black nigga on the block"

"Not anymore. I'm gonna see to it that you die in this jail"

Cam laughed hysterically as Gaines stormed out of the interrogation room. He was headed toward interrogation room number two where Antonio was.

"Mr. Hall? It's so glad to see you again so soon" he said, upon entering the room.

"Fuck all that cordial shit, Gaines" he said, waving his hand. "Why the fuck you got us up in here? You know we ain't do shit"

"That's where you're wrong. We found those guns in your truck so you're going down. All three of you"

　　　　　　　　　　　　　　Gemini Betrayal

"Bullshit" he replied with a straight face. "How I know you ain't plant that shit there yourself? Y'all pigs always fucking with me and my family"

"I know they're yours" he said, without responding to Antonio's accusations. "Your boy, Cam, just told us everything we wanted to know. He told me those were you and your sister's guns"

Antonio shook his head in disbelief. *Ain't no way Cam snitched. He wasn't that weak. Or was he?*

"Why you get all quiet, boy?" Gaines asked with a smirk on his face. "Family ain't as tight as you thought, huh?"

"My family is tight. Tight as virgin pussy" I said with a laugh. "Look, man, do what you gotta do. I know we ain't do shit so I'm good"

"We'll see" Gaines exited the interrogation room. He stood outside with his partner before heading to Tia's interrogation room.

"This is bullshit, Wilson. These bastards aren't gonna turn on each other."

"But they will, though" he said with a sly grin.

"What you thinking, Wilson?"

"How about we just arrest the Hall girl and Cameron?"

"What about Antonio Hall?"

"We're gonna make it seem like he turned them in. He walks for now"

"I don't know. That seems kind of risky. I want his ass so bad I can fucking taste it"

"Calm down. We gonna get his ass, too. Don't worry. Just trust me on this one"

Gaines eyed him like he wanted to be against it. He brushed it off and agreed. They both headed into the room where Tia was, wearing smiles.

"How you doing again, Antonia? Its not a pleasure to see you as usual" Gaines said, sitting across from her. Wilson stood next to her chair.

"Likewise you bastard" she spat. She looked Wilson up and down. "I see you gonna always be his bitch" she said, laughing.

"I will fuckin-," Wilson started but Gaines interrupted.

"I got this, Deputy. Is there anything you have to say" he asked calmly.

"Just when can I go the fuck home?"

He laughed and Wilson joined in. She eyed both of them suspiciously.

"What the fuck is so damn funny?" she yelled at them. They calmed their laughter before speaking again.

"Oh you're not going home, my chocolate love. They snitched on you so they could walk" Gaines said standing to his feet and adjusting his belt.

"What the fuck you talking 'bout, Gaines?" she yelled again standing up too.

"Wilson? Cuff this bitch and book her" he said, walking past Tia.

"What the motherfuck?" she said, turning and punching Gaines in the back of the head. Wilson grabbed his nightstick and hit her across the head. She fell to the floor instantly. Gaines grabbed a handful of her hair and lifted her head from the floor.

"I got your ass, bitch" he replied, then spit in her face. "I will see you in a little bit, Wilson. I gotta go finish in the other room"

"Got it, boss" he said. He handcuffed Tia and mirandized her. He threw her ass in the back of his squad car and escorted her to the women's facility. He was smiling hard as shit on the inside because he had finally gotten her ass. He was gonna remember this arrest for the rest of his damn life.

While he did that, Gaines did the same to Cam.

"Why the fuck I'm not being released?" he asked angrily.

"Because your boy and your girlfriend turned you in to save their own asses"

"What the fuck?"

"Yep. I told you not to trust they ass. See how they did you? Now you shit outta luck" Gaines replied as he took Cam through booking. After he got him through the booking process, he led him to his cell and told him to sleep tight.

"Fuck you, nigga" Cam said to him.

"You better worry about who gonna try to fuck you" Gaines said, locking the cell and retreating back down the hall. Cam could hear his annoying laugh echo throughout the cell block.

"I'm gonna kill that bitch ass nigga" he mumbled to hisself. He got on the bunk and laid down. Crazy thoughts ran through his mind about what Gaines had said.

Ain't no fucking way they snitched on me. I know Antonia wasn't that fucking pissed at me that she would turn me over to the feds. What if Gaines was lying though? If he were, then I wouldn't be in here, right? And Antonio? Really? I couldn't fucking believe that shit. He was like my fucking brother. Hmm. Brother my ass. Guess friends that call you family is just as shady as the motherfuckers that really are your family. Fuck it.

He pushed his thoughts out of his head and closed his eyes for the night.

✶✶✶✶✶

Over at the women's facility, Tia was booked and placed in one of the rowdiest cell blocks in the prison. She entered the block and all the females were yelling and reaching between the bars trying to grab her.

"Y'all bitches better stop fucking playing with me" she snapped.

"Fuck you, bitch. I know who the fuck you are" one female yelled.

The CO escorted Tia to her cell and pushed her inside it. "Bitch, don't shove me" she said.

"Don't give me shit, Hall" she said as she closed her cell door. "Put your fucking hands through here" She unlocked the cuffs and walked away. "Fucking bitch" she mumbled.

"Your fucking mother is a bitch, Jenkins" Tia yelled back. She turned and saw that she wasn't alone in her cell. Her cellmate jumped down and stepped up in her face.

"You real cute, Baby" she said, touching Tia's hair.

"Bitch, don't put your fucking hands on me" she said, smacking her hand away.

"Oohh you feisty. I like that. My name Redz" she said. "What's your name, Baby?" she asked stroking the side of Tia's face.

"I told you not to fucking touch me, bitch" Tia said, through clenched teeth before knocking her hand away again. This time she fucking lost it.

She hit Redz in the throat with a left hook. She grabbed her neck just like Tia knew she would. She seized the opportunity and threw blow after blow to her midsection. Redz dropped to the floor holding her stomach. Tia kicked her in the face, back, and in her stomach area. Once Redz moved her arms, she continued to kick her. Eventually, she got worn out.

She hopped up on the top bunk and looked down at Redz on the floor. "Hope you remember this the next time you try that shit with me or anybody else. Fucking stupid bitch" Tia turned on her side and closed her eyes.

Redz was still on the floor. She looked up and saw no motion from Antonia. She knew it was safe to get up from the floor. She wiped the blood from her busted nose and lip with the sleeve of her jumpsuit.

"I can't believe you let that new bitch do that to you" said Mecca. She watched the entire ordeal with her lover and cellmate Brandy.

"I know, right? How could you do that, Redz?" Brandy asked.

"Look, fuck both of y'all. This shit ain't over" she said, more to herself than them. She walked over to the bottom bunk and laid her sore body down. She closed her eyes and dreamt about her retaliation.

✳✳✳✳✳

Antonio was so pissed off that he couldn't get his car back until later that morning. They took his truck to the impound lot. So, once again, he had to catch an Uber home. This time he had a dude.

He rode an entire thirty minutes in dude's car that smelled like grade A loud, cigarettes, and cheap whores. Then dude had the nerve to have the radio turned up to like twenty-five bumping Kevin Gates. Antonio didn't mind but like damn. It was like six in the motherfucking morning!

He tried multiple times calling his sister and Cam. No answer from neither. *What the fuck they doing? he thought. Oh yeah. They probably made up and doing each other.* He laughed to himself just thinking about it.

He checked his missed call list. Thirty missed calls and seventeen voicemails and they were all from Destiny. "This bitch is psycho" he said, aloud to himself. He didn't even bother to call back. He sat back and tried to enjoy the rest of his ride.

"Aight bruh, we here" the driver said as he pulled up to Tony's house.

"Thanks man" he said.

"No problem. Aye" he said stopping Antonio.

"What?"

"You smoke loud? I got that good shit" he said, holding up a clear box full of weed bags.

"Yeah. I can try it out. How much?"

"First one on the house," he replied, passing him a bag and his business card.

"Good looking" Antonio said. He gave him a pound and got out. Walking towards the front door, he rated his driver. Instead of giving him a one star like he anticipated on doing, he thought he'd be

Gemini Betrayal

generous. So he gave him three stars. He put his phone back in his pocket and headed in the house.

The downstairs of the house was pitch black. He put his key on the table by the door and headed upstairs to the room. He walked in the room and saw Destiny wide awake lying in bed. He said nothing to her because he could see anger written all over her face. He wasn't with the shits tonight. So he just took his watch and chain off and laid it on his bedside stand. He took his shoes off, put them in the shoebox on his closet shelf and grabbed a towel. He headed towards the bathroom, still not uttering a word to Destiny.

He turned on the shower water and removed his clothes. He took his cell phone out of his pocket and tossed everything in the hamper. He checked his phone to see if Tia or Cam called and they hadn't. He shrugged it off and hopped in the shower.

The steamy hot water rained down on his chiseled tatted up body. The beads of water were slowly relieving him of his stressful day. His body still ached but for some reason, the water was helping ease that pain as well.

He felt a cool breeze enter the bathroom and knew Destiny came in there. He still didn't say anything as he washed. He wondered how long she would stand there in silence. He laughed to himself, imagining how her face probably looked on the other side of the shower curtain.

After he finished washing from head to toe, he turned off the shower and pulled back the curtain. Just like he figured, Destiny was standing there. Hands folded across her chest, mouth poked out and leg shaking. *"I don't understand how women can be angry and sexy as hell doing it all at once"* he thought.

"What is it, Destiny?" I asked, exasperated.

"So you just gonna come home like ain't shit happen. I know you seen me blowing your fucking phone up, nigga" she said, rolling her eyes at me.

"Yeah I saw" I said, making my way past her to the sink. I got my toothbrush and began brushing my teeth.

"So you didn't think to pick up or call me back?"

I didn't respond. I just looked at her in the mirror standing behind me.

"Uh, hello? You can't hear now?" she asked, yelling a little.

Still no response. I continued to brush my teeth. I rinsed my toothbrush off then gargled some mouthwash. I could see her getting more and more frustrated by the minute. I didn't care. I was busy at the moment. So, if she wanted a response she would have to wait. When I finished, I brushed past her again leaving out the bathroom. She was right on my heels as I entered the room.

"So you're not gonna answer me, Antonio?"

"If you must know, I got arrested a few hours ago. If you didn't nag so motherfucking much and just ask, you would've known. You always being o.c. with shit, man"

"Fuck all that. When you got released, why didn't you call back? I know you saw me calling then because your phone was ringing and you kept sending me to voicemail"

"I didn't find a need to since I was already coming home to your bullshit anyway" I said, throwing the towel over the closet door.

Destiny didn't even respond back. She just examined the chocolate specimen of a man standing before her. His back was still to her as she grabbed the baby oil from the nightstand. She walked over and grabbed him by the hand. She led him over to the bed and he laid on his stomach.

113   Gemini Betrayal

She sat on his back and rubbed oil all over his shoulders and back, making her way down his legs and feet as well. He turned over on his back when she instructed him to. She sat on top of him and continued to rub the baby oil all over his chest and stomach.

When she reached his penis, she massaged the oil all over it to make it erect.

"Oh, baby" I moaned, "put it in your mouth. Show daddy how much you missed him"

"Okay, daddy" she replied.

She flicked her tongue across the tip of his dick. She could feel him shifting which means he was getting more turned on. She rolled her tongue all over his manhood. Up the shaft. Down the shaft. All around; just how he liked it. She took him into her mouth inch by inch until it was all in her throat. She sucked and deep throated that joint like her life depended on it.

Antonio let her go a little longer before telling her to sit on his face. "Bring me my pussy" I said, seductively. She did as she was told and sat her pussy right on my lips. I flicked my tongue back and forth across her pussy and sucked on her clit. It didn't take her long to cum and have her juices cover my lips and goatee.

She moved from my face and laid down on her back. I got on top and was about to enter her before she stopped me.

"What's wrong now, Babe?" I asked.

"Nothing. Don't you wanna put a condom on?"

"Fuck that condom, Boo. I'm hitting that shit raw dog"

"I'm not on the pill or anything anymore"

"Oh fucking well" I said. "Looks like you getting pregnant tonight"

"I love you, Antonio" she said, a little above a whisper. I looked down at her.

"I love you too, Destiny" I said. I kissed her as I entered her dripping wet paradise. We made love until around nine.

We passed out covered in one another's sweat.

Chapter Thirteen

Days went on and Antonio was starting to get worried. He hadn't heard anything from Cam or Tia. Hell, he ain't heard from nobody for that matter. Not Sienna, Leana, Twan, Reggie, or Rocky. Everybody was fucking M.I.A.

He tried calling his sister phone again. This time it was going straight to voicemail. The same with Cam's cell. *"Did them motherfuckers block me? If they did, that's some straight bitch shit; especially on Cam's part"* he thought to himself. He blocked his number and dialed their numbers again. The same thing happened so that wasn't it.

He tried calling the rest of the crew. Unlike Tia and Cam, everybody else's phones rang. They just didn't answer them. Motherfuckers!! *"What the fuck was going on with everybody?"* He called Destiny in the room and asked to use her phone. Nobody knew her number so they would probably answer it, thinking it was a customer.

"Yo" Twan said, when he picked up the phone.

"What the fuck you mean 'yo'? Why the fuck ya'll ain't been answering my motherfucking phone calls, motherfucker?" I yelled into the phone.

"Tony?" he asked, in a surprising tone. "What's up, fam?"

"Don't give me that fam bullshit, Twan. What the fuck is up with y'all? We got beef or something? Tell me something" I rambled on. The phone got quiet. "Hello?"

"I'm still here"

"Then let it be known, nigga. You speak when you're fucking spoken to"

"I can't talk right now Antonio. Meet me at my house in an hour" Twan said, before abruptly hanging up the phone.

Antonio was pissed! He sent out a mass group text to all the crew members and the drug runners for an emergency meeting at Twan house in an hour. Nobody responded back.

"Is everything okay, baby?" Destiny asked, rubbing my back.

"I don't know, boo" I said, looking stressed.

"Is there anything I can do to help?"

"Naw, Destiny. Here" I said, handing her a stack of one hundred dollar bills wrapped in rubber bands. "Go out and enjoy yourself today. Don't stress about me and my problems, Babe"

"You sure?" she asked for reassurance.

"Yeah. Go ahead. I will see you later on tonight"

"Okay, daddy" she replied. She stood in front of him with her hand out.

"What?"

"I know you don't expect me to catch Ubers all damn day, nigga" she said, smiling.

"Oh yeah. Here you go" he said as he pulled her car key from his drawer. She kissed him deeply before grabbing her purse and phone and heading out the door to the mall.

Antonio got his guns and made sure they were loaded and ready for whatever may go down at the meeting. He didn't know why everybody was avoiding him like he did something. But best believe he was gonna find out today. No matter what.

✳✳✳✳✳

He pulled up outside Twan's house exactly an hour later. He didn't see any cars parked out front other than Twan's. He shook his head in dismay. He knocked on the door and it opened. Instead of Twan opening the door, it was some big booty girl.

"Hey I'm Dana. You must be Tony. The big man on campus" she said, looking me up and down, from head to toe.

"Yeah" I said, as I looked her over as well. She wasn't wearing nothing but a wife beater and some little tight ass hugging shorts. Her ass was practically falling out the motherfucking shorts! They looked like boy shorts more than anything.

She closed the front door and led me to the kitchen. "Twan will be down in a minute" she said. "Can I get you something to drink?"

"Naw, shorty. I'm good"

"Suit yourself" She opened the fridge and bent all the way over, scanning shelves until she was level to the bottom shelf. I never took my eyes off that ass. Didn't even blink. She grabbed a bottle of water and closed the fridge.

She opened the bottle and took it straight to the head. In no time at all, she had gulped down the entire bottle. I sat there with my jaw dropped. That's when Twan caught me when he came in the kitchen.

"What the hell going on in here?" he asked as he walked over to Dana. "What you doing, Dana?"

Gemini Betrayal

"Oh, nothing, baby. I was just showing your friend my skills" she replied.

"Well, you can show me your skills in a little bit. Right now get your ass upstairs and get naked for me"

"Okay, baby" she said. He slapped her ass then she did what she was told. She made eye contact with Tony again as she sexily licked her lips. She ran her hand across his jeans and then left out the kitchen.

"That damn girl is too damn much" Twan said, shaking his head and smiling from ear to ear.

"Where you get her from?"

"I met her at this restaurant I went to"

"Cool. Now down to business" he said with all seriousness. "What the fuck is up with everybody?"

"Well" Twan started before taking a deep breath. "Word on the street is that Tia and Cam got locked up the other night when y'all came back from doing that thing"

"What the hell? I thought they got released too?"

"Nope"

"But that still don't explain everybody else"

"Also, on the street, people saying you the reason they locked up"

"What the fuck?" Antonio yelled, standing to his feet. He walked over and got in Twan face. "Are you calling me a snitch, nigga?"

"I ain't calling you a goddamn thing Tony. That's what the streets saying"

"Man that's bullshit. I ain't no motherfucking snitch"

"I know you ain't, bruh; I know" Twan said. Antonio looked at Twan's facial expression as he said that.

"I don't think you believe me Twan"

"What? Naw, man, I do. I do" he said, stumbling over words. "You my dog"

"Nice to know" I said, still looking at him. Twan seemed too fidgety for me. Maybe I was just being paranoid. "Well, I'm out"

"Where you headed to?"

"I guess I'm about to go visit my sister and Cam to see what their deal is"

"Cool. What about the rest of the crew?"

"Tell they ass they better pick up their product tonight at midnight. If they not there, they might as well never come back. They ass is gonna be dead to me. Send the message to everybody now" he demanded.

"I'm on it" Twan replied as his fingers tapped on the screen.

He walked Tony to the door, dapped him up and sent him on his way.

Tony got in his truck and headed up the road to the women's correctional facility. Hopefully, his sister didn't think that he would actually snitch on her and Cam. Like really? That's like burning his own ass in a sense. Whether he was in charge or not, he was going down with everybody if they ever got caught.

✶✶✶✶✶

He waited patiently for his sister to come out the back. He looked around at all the families. There were hugs and kisses being exchanged among the loved ones. Children playing with their imprisoned mom or whomever the females were they were visiting. He looked back towards the door and saw his sister coming out. They made eye contact and she did not look excited to see him.

"What's up, sis?" he said, standing to hug her. Her arms remained by her sides as he threw his arms around her. Not feeling the love back, he pulled back and sat back down.

"You got some nerve coming here, Antonio" she said in a low voice dripping with slight anger.

"Why would I not come here? I didn't even know you were here 'til this morning when Twan told me"

"Mmhmm I bet. You can tell me anything"

"He told me you think I snitched on you" I said, skipping to the subject at hand.

"Yeah and what if I do?"

"I'm telling you, Sis, it wasn't me. I would never snitch on you. You know me better than that"

She looked at him without uttering a word. This was her brother. Other than their father Big Tone, he was all she had. "I'm sorry, Tony. You're absolutely right. I know you wouldn't do that to me. I'm just tripping" she stated sincerely.

"Thank you for the apology. Don't worry I'm gonna get you out of here as soon as possible"

"Okay. How's Cam?" she asked out of the blue.

"I don't know. He's locked up too."

"What?!!!"

"Yep. At least that's what Twan told me. I'm gonna go over to the men's jail after this to see if he there"

"That's fucking crazy" she said, shaking her head. "You know what else is crazy?"

"What?"

"How did Twan know all of this shit in the first place? I'm not sure if they let Cam call anybody because they damn sure didn't let me use the phone yet. Fucking bitches" she said, looking over at Officer Jenkins.

"What you getting at, Tia?" he asked with raised eyebrows.

"Nothing but just hear me out. If I didn't contact anybody, how did he know I was locked up?"

"He said he heard on the block"

"That may be so but keep an eye on him, Tony. He can't be fully trusted. That's my honest opinion"

He sat there and thought about it. *It was kind of strange that Twan got wind of what happened and not me. But so did the other crew members. At least that's what I was told.*

They sat and talked a little while longer. They called for all the inmates to line up. Tia hugged her brother tightly and told him to be careful.

They parted ways but continued to look back at one another until Tia was no longer seen as she walked back behind the electric door.

Tony left the jail and headed to his car. He had to make a stop at the men's jail before visiting hours were over. He arrived there and went through all the security checks and everything. And guess who he bumps into while entering?

"Hey, Mr. Hall" Gaines said.

"Don't hey me" I said back.

"Don't be too mad at me. Look at the bright side, you're gonna be his bunkmate as soon as possible"

Antonio didn't even have a chance to say anything because he walked away. He sat in the waiting area for over an hour before they let him in the back. Cam was already sitting at the table when he walked in.

"What's up, bro?" he said to me when I reached his table. We grabbed each others' hand and embraced into a brotherly hug.

"How you holding up in here?" I asked him as we took a seat.

"I'm hanging in there" Cam said. Antonio noticed his face but didn't say anything. He knew if it wasn't a scuffle with another inmate, it was definitely from Gaines.

"I'm gonna get you out of here. I gotta bail Tia out, too"

"I know" he said.

"You know I love you like a brother, right, Cam?"

"Yeah I know" he replied, not knowing if he was being real or not. It didn't matter because right now, he just needed Antonio to get him out of here. "Aye, you know who I ran into in here?"

"Who?"

"Your pops"

Antonio didn't say anything about it. He just nodded his head.

"You should come see him sometimes. He mad cool yo. He reminds me of you" he said, chuckling.

"I don't know how many times I have to tell you that I don't fuck with him like that" I replied sternly. That was the end of that conversation.

We talked for thirty more minutes and parted ways. While Antonio was thinking about how fast he could get them out of jail, Cam was plotting on how he could kill him.

I left the premises of the jail thinking about how all this shit been happening lately. That's why I wanted to get out before it was too late. But I couldn't just sit around and not help out the family. There was no way I could let Tia and Cam just sit behind bars any longer than they already have.

I was so deep in thought that I drove right through a red light and almost got hit by a UPS truck. I pulled over to the side of the road to decrease my heart rate. I looked through the window and saw Christian. "*Damn!! she still look fine as hell*" I thought to myself. I beeped my horn to get her attention. I rolled the window down as she walked towards the car.

"Oh my god, Antonio" she said excitedly, as she got in the truck. She threw her arms around my neck and we hugged one another. "It's so good to see you"

"Same here" I said. "How you been?"

"I been good. And yourself?"

"Same old same old" I replied. I looked her over and I noticed her hand. "Damn, that's a big rock. You engaged?"

"Married"

"Wow. That was fast"

"Well, I was engaged when I met you. I just didn't wear my ring when I went to the gym"

"So why the fuck you didn't tell me?"

"Why the fuck didn't you ask?" she snapped back.

We were so busy going back and forth that I didn't notice that Destiny was headed right towards us.

"What the fuck?" she said, as she snatched open the passenger door and pulled Christian out by her hair. Christian didn't even think twice as she landed a blow to Destiny's right cheek. Her hair got released quickly. Destiny punched back and hit her in the temple. Christian stumbled a little but not too much. She punched Destiny in her nose and she flew back onto the sidewalk.

Nosey bystanders had gathered to see the commotion. Some people were taking pictures while others were either recording or busy trying to put the ladies on facebook live. Antonio didn't even break it up. He put his car in drive and slowly left the scene. He didn't have time for the bullshit.

Once he got home, he took his pain meds and washed them down with a shot of Hennessy. He went upstairs and laid back on the bed. His life was so out of control right now. He needed somebody to reassure him that everything was gonna be okay. He needed his mom.

He laid there thinking about his mom. He remembered how beautiful she was and how much he and Tia favored her. She always referred to them as her prince and princess. Never in a million years did he ever think she wouldn't be around for him. Let alone did he think he would lose her so tragically. At least, he got his revenge so he was a little at peace. He promised that he would visit her soon. He thought about her favorite champagne and smiled. He made a mental note to get a bottle for her and have a drink with her when he go visit.

I heard a car pull up in my driveway. *That must be Destiny.* I didn't even budge as I heard the door slam. I could hear her running up the steps coming full speed like a damn bull. She busted up in the bedroom like she was motherfucking S.W.A.T or some shit. And I still stayed the same way.

"Who the fuck was that bitch, Antonio?"

"What bitch?"

"Don't fucking play with me. You know exactly who I'm talking about. That bitch that was in your fucking car, nigga"

"Oh, Christian? She's an old friend. You don't have to worry about her"

"I don't fucking believe you"

"If you don't, then leave" I said, nonchalantly.

She pumped her breaks and didn't say anything else. In reality she had nowhere else to go and knew he would throw her onto the street without hesitation.

"Ughhhh," she yelled as she left out the bedroom. She went down the hall to the other bathroom to shower and clean herself up. She changed into a new outfit and headed back downstairs to start on dinner. Antonio didn't hear anything out of her the rest of the evening which was perfectly fine with him. He needed some peace and quiet for a change.

Later that night, they were up watching tv and laughing at re-run episodes of Martin. They heard a hard knock at the door. They both looked at each other crazily because it was late. *Who the hell was knocking on their door at eleven at night?*

Antonio grabbed two of his guns and handed one to Destiny. They slowly descended the stairs together. Destiny stood at the bottom of the steps with her gun aimed at the front door as he walked over to it. They both cocked their guns and Antonio snatched the door open.

"Whoa, whoa, whoa" Rocky and Twan said, as they ducked for cover.

"What the fuck is going on?" Twan asked.

"Our bad man" Antonio said, as he put the safety back on. He welcomed them inside and they went into the living room to have a seat. While they did that, Destiny went and got them all a beer and passed an already rolled blunt to Antonio before heading back upstairs.

"So what's goin' on?" Antonio asked. They both just looked at each other instead of responding. Twan stood up to answer.

"It's like this Tony. We know your sister is gonna flip on you as soon as she get out"

"Why you say that?"

"You know how your sister is. If she think somebody trynna fuck her over, she goes off and wants blood. So I'm just letting you know I will take her out for you. Just say the word"

Antonio sat there stunned. He stood and towered over Twan a little. "Tia was right about your ass. You know that?"

"What you mean?"

"Your punk ass can't be trusted. How the fuck can you come in my house and disrespect me like that? As a matter of fact, your ass is dismissed"

"Dismissed?"

"Yeah, motherfucker. Get the stepping. Get the fuck outta my damn house"

"I'm serious. She told me"

"When?"

"When she called me earlier" he said, pulling out his phone to show the number from the jail. He even called the number so he could see he was telling the truth.

Antonio got quiet and sat back down. *This shit didn't make sense. I thought my sister trusted me but I guess not. Maybe blood ain't thicker than water after all.*

"Man I got you. You know I got your back through whatever. Trust me" Twan said.

Antonio nodded his head in agreement. They discussed who was gonna be in Tony squad and who wasn't as they drank and smoked. Twan and Rocky didn't leave until after 1 in the morning. By the time Antonio went upstairs to Destiny, she was in the bed butt ass naked.

He stripped out of his pajama pants and boxers and got into the bed. She turned over once she knew he was all the way in the bed.

"I thought you asleep" he said, stroking her hair.

"Nope. Was lying here waiting patiently for you" she replied. She went underneath the cover and began to stroke his manhood. It didn't take long to become erect.

She stroked and slurped. Slurped and swallowed all over his penis. He told her he was ready to come so she moved to a better position. She climbed in between his legs and deep throated every inch as her forehead touched his abs. She kept a steady pace as he held her head in place and nutted all in her mouth.

The hot fluids warmed her throat as she swallowed each drop. After it all was released, she stroked his dick to get out the extra cum. She then licked the tip and kissed the head of his penis goodnight.

She laid back next to him and cuddled under him. He kissed her forehead and they fell peacefully asleep.

✳✳✳✳✳

The next day Antonio woke up feeling relieved. The sun was shining through the window as he stretched in the bed. He turned over and saw Destiny still asleep. He kissed her shoulder and she pushed him away. He chuckled then turned over to his night stand. He picked up his phone and saw that he had several missed calls. He checked the voicemails.

Aye, Bro, I'm out. I'm gonna be at the crib if you need me. Thanks for everything. I owe you. That message was from Cam. Message two was from Big Tone.

Antonio I don't know what the fuck going on between you and your sister but y'all better get y'all motherfucking shit together. Don't make me fuck y'all up. Shit. Y'all motherfucking mother probably turning over in her grave because of y'all two. Delete. *The last was from my sister.*

Hey, Bro, I'm letting you know that I'm out but I need a couple days to myself. So I will be ready and back to business in a couple days. Talk to you later.

What the fuck was that? Antonio thought to himself. What the fuck did Tia mean with that bullshit? And then my fucking father. That nigga got fucking issues. I don't know what the hell Cam said to him but I for one don't give a fuck. He have no right to say shit about my mother. He done lost his fucking mind. And Cam, I will just deal with him later on today. I don't feel like being stressed out right now. I shot my sister and Cam both a text and told them I'm glad they out now and will see them when I got a chance to.

I wasn't gonna let this shit get to me though. It wasn't worth it. I got up and threw my boxers on. I went to the bathroom to clean my face and brush my teeth. I looked at my reflection in the mirror.

I didn't even look as if I was in my late 20s. I could still pass for a 22-year-old. I had tattoos, tight abs, muscles, and a handsome face. Damn I looked motherfucking good! Any bitch would be lucky to be on my arm and Destiny crazy ass the one that caught me. I shook my head and laughed.

Gemini Betrayal

I headed downstairs to the kitchen. I rummaged through the fridge looking for something, anything, to cook for breakfast. I grabbed a banana from the fruit bowl as I continued to look. I found a pack of turkey bacon so I decided to cook that with the little bit of pancake mix I found. I finished my banana and threw the peel in the trash before heating the oven for the bacon.

It was so long since I actually cooked breakfast. I think the last time I cooked breakfast for a woman was for my mom. God, I missed that woman. I remember the happiest day we spent together was when Tia and I both graduated high school.

Our mother had surprised both of us with matching Dodge Chargers. I had a black one with black tints and Tia had a purple one with black tints. She made sure we had our licenses before graduation day; she ain't play no games. Then she let us drive them to our graduation party her that our father had planned for us. It was at some hall in Bowie and it was lit. Luckily, they didn't stay and cramp our style. They kicked it for a little over twenty minutes then left. She told us to be careful and no drinking and driving. We promised her we wouldn't. She snatched our diplomas from our hands after we took a billion pictures and told us they were going home with her. She walked away with tears in her eyes and a smile spread wide across her face. I had never seen my mom so happy in my life.

I went back to cooking. I made enough breakfast for both Destiny and me. I called upstairs to tell her breakfast was almost ready and I heard her practically fall out of the bed. I laughed to myself as I could hear her footsteps hit the floor and travel across the floor to the bathroom. Moments later I heard her running down the stairs.

"Damn, was it a fire upstairs or something? You hauled ass down here"

"Shut up and feed me nigga" she laughed.

I gave her a kiss on the lips as I sat a plate in front of her along with a glass of orange juice. I grabbed my plate and the syrup and sat down across from her.

Gemini Betrayal

We were enjoying our breakfast and joking around. It felt good to be able to do this with her and I hope it stayed like this. I was tired of the dumb arguments and all the bullshit.

We heard the doorbell ring.

"I'll get it, babe" I said, wiping my mouth with a napkin and getting up.

"Don't worry, baby. I got it" she said and headed towards the door.

I could barely see from the kitchen where I was but she was standing there talking to somebody.

"Who are you?" Destiny said.

"I'm Janae"

"Well, what do you want?"

Janae pulled a little boy that looked to be no more than two around from behind her. "He's here to see his daddy"

"And who is his daddy?" she asked, not wanting to hear it aloud.

"Who do you think is his daddy, you dumb bitch? Where's Antonio?"

Gemini Betrayal

Chapter Fourteen

I was putting away our breakfast dishes when I saw Destiny coming back to the kitchen.

"Who was at the door, baby?" I asked with my back to her.

"Your baby mother and your son"

"My what?" I asked turning around, with a chuckle. I saw Janae's little thieving ass walk into my kitchen with a little kid.

"You heard her right" Janae said. I looked back and forth between Destiny and Janae. Janae and the little boy.

"Bullshit. Bitch if you don't get your hoe ass outta my motherfucking house, I will kill you"

"You ain't gonna do shit, motherfucker. And stop talking like that in front of our son"

"Bitch, that's your son. I don't have no motherfucking son"

"Yes you do, Antonio. Meet your son Antonio Desmond Hall III" she said with attitude.

I looked at the little boy. Really looking at him this time. He did favor me a little bit. He had hair like mine but eyes like Antonia. Was it possible that I was a goddamn father? I wasn't ready for this.

"You tripping, Janae. That can't be my son. I ain't even been with you or seen your ass in almost two years"

"Okay dumbass, he will be two next month. I was pregnant before you broke up with me"

"You mean before you stole my fucking money and rolled out?"

"Whatever. That's neither here nor there. You got a son and you need to help me take care of him"

"How sure are you that this is even Antonio's baby?" Destiny jumped in. I almost forgot she was in the room. She was so quiet. She was probably just as shocked as I was.

"I'm sorry but who was talking to you? I'm talking to my baby daddy. Not you"

"I don't know who you are nor do I care. But you need to get the fuck out of our house!" Destiny yelled.

"Y'all house? Wow okay. Antonio I guess you did finally settle down with somebody" she said. She looked over at Destiny. "I guess it is possible to turn a hoe into a housewife" she said as she threw her head back in laughter.

Destiny was getting ready to attack but I jumped between them. I grabbed Janae by the arm and pulled her towards the front door.

"Get the fuck outta my house and don't ever come back"

"What about your son?"

"Until you bring back proof, that's not my fucking son!" i yelled.

"But we need money" she cried as I pushed her out the door.

I grabbed his wallet off the coffee table. I pulled out a twenty dollar bill and threw it at her. I slammed the front door and was heading back to the kitchen but stopped when I saw Destiny standing before me.

"I'm sorry, baby" I said.

"Don't be" she said in a low voice. "You didn't know and you still don't" She kissed me and we embraced. We separated and she went upstairs to run me a shower. I headed upstairs behind her.

I got in the shower and hoped that the hot water and steam would relieve my stress. *Who the fuck was I kidding?* I thought. *That could just possibly be my baby. But knowing Janae that bitch was probably lying. She was always money hungry. So why would it be any different now? Whether that's my baby or not, that bitch wasn't getting a dime out of me until she proved it. She had the game fucked up. Who she thought I was? Boo Boo the fucking fool? I don't even care. That bitch was still gonna die.*

I got out the shower and wrapped my body in a towel as I looked for something to wear. I decided on a pair of Jordans, some distressed jeans, and a plain white tee. I was just gonna be basic today. I grabbed my chain and bracelet from my top drawer, kissed Destiny and left out. I didn't know where I was going but I needed to go and clear my head.

I called my sister about twelve times and she never answered. "This bitch gonna make me fuck her up" I said aloud. I called Cam and he answered on the second ring.

"Yo, what's up?" he said, when he picked up.

"What's up, homie. Where you at?"

"Out on the block. You know me. My money never sleep"

"Right. So why should you?" I finished the slogan.

"You damn skippy" he said. It's funny that we have been saying that shit since we were teenagers.

"How long you been out there?"

"A couple hours now. I got an early start. You coming out?"

"You know the king don't run corners no more. But I'm gonna come to you. Where you at?"

"My usual spot around 54th"

"Be there in twenty"

"Peace"

"Peace"

I headed toward Cam's spot but decided to stop by the barbershop right quick.

I arrived at Special Cutz Barbershop in less than five minutes. I went in to get my beard shaped up and shit. I saw my barber Donnie and thankfully his customer was just getting out the chair, so I made my way over and sat down.

"Hey Tony, what's up?" he said, as he threw a cape around my neck.

"Nothing much, man" I said, exasperatedly.

"What's wrong with you?" he asked as he began to cut my face.

"Bro, you remember that bitch Janae?"

"From around Butler? Yeah"

"Well, that bitch popped up at my crib this morning talking about I'm her baby father"

"What the fuck? Damn, dawg. I didn't know you was still hitting homegirl"

"Nigga, I'm not. She said the little boy was two or turning two. I don't fucking know. I was too busy stuck on what she said. Destiny was pissed the fuck off though"

"What she say?"

"Nothing really but was about to glass Janae ass. But I stopped her"

"Boy you dumb. I would've let they ass fight to the finish" Donnie said, laughing. I joined him in laughter over his crazy joke. He finished cutting my beard and I headed into the office to meet with the boss.

I knocked on the door in our secret code. I heard him shuffling toward the door then five locks unlocked.

"What's up, Boss?" J.R. said as he closed and locked the door back.

"Nothing much. Where's Zay?"

"In the back, finishing up the bags for you."

"Cool"

"I'm gonna go help him hurry up" J.R. said.

"No problem" I said as I took a seat.

I been knowing J.R. and his brother Zay all my life. We literally grew up together. J.R. reminded me of myself and Zay and Tia were just alike. They were some crazy hot headed motherfuckers while J.R. and me were semi-sane. I looked around their office. They had pictures of them with celebrities and their family members. I noticed a picture on his desk and picked it up. It was a picture of me, Tia, Zay, and J.R. when we were teenagers. I don't know why he had it but it surely did make me smile, knowing how much we got along with one another. The only difference is that they got in the game three years ago while we had already been deep in it. I was definitely trying to get out but my sister wanted to die living this life. That shit wasn't for me.

"Here you go" Zay said, as he and J.R. came from the back with four duffel bags. I looked through the bags as they put them on the desk. I gave both of them their cut of the money and dapped them up. I told them I would be back next Wednesday and then left. Next stop was to Cam.

$$*****$$

I pulled up to Cam on the corner and he finished his sale before getting in the passenger seat. He handed me an envelope full of money and I securely counted it in my lap. I handed him his portion and we talked for a few minutes.

"How is it out here today?" I asked him.

"Some slight shit for real, Boss. I think I'm gonna head in the crib in a little bit. I probably come back out later on tonight and be on call"

"True shit. You make sure you be careful out here and watch your back"

"Come on, Bro. Ain't nobody fucking with Killer Cam" he laughed.

"I know but I'm serious though. Watch your back for everybody"

"What the hell going on?"

"Some beef going on between my sister and Twan. They telling me not to trust the other. I don't know man, I'm so fucking confused"

"Don't be. Family over everything. Remember?"

Gemini Betrayal

"Yeah, I remember"

"Okay then. There should be no confusion"

"You right" We slapped fives and he got out the car and stood back on the corner. I drove down the block and decided to head to my sister's house.

$$*****$$

I pulled up to Tia's house and parked behind a white Beamer. I hopped out my car and jogged to the front door. She came to the door moments later.

"What do you want, Antonio?" she said, in a snappy tone.

"Well damn" I said, placing a hand on my chest. "I can't see how my sister is doing?" I asked making my way inside. Reluctantly, she let me in.

"I'm kind of busy right now" she said, following me into the living room.

Her place looked like a goddamn military base. She had guns of all sizes spread across her coffee table.

"Um, are you getting ready for war or something?" I asked her more as a serious question than a joke.

"You never know what's gonna happen. You gotta always be prepared, right? Ain't that what daddy taught us?"

"Yea he did. He taught us a lot" I replied sarcastically.

I watched her body movement as she kept busy cleaning her guns and loading each one patiently. I couldn't read her thoughts for the life of me. You know how people say that one twin can always know what the other is thinking? Well, not in this case. Hell no! Tia was the hardest person to read and figure out.

"Aye, we cool right, Tia?"

She paused from loading her .45 and hesitated before responding. She looked up to me. "Yeah we okay. No hard feelings right?"

"Why would there be hard feelings?" I asked through squinted eyes.

"Nothing. I'm just tripping again"

"We need to talk, Sis"

"There's nothing to talk about, Tony" she said, pushing me out towards the front door. "You have to go so I can get back to work"

"Fine. Be stubborn like always. Just remember I'm here if you need me, Tia" She closed the door on me and I walked back to my car. I got in my car and just sat there for a couple minutes.

Tia ass was tripping. And I mean hard as a motherfucker. She wasn't trusting me or believing me for whatever fucking reason she had. Oh well. She wanted to handle shit on her own, I'm gonna let her. She gonna be running back looking for help and I won't be here. Guess I gotta do my own thing now.

I drove around, not going anywhere in particular. I just wanted to have some peace with myself. I pulled out my phone and called Janae's trifling ass.

"Hello?" she said.

"Yo" I replied.

"Who is this?"

"Don't fucking play with me, bitch. You know exactly who this is"

"Oh is this my baby father?" she asked.

"Kill that 'baby father' shit, slim. I'm not fucking playing with you"

"You could be"

"Ain't nobody got time for your games, Janae"

"Who said I was playing games, Antonio? I want you. I know you miss this pussy"

I didn't respond.

"I will take that as a yes" she said softly.

"Look I didn't say-"

Click.

That dumb bitch hung up on me. I was about to call her back but I received a text message. I opened it up and it was an address from Janae. I copied the address and put it in my Waze GPS app. Wherever she was, it was fifteen minutes from me. I turned up the music and listened to Shy Glizzy new track as I headed towards her.

When I arrived, I pulled up to a little red house. This neighborhood looked so familiar. I got out the car and looked around. This was our old neighborhood. It looked totally different because of the new developments and all. They were doing their best trying to move all the blacks outta this neighborhood. I walked up to the door and it swung open before I even landed on the front porch.

"Hey, baby daddy" Janae said, opening the door wider so I can come inside. This chick had on a little ass mini dress.

"Don't make me fuck you up" I said, stepping in her face when she closed the door.

"Oh calm down. I'm just trying to lighten the situation"

"You know what would lighten the situation a lot? If you had my motherfucking money you stole"

She rolled her eyes at me. "You still talking about that? I thought we put that in the past?"

"And I thought I left your ass in the past. But I guess we were both wrong as fuck" I said as I sat down on the sofa. She came over and sat beside me.

"Look, Antonio" she began. "I wanted to tell you about the pregnancy but I knew you wasn't gonna believe me"

"So you thought waiting two years was gonna convince me? Bitch, you dumber than you look"

"Whatever. Anyway here's the address you can go to take a blood test for your son" she said, handing me a business card. "You can do a walk-in and tell them you want the results as fast as possible"

"Sure, whatever. Where's the kid at anyway?"

"Oh, he's at my mama house"

"Oh okay."

"Yep. That means you get to have some fun with me before you go home to your girlfriend Diamond" she said, climbing onto my lap.

"Her name is Destiny" I said.

"Like I really care" she responded.

She kissed on my ear and my neck before moving to my lips. Damn. I did forget how soft her lips were. She rotated and gyrated her hips on top of me as she continued to kiss me. I grabbed her ass and held her down tighter on top of me. I started to suck and bite on her neck. She threw her head back as I sucked on her neck harder. I felt

Gemini Betrayal

like a vampire trying to get a taste of blood. I managed to pull her dress up over her head. Her titties bounced and I noticed she didn't even have on underwear. That bitch knew what she was doing. This was all a trap. I didn't care though.

I laid her on her back on the chair and unzipped my pants. I pulled my dick through the hole of my boxers and out my jeans. "That pussy still as good as I remember?"

"See for yourself" she said, opening her legs wide.

I pulled a condom out of my pocket and slid it on. I fingered her pussy to get her wet before entering. Once I could feel her juices start to form, I positioned myself and dove deep inside her.

"Aaaahhhh" she screamed loud in my ear. She reached under my shirt and dug her nails in my back. It felt like she had Freddy Krueger fingers as she ran her nails up and down my back. This didn't do anything but cause me to go deeper inside her wetness.

I sat up and grabbed her by the ankles and deep thrusted in and out of her. I played with her clit as my strokes became faster. I looked down at her and she was squeezing her eyes tight and making crazy faces. I looked back down at her pussy and I got sprayed. She squirted all over me and my tee shirt. I finished up a few minutes later as I went balls deep and ejaculated.

I stood up and walked to the bathroom. I flushed the condom down the toilet and grabbed a rag to wash my dick off. I wasn't worried about my shirt, however, because I always had an extra. I went back to the living room and she was lighting a blunt while she was naked.

"Wanna hit this?"

"I just did" I said, laughing.

"Don't play with me, nigga"

"Naw, I'm good. I gotta get home" I said, adjusting my clothes.

"Oh, you gotta get home to wifey?"

"Don't antagonize me, woman"

She just laughed at me and didn't pay me no mind.

"I'm going to that place tomorrow"

"Cool"

I left out and jumped in the car. I saw that it was already after 5. I wondered why Destiny hadn't called me all day. I called her and the phone went straight to voicemail. I called a few more times after that and the same results. *Fuck it. Guess I was gonna see her at home later.*

✷✷✷✷✷

I pulled onto my street and noticed police cars in my driveway. I slowly crept pass by and saw there were two cars and one unmarked car. That must've been Lieutenant Gaines. *What the fuck is going on here? I* called Destiny's phone again and the call got sent straight to voicemail. *This bitch really looked at the phone and sent me to voicemail? She tripping big time.*

I eased around the corner and headed over to Twan's house since he lived the closest. I parked my car and looked around before hopping out the car. I ran up the steps and quickly knocked on the door. The door flew open and I practically jumped inside and closed the door. I looked through the window to make sure the coast was still clear.

"What the fuck is going on?" Twan asked as he looked out the window with me.

"I don't know what the fuck going on, man. I was on my way to my crib but when I got there, it was cops there"

"Oh shit. What the fuck you done did now, Bro?"

I looked at him crazily. "I ain't done shit, nigga. You know I been trying to keep my name out the streets"

"Yeah I know. What about ol' girl?"

"I don't know. I called her phone so many times and I got no answer"

"Aight, just chill. I'm gonna call Leana and Sienna to go by your spot and see what's going on"

"Cool"

He stepped off and called Sienna and told her to go grab Leana and go to my house. They obliged and said they would get back to us in thirty minutes.

I paced the floor back and forth thinking about what the fuck could have happened. Did Destiny get hurt? Did she turn me over to the feds? Did somebody get killed on our street and they asking questions? So many questions with no answers at the moment. I was so nervous and panicking. I called my sister to calm my nerves.

"What you mean the police at your house?" she asked, once I gave her the rundown. "What kind of mess you got us in this time?"

"Us? What the fuck you mean 'us'? They at my motherfucking house not nobody else's"

"Not yet" she said.

Damn maybe she's right. Maybe that bitch Destiny did call the cops on me. But why would she do that? Oh, shit. Probably that shit with Janae. Goddamn it.

"You still there?" she yelled into the phone.

"Yeah I'm here. I gotta go. I will call you back" I said, as I hung up the phone.

Twan came from the kitchen carrying two beers and handed me one. I cracked it open and took a big swig.

"You need to calm your nerves" he said, as he passed me a freshly rolled lit blunt. I inhaled deeply and exhaled. It did make me feel a little better. I continued to switch between the brew and the jay. That is until he snatched the blunt from me. I snickered at him. I was definitely on the verge of being high.

"I think that's Sienna and Leana pulling up" I said, when I saw headlights. The car parked and moments later, there was a heavy knock at the door. *"That's not them"* I thought.

I sat down the beer and hid behind the wall in the living where I couldn't be seen by anybody. I pulled my gun out and took off the safety.

"Who is it?" Twan yelled toward the door.

"It's the police" one of the officers replied through the door.

Oh shit.

Twan walked over to the door and opened it. "What's up?"

"Good evening sir, we're looking for a person by the name of Antonio Hall."

"Okay and?"

Gemini Betrayal

"Let us finish, asshole" the other butted in. "We know you two scumbags hang together. Have you seen him?"

"Nope"

"You said that awfully quickly. Makes me think you're lying to us"

"Why the hell would I lie? You asked me a question and I answered it. Now, if you two gentlemen don't mind, have a good night" Twan said, closing the door. The door flew back open by the second officer.

"Look jackass, don't play games with us. It would make all our lives easier if you would tell us where your friend is"

"I already told you I don't know"

"Here's my card. Call if he contacts you"

"Yeah whatever" Twan said. "What are you fuckers looking for him for anyway?" I heard him yell from the porch.

"Murder" I heard one of them say before walking away. They got in their squad car and drove off.

Murder? What the fuck?

Chapter Fifteen

Leana and Sienna showed up ten minutes later at Twan's house. They burst through the door looking wild.

"What the fuck did you do, Tony?" Leana asked me. She had apparently been crying a little because her eyes were red.

"I ain't done shit. I wish everybody stop fucking asking me that"

"Then what happened at your house?" Sienna asked, placing her hands on her hips.

"I don't fucking know. I haven't been home all damn day. When I saw them at my house, I never stopped. I just came here and I been here"

"So you don't know?" Leana asked.

"Know what?"

"Destiny got killed. That's why all the police were at your house"

I got taken aback a little. I stumbled back and fell onto the sofa. My mind was racing. *Who the fuck killed Destiny? Why the fuck did they kill her? And more so, why did the cops think I did it?*

"I need to get to my house" I said, after I calmed down inside.

"We got you" Twan said, in a reassuring tone. We all left his house and piled in his truck. We headed down the block towards my house.

We got there and it was free of cops. We all looked around and there were no neighbors in sight either. We exited the car and went to the door. Surprisingly, it was still unlocked.

The outside as well as the inside were covered in yellow tape. I saw traces of blood on the steps leading to the kitchen. So we followed them. The spots of blood turned into bloody footprints as well as bloody shoe prints.

My eyes started to water at the thought of what may have to happened to Destiny. The prints led to the basement door. I opened the door and turned on the light. I crept down the stairs with my gun drawn. I looked back and my crew was right behind me locked and loaded as well.

We reached the bottom of the steps and smelled a foul odor.

"Oh god" Sienna said, as she covered her nose.

"What the hell is that smell?" Leana asked.

"What you got in your basement, Yo?" Twan asked covering his nose as well.

"I don't know what the fuck that smell is" I said. I sniffed trying to find where the odor was coming from. I walked around until the smell seemed to be getting stronger. "I think I found where it's coming from, y'all" They all joined me over to the deep freezer I kept in the basement.

I opened the freezer and the stench hit me harder. I peeped inside along with the others and it was my mother's corpse along with a bunch of dead fish.

"I think I'm gonna be sick" Leana said, as she covered her mouth and ran upstairs. Sienna ran right behind her to be her protection.

"Ain't that your moms, Tony?" Twan asked.

"Yeah, man" I said. My tears came back with a quickness. But they weren't from sadness. It was from anger. Whoever did this has no respect and was definitely going to die. There was a note laying on top of my mother's dead body. I picked it up and read it aloud:

I'm sorry it had to be this way but I told you not to fucking play with me. Now your ass gonna end up swimming with the fishes. Don't worry, though I promise to kill you slowly and then lay your remains next to your mom. I will be seeing you soon enough.

"Do it say who its from?" Twan asked.

"No and I don't know who it could be" I said, thinking hard. *Who would want me dead? Why would someone dig up my mother's grave? Was they sending a message when they killed Destiny?"*

"Well, I think I know who it is" he replied. I looked over to him strangely.

"Who do you think it is, Twan?"

"Your sister"

"My sister? Really, nigga?"

"Yeah, really. I told you her ass didn't trust you and was trying to get back at you"

I thought about it. "I don't think so, Twan. I mean that's our mom, man. She wouldn't do that"

Gemini Betrayal

"And why wouldn't she? Your sister is fucking ruthless and gives no fucks about nothing or no one. All she cares about is her money and the game"

He was right. That's all Tia thought about. Drugs, money and sex. I couldn't wrap my mind on this and think she would do this. *I know she was crazy. But her own mama, hell naw, man. She wouldn't do that. Would she?*

I heard the upstairs door close and footsteps cross the living room floor. I thought it may have been Sienna or Leana but whoever it was was tiptoeing. Then I heard Sienna's voice,

"Aye yo, what the fuck?!" I heard her yell before gunshots rang out and echoed throughout the house. Me and Twan hit the stairs two at a time towards where we heard the footsteps. We had our guns out and ready. We saw Leana and Sienna standing over a body.

"What the fuck happened?" I asked, pushing between them. I looked down at the masked figure that was bleeding out a little.

"Whoever this is just came in here and tried to stick us up. They hit Leana over the head with the butt of their gun and she dropped beside me. Then I shot them and they tried to run so I clocked they ass" Sienna said.

I laughed to myself, picturing the entire scenario in my head. I picked the person up and sat them down on the chair. Twan snatched the mask off and we were all fucking surprised.

"What the fuck?" we all said in unison. We couldn't believe our eyes.

"Rocky? What the fuck?" I asked.

"I don't wanna hear your shit Tony" he said. He tried to stand up but Leana knocked him back on his ass with a left hook. She spit right in his face before walking away.

"Get the fuck up nigga" Twan said, snatching him up from the floor.

"You not appreciative of me Rock?" I asked.

"Fuck no. I been starving like a motherfucker in these streets"

"Starving? Nigga, how the fuck you starving but nobody else is?"

"I been needing more money but I knew you wasn't gonna give me more work"

"So, you thought you would come up in here and fucking rob me?" I said, finishing his sentence and stepping in his face.

"I damn sure was. You sitting pretty while all the rest of us doing your fucking dirty work and getting paid fucking minimum wage"

"Minimum wage? Y'all getting minimum wages?" I asked everybody. They all shook their head no.

"Shit, I get paid quadruple minimum wage. Probably more than that Boss" Twan jokingly said.

"See what I mean? Nobody complaining but your bitch ass. So you know what? You're dismissed. You are no longer part of this family" I said as I walked away.

"I don't give a fuck Tony. Man, fuck you and your whole fucking squad. Y'all motherfuckers were holding me back anyway. Shit. Fuck all y'all"

"Sienna?"

"Yes, Boss?"

I didn't say another word. I snapped my fingers and she knew exactly what that meant. She shot Rocky in the back of the head, execution style. Leana got her gun and emptied the clip as she turned his body into Swiss cheese.

"Y'all clean this mess up. Y'all can crash in the guest rooms for the night if y'all want. I'm going to bed"

"You got it big man" Twan said.

I headed upstairs to get in the shower and relax my body. I was in there for about a good thirty minutes before I got out. I threw on a pair of boxers before hopping into bed.

For once in a long time, I didn't have the tv on as I laid down. My mind only replayed memories of Destiny. From the first time we met, all the way up to now. I wish she didn't have to go the way she did. In my mind, it was all my fault. They were probably looking to kill me and she happened to be here instead. A bad case of being at the wrong place at the wrong time. I'm not sure how late I was up but I eventually dozed off to sleep.

✳✳✳✳✳

I felt a hand rubbing on my legs. Then they traced my body all the way up to my neck. I felt soft kisses being placed across my chest and neck. I didn't move because I was really enjoying it. I wasn't sure if I was dreaming or not but I was loving the attention to my body. Whether it was a dream person or somebody in real life, they were headed down south.

I could feel the inside of a warm mouth. They sucked on it softly and gently. They acted like it was a prized possession or something. My eyes eased open and I saw that it wasn't a dream. Somebody was real live in my bed, in between my legs, sucking my dick! I turned on the bedside lamp to see who it was. It was Leana and she had a finger up to her lips telling me to be quiet. I nodded my head and she continued.

I watched as she sucked my dick and brought it to life. I cut the light off as soon as it was stiff and standing tall like the statue of liberty. She put a condom on me using her mouth. I was quite impressed. She got on top without me having to ask. She started off riding slow and kissing me. It was a little weird at first when our lips touched for the first time. After a couple kisses, you would thought we have kissed like a million times before.

Her pace started to quicken and so did mine. I grabbed her by the hips and held her tight to my pelvis. She was scratching up my chest with her nails and kissing all over my neck. I wouldn't be surprised if she would have left marks on me. I flipped her over on her back and got in as deep as I could. I wanted to feel her guts and everything.

She arched her back and I fucked her harder as I placed my hand under her ass and pulled her toward me. She fucked me back and moaned loud. I couldn't believe how good she was taking my dick. This bitch was the real MVP. She pushed me off top of her then got on her knees. She put her ass high up in the air and I just stared at it for a second in the dark room. It looked beautiful even in the dark.

I stuck my dick back inside her wetness and gave her deep strokes. I started going faster and faster. And she was taking it like a beast. This shit was insane.

"I'm 'bout to cum" I said to her between deep pants.

She pushed me away and turned around on her knees. She sucked and slurped my dick until I busted my nut. She swallowed most of it then let the rest shoot onto her face. She sucked the tip and sucked out the excess cum and swallowed it.

"Can I use your bathroom, Boss?" she asked.

I laughed as I told her 'yeah' She really asked me that but couldn't come and ask me politely if I could blow her back out for her? This was madness. She came back and got back in the bed with me.

"So?"

"So, what?" she asked.

"So what the hell was that?" I asked.

"I don't know. I was in the other room and was wondering how good your dick was"

"Uh huh. I guess. Well, how was it?"

"It was better than I imagined" she giggled.

"Well, I do try" I said, laughing with her.

"I think I better get back to the guest room. Don't need nobody getting any ideas"

"Like what?"

"Like anything. But I would like to do this again. Very soon" she said, as she put her clothes back on.

"Anytime you ready, just let me know"

"Cool" she said. She leaned over and tongue kissed me for a few more seconds before leaving my room and closing my door behind her.

I laid back down and thought about what had just gone down. Me and Leana? Who would've ever thought we would ever end up in the same bed? I didn't even trust her at one point. The shit was wild but I liked it. I wouldn't mind hitting that pussy again. It never crossed my mind to even look at Leana like that. Especially since I thought she was a full blown lesbian all these years anyway. I went back to sleep and hoped that I wouldn't wake up and catch Sienna sucking me off next.

✳✳✳✳✳

I got up early the next morning to the smell of breakfast cooking. I went into the bathroom to brush my teeth and wash my face before heading downstairs. I walked into the living room and Twan was stretched out across my couch knocked out sleep.

"I said pick a guest room, motherfucker" I said, punching him in the shoulder and startling him awake.

"Man, what the fuck?" he yelled.

"What you doing sleeping on my couch, Bro? I got four extra rooms you could've slept in"

"I know but this couch was way more comfortable"

"Nigga" I decided to not even continue to go back and forth with him. I headed to the kitchen to see who was cooking.

To my surprise, it was both of the girls in my kitchen; another surprise. I didn't even know either of them could cook. Especially since they both remained single all the time and always ate out. They claimed they didn't have time to deal with a relationship or trying to explain their job to anybody.

"Morning ladies" I said, as I entered the kitchen.

"What's up, dawg?" Sienna said to me. I looked at her like she was crazy. Yeah, she was definitely a lesbian. I snickered to myself as I sat on a stool next to Leana.

"Morning Tony" she said.

"Good morning y'all" I said back, politely. I looked over at Leana and she was staring back at me. Weird. She snuck a kiss on my cheek and got up to go over to the stove.

"I hope you don't mind us tearing up your kitchen" Leana said.

"Yeah Boss. We didn't think you would mind" Sienna added.

"It's perfectly cool. I just hope y'all don't burn down my kitchen or kill me with y'all cooking"

They looked at me with deadly stares. *Damn I see they couldn't take a joke.*

"Go get that punk ass nigga, Twan and let him know we made enough for him too" Sienna barked at me.

"Got you" I said. I walked back into the living room to get Twan but he wasn't there. I jogged up the steps to see if he was up there.

I could hear someone talking in a low voice in the hallway bathroom. I walked slowly down the hall towards the bathroom, trying to hear what was being said. I stepped on a floorboard and it made a loud squeak. I froze instantly. I heard the toilet flush and the water start running. A few seconds later, Twan emerged from the bathroom, looking nervous. The look on his face was priceless. He looked like a pussycat that just got caught eating a canary.

"What's up, Bro?" he asked.

"What's up with you?" I asked him back.

"Nothing. Nothing at all"

"Who was you on the phone with?"

"The phone? When?"

"Nigga just now"

"Oh. That was my mom" he said nervously.

"Oh. How she doing?"

"She doing good. She said to tell y'all 'hello'"

"Next time you talk to her, tell her I said hello. Matter fact, call her back so I can talk to her."

"Oh no"

"Why not?"

"She said she was about to go run some errands"

"Oh well, breakfast ready"

"Cool, I'm starving" he said, heading down the steps. He looked back at me. "Yo, you coming?"

"Yeah in a minute. Let me grab my phone" I went in my room and snatched my phone off the nightstand. Then I walked into the bathroom to see if he had dropped anything. I looked all in the trash can too. Nothing. *What the fuck was this nigga hiding from me? From us?*

I went back to the kitchen and everybody was already eating. They passed me a plate and I dug in. The taste of this good food took my mind off of Twan's suspicious behavior. I guess my sister was right. I did need to keep an eye on him.

Chapter Sixteen

I called Destiny's mother from her phone to tell her what had happened.

"Who is this?" she asked after I broke the news to her.

"I'm Antonio. I was dating your daughter"

"Antonio? Oh you must be that damn thug she was telling me about. Well, you tell me what kind of thug doesn't protect his home? Where the fuck were you when my baby was being killed?" she asked. I didn't even know how to respond nor did I want to for that matter. This lady was tripping. She didn't even sound broken up about the news in all actuality.

"I was working when this went down"

"Working, huh? Young man selling drugs is not a goddamn job. It's an excuse for you motherfuckers that don't want to make nothing better for yourselves. All y'all damn high school dropouts and shit. Y'all make me fucking sick!" she yelled at me.

"Look lady," I said sternly. "I don't know who the fuck you think I am or what the fuck Destiny done told you but I am far from being a high school dropout. I finished the top of my high school class and I finished college. So you can go ahead with all that shit"

"A college grad selling crack on the streets? Wow!! I guess they give anybody degrees nowadays"

I hung up the phone in her ear. I was tired of her insults. "That bitch don't know shit about me" I said aloud.

I got up and headed out the house for a while. I texted Leana to see what she was doing in a couple hours. She told me she was free for whatever and I told her 'let's hangout'. She agreed and I told her I would pick her up around seven and we could go out to T.G.I. Fridays for food and drinks. I looked at my watch. That gave me three hours to kill doing nothing as usual.

I decided to just face a jay full of purp and relax for a bit. I sat there puffing and letting all the bullshit out of my body. I pulled out my phone and called my sister.

"Yeah" she said, when she picked up.

"Damn!! what's all that for?"

"Nothing. What's up?" Tia asked.

"Nothing just checking on you. I haven't heard from you in a week. Just wanna make sure you're okay, that's all"

"I'm fine"

"Cool"

Click.

That was basically how we've been communicating lately ever since she's been home. My sister has been distant before but never like this. I wasn't gonna bother her though. She would come around eventually.

I sat in my car, in my cloud of smoke, just thinking about my sister and me.

Ever since we were little, we had been inseparable. Even when we were seven years old, our my mother had bought us bunkbeds and we slept in the same bed. Most people thought it was weird, but I always knew as long as my sister was next to me, she would protect me. Now, even older, I need her as much as she needed me. We were like

Gemini Betrayal

two peas in a pod. It seems like since our mom got murdered and our father went to prison, she has been acting like a whole new person. She has her moments when she wants to be the loving sister and other times she just act like a dumb bitch. But nonetheless, I loved her so much and that would never change.

I was pulled out of my thoughts by the ringing of my cell phone. I looked down at the caller id and I didn't recognize the number so I sent it to voicemail. I hit my blunt a couple more times and my phone had rung again. The same number popped up so I decided to answer it.

"Yo, hello?"

"You have a collect call from an inmate at a federal prison" the recording began. I heard my father's voice then prompts followed. I hesitated before hitting the button to accept charges. We were connected soon after.

"What do you want man?" I asked my father.

"Motherfucker, you better show me some respect"

"Yeah, when you earn it"

My father got quiet momentarily. "Look, I was just letting you and your sister know that I was coming home soon"

"And what that gotta do with us?"

"I need you all to let them know I'm coming to stay with one of y'all so they wont put me in no motherfucking halfway house"

"Fuck no! You better call Tia and ask her"

"You think I didn't? She didn't answer her phone as usual. So I need your help son"

"Whatever, man. I will tell them whatever but your ass not staying in my crib"

"I guess so" he said, laughing.

"When you getting out anyway?" I asked.

"Not sure yet. They undecided. Maybe a couple days. Maybe a couple of weeks. Who's to know?"

"Whatever, bye" I said, hanging up. I didn't even give him time to interject.

Now this bullshit. I was not anticipating on my father ever getting out of jail, honestly. They said that nigga had life without the chance of parole. I swear our legal system is fucked all the way up.

I finished off my blunt as I rolled through my city waving and nodding at my peeps and bystanders. It was crazy how much my city had changed in the past fifteen years. The grass seemed greener. The buildings looked more cleaner; at least the outside of them did anyway. But the best thing out of all these changes was the fact that white folks were moving in. They became great customers for my business as well. I think I probably see them more than I see folks of my own skin color. I laughed as I pulled up at the mall.

I was like a female sometimes. When I was down about something, I would go shopping. My mother always joked about that because I did it when I was younger too. I headed into the mall and the first place I see is a Foot Locker store. I go in there and I see my homeboy Russ.

"What's up, son?" he said, giving me a dap.

"Nothing much, fam. What you got new for me?" I asked. He looked around then led me to the back of the store. He pulled about six shoes boxes out from a locker.

"I got these" he said, opening all the boxes for me. I examined them all and told him to bag them up for me. He took them up to the front while I went to the bathroom.

I didn't even knock before opening the door and I walked in on one of the female employees.

"Damn nigga" she said. I wasn't sure if she was more upset that I walked in or the fact that I walked in while she was playing with her pussy on FaceTime.

"Who the fuck is that, Brittany?" the dude on the screen said.

"My bad, Boo. I didn't know anybody was back here." I turned to walk away but she quickly grabbed my hand. She hung up her cell phone and pulled me back in the bathroom, this time locking the door.

"What are you doing?" I asked.

"You look good. So I know your dick probably looks good too" she said, tugging at my jeans. She had managed to release my dick and looked at it with a smile on her face. "Wow!! that dick looks beautiful" She sucked it one good time. "And it tastes delicious. Do you mind?" she asked.

"Do whatever you want" I said, giving her a green light.

She sucked and slurped on my penis and didn't miss a beat. She put the entire thing in her mouth without even gagging. *Holy fuck.* I threw my head back in ecstasy. I could feel my cum building up to be released. I warned her and her pace increased. Not even two minutes had passed before I ejaculated all in her throat. She got up and washed her hands and rinsed out her mouth.

"Damn that was good" I said .

"Yeah it was" she replied. She dried her hands, touched up her lipstick and hair, then left the bathroom.

I straightened my clothes then headed up front to where she had gone. Once I got up front, Russ had already totaled my stuff. I handed him a stack of money for the purchase and some extra for looking out. We dapped again and I headed back out the store.

I strolled through the mall a little more. I bought a couple new pieces of jewelry, some clothes, and even a new ipad. Eventually, my stomach started to grumble so I decided to grab me something in the food court.

I got to the food court and looked around at the choices. I decided to go grab some panda express. I ordered me a plate of orange chicken, fried rice, kung pao chicken, two chicken egg rolls, and a large lemonade. I found a table in the middle of the court and headed over to it. I sat down and was getting ready to crush.

I dug into my food and ate like I hadn't eaten in months. You would have thought I had spent days in a dungeon or something as fast as I ate. I was so busy enjoying my grub that I hadn't noticed the group of four guys heading my way. One sat down across from me and the others took seats on each side of me.

"Can I help y'all?" I asked, looking at all of them.

"Naw you can't , but we gonna help ourself to yo' shit you got in them bags though, cuz" the one sitting across from me said.

I threw a menacing look at him. "No you're not" I said simply and continued to eat.

"I don't think the man asked for permission" the guy to my left said.

I grabbed my napkin and wiped my hands and mouth off. "I think y'all better leave before y'all get fucked up" I said in a low tone as I leaned across the table.

"Nigga please" he responded loudly. "Y'all get that shit and let's bounce" And they did just that. As they grabbed at my bags, I prepared myself.

I stood up without them noticing and picked up the chair next to me. The two that were on my right were the ones I took out first. I cracked one over the back of the head with the chair and the other I had grabbed and slammed through the tables. The one that was on my left dropped the bags he had and came to their aid. He ran towards me and got hit with a right hook. I stomped him out a few times until I seen a tooth fall out. I looked across the room at the leader.

He was staring at me in astonishment. Forgetting where I was for a moment, I pulled out my gun and opened fire. Everybody in the food court ducked and hid under the tables for cover. I had missed him and he ran. I chased after his ass without hesitation.

He ran through crowds of shoppers and I was right behind him. Once I got a clear space, I shot at him again. Once again, everybody ducked down. I happened to hit him in the shoulder but his ass didn't drop. I seen him run through a set of double doors so I ran in there too.

I got in the empty hallway and the door closed behind me. I slowly crept through the corridor with my gun cocked and ready to blow at the slightest movement. I turned a corner and still didn't see his ass. I went into the stairwell and could hear heavy breathing. I listened intently to see where it was coming from. The lower level. I looked between the railings and saw him leaning against a wall. I shot my gun and had just missed him. He opened the door to the underground parking garage and I went right behind him.

I got into the parking garage and heard an engine starting. I quickly ran into the direction of the car and came up on a black chevy impala. He was so busy trying to stop the bleeding he didn't see me. I pulled the handle and the door popped open. I pointed my gun at him and he stared down the barrel of my gun.

Gemini Betrayal

"Next time you try to rob somebody, make sure it's a bitch ass nigga and not a motherfucking gangsta" I filled his ass with three bullets before closing the door back and fleeing the garage.

I went back to the food court and everybody was staring at me. I was surprised that the fake thugs were still there bleeding and shit. I laughed to myself and grabbed my bags. I headed out the mall and to my car. I threw the bags in the trunk and hopped in my whip. I sped off and headed towards my house.

I was riding peacefully towards my house. Just bopping my head to the music, smoking a little more weed, and enjoying my day. It all changed once I turned onto my street though. It was always some shit.

✳✳✳✳✳

"Antonio Hall step out of the vehicle" Gaines said, through a bullhorn.

I looked all around me and I was surrounded by half of the motherfucking police department. They were all standing and aiming guns at me. I just sat inside my car and continued to hit my blunt.

"Out the car now, motherfucker" he repeated. And still I sat there. I wasn't gonna move until I finished my goddamn jay. He had me fucked all the way up.

I finished my weed a few minutes later. I turned off my ignition and sat still in my car.

"Put your hands in the air so I can see them" Gaines said to me. I reluctantly obliged. "I want you to reach over and open the door with your right hand but keep your hands where I can see them" I did as I was told.

Gemini Betrayal

I got out of the car and heard a series of guns click and place bullets in their chambers. Gaines rushed over to me and roughly handcuffed me.

"Damn what the fuck happened to reading me my rights, man?" I asked him, laughing.

"Fuck your rights you piece of shit. I've been waiting for this day" he said, as he led me to a squad car.

"Fuck you" I said. "Y'all pigs ain't got shit on me, moe"

"That's what the fuck you think. I'll see you down at the station" He slammed the door and stood there grinning from ear to ear as the officer pulled off down the street.

What the fuck do this cracker think he got on me now? I thought to myself. *Oh shit! The incident at the mall. I was so motherfucking stupid to do that shit there. But he wouldn't know about the body in the garage; at least I don't think so. It wasn't no cameras down there or anything. I don't know and I wasn't gonna try and wreck my brain, trying to figure out anything.*

I laid my head against the window and closed my eyes. I wasn't about to let these pigs think they had anything on me. I was just gonna enjoy my ride and see what happened when I got down to the precinct.

Gemini Betrayal

Chapter Seventeen

"I don't have time for your shit today, Hall! Just answer the goddamn questions!" Wilson yelled at me. I looked at him and shook my head. "Answer me boy!" he yelled again; this time in my ear. Hell I might have lost a little hearing in my left ear I swear. Gaines pushed me back a little and replaced the spot with himself.

"Looka here, boy. Just tell us what we wanna know so you can go" Gaines said.

I cut my eyes at him. "I told you I don't know what you are talking about. I wasn't around no Minnesota Avenue no damn two weeks ago"

"You really expect me to believe that when we found your fingerprints at the scene?"

"That's bullshit. You could only have my fingerprints if I was there. Unless you stole my fingerprints"

He backed off a little and left. Moments later, he reentered the room carrying a box. He slammed the box on the table and pulled out a folder. He slung it across the table and it landed in front of me. I looked at him.

"Those are the pictures from the crime scene on Minnesota Avenue."

I focused my attention on the folder in front of me. I took a deep breath before looking at the contents of the folder.

Gemini Betrayal

The first picture was of a guy whose face was beat in really badly. I couldn't even make out what his face originally looked like. I went to the next picture and it was a picture of another man lying in a pool of dark red blood. He had no arms or legs attached to his body. I practically threw up in my mouth. I got to the third picture and it was the most gruesome. It was of a man and a woman whose body parts were cut up as well. The man's penis was in his throat and the woman's breasts were cut completely from her body and lying between the two. Their fingers were all cut and stuffed in the woman's mouths like pretzel bites or some shit. I couldn't take anymore! I threw the pictures and folder onto the floor.

"What's the matter, Hall? You can't believe your eyes?" he said, picking all the pictures up from the floor and shoving them in my face. "Well believe it, motherfucker! This is what you and your gang do to innocent fucking people. And I got your ass. I'm gonna get all of y'all asses, no matter how long it takes. Even if it fucking kills me!" he yelled at me.

"I didn't do none of that shit, man. I keep telling you that"

"Bullshit! Your fingerprints are at all these crime scenes. Doesn't matter if you did it, your motherfucking sister, or any of you bastards! Y'all all going down one by one" he said, all in my face and banging the metal table. "And your ass is first" He looked over to Wilson as he was leaving out the door. "Book his ass and don't give his ass a bond hearing neither. His ass is mine"

"Yes sir" his little helper monkey replied. He pulled me to my feet and cuffed me again. He slowly walked me down to the holding cell.

I couldn't believe this shit. I was trying to get out the game but somehow it feels like I'm in deeper than ever. I could see my life quickly passing me by. I was tired of going the fuck to jail. Especially going and I didn't even do a motherfucking thing! This was some straight up bullshit.

Gemini Betrayal

He led me into the holding cell and removed the cuffs from my wrist. I rubbed my wrists to try and soothe them as he closed the metal bars in my face. I watched as he headed back down the long hallway. I looked around at all the other holding cells that housed convicts. All different shapes, sizes, and nationalities.

I don't think I could get used to this. According to Gaines' ass, I didn't have much of a choice now. I stood there with my head hung as the lights went out and darkness surrounded me.

$$*****$$

I was going crazy sitting behind these four walls. You would have thought I been in here for years, maybe even months. But in all actuality, it has only been two weeks. Two long motherfucking weeks.

I had been to jail before but these niggas was on some new jail shit. I done seen a dude stab somebody with a sharpened piece of tile from the damn shower floor. One dude had hung himself using the metal bunk, the second night I was in here. And I done seen these niggas get into a physical altercation which turned out to be staged just so they could kill one of the guards. This shit was madness!

I had been calling my sister and all my so-called homies. Not a goddamn soul answered. It seemed like they had fallen from the face of the earth or some shit. Maybe I shouldn't have put that much trust in niggas and bitches. That was the first rule my father had taught me and Tia about the game. But even she's turned her back on me. I always thought blood was thicker than water. Guess I was wrong; and so was the motherfucker that came up with that bullshit ass saying.

I was standing in the chow line getting ready to eat whatever it was that they fed us on Tuesdays. I looked and saw this dude that was about my size come over towards me. He jumped right in front of me.

Gemini Betrayal

Not that I was pressed for this crap or anything, but the fact of the matter was this nigga thought I was sweet for it or something.

"Aye, big homie, what is you doing?" I asked, tapping his shoulder hard. He looked at me with a grim face.

"Don't ever put your fucking hands on me, dawg. And if you must know, I'm 'bout to get my grub on" he said, laughing.

"I understand that on the real but you got me fucked up" I said, maneuvering around him to get back ahead of him. I grabbed a tray of food from the dude serving food and picked up a drink. I looked back at the dude, "Don't ever do no shit like that again, my nigga. I'm forewarning you" With that, I walked away and headed toward a table in the corner.

It was always a thing for me to sit far away from everyone else and being in this cage ain't make no difference. I looked at everybody sitting around me. They were all grouped together in their own gangs. Hispanics with the Hispanics, the whites with the whites, crypts, bloods, and so and so on. You get my drift. I discovered that I was one of few that were sitting alone. Not sure if they were new here or people didn't really fuck with them. In my case, I wasn't here to make friends. I just wanted to get the fuck out of this hell hole. I looked down at the monstrosity on my tray. That shit looked like straight chewed up dog chow. I ate a little and surprisingly, it didn't taste that bad. I mean it wasn't Ruth Chris's but it was food. Or something like food anyway. I looked up and I had company approaching.

The dude that had cut in front of me walked over and sat down at my table. I don't understand why guys did this. Did they think they could intimidate somebody? They damn sure didn't intimidate my black ass. I didn't have not one bitch bone in my body. Guess some people had to learn the hard way.

"What the fuck do you want, slime?" I said, putting my fork down.

Gemini Betrayal

"Slime? You got me fucked up, dawg"

"Oh really? How so?"

"See I know who you are. You run the Southside and some other parts too. And you got a fine ass twin sister that run shit with you, right?"

"You keep my fucking sister out your motherfucking mouth" I said, sitting up straight in my chair.

"Man, shut your punk ass up. You ain't gonna do nothing. Your ass right in here with me so you can't run from me. I think I'm gonna make you my new bitch" he said, with a heavy laugh.

"Punk? Never me. And as far as a bitch, that's what the fuck you gonna be. If I wanted a bitch, you would be the first on my list. Lucky for you I don't roll like that. But I advise your ass to stay the fuck away from me if you know what's good for you" I got up from the table and never lost eye contact as I walked away. I went and threw my food and tray in the trash across the cafeteria.

I felt something slightly heavy hit the back of my head as I dropped to the floor. I turned over to see this nigga standing over top of me ready to hit me with the metal tray again. As the tray came down towards me, I had managed to kick him right in the nuts. I jumped up and two pieced him. He stumbled but didn't fall. He charged me and knocked me back down. All the other prisoners moved back a little and formed a circle around us in the middle of the room.

He was on top of me pummeling me but I wasn't gonna give in. As he continued to punch me, I continued to punch him in the midsection. I'm not sure which blow caused it but he rolled off top of me and I seized the opportunity. I stood up and stomped on his head. Moments later, I was grabbed by two guys. At first I thought it were the guards but it was two other prisoners coming to this nigga's rescue. They threw me on the ground and jumped me. They were both

Gemini Betrayal

punching me and kicking me in my face and stomach. I couldn't do shit because I was outnumbered.

In the distance, I could hear the alarm and guards rushing down the metal stairs to come break up the commotion. All the prisoners scattered around the room making it more impossible for the guards to get through. I heard somebody yell out "tear gas" and everybody hit the floor or hid behind something, covering their faces. I managed to make it to my feet again only to be tackled by the dude once again.

He had gotten me on the floor in the midst of the room being filled up with gas. He reached in his pocket for something as he held me down. I could barely see anything because I was being blinded by the harsh gas in the air. I felt I burn on the side of my face and I yelled.

Guards made it to where we were and grabbed both of us from the floor. I felt blood trickling down my face and a couple of drops hit the floor.I was immediately rushed to the infirmary by three guards while everybody else was escorted back to their cells. Except for the dude that I was fighting. They led him through the doors leading to solitary.

$$\text{*****}$$

Hours later, I was just finishing up in the infirmary. On top of my cut being stitched up, I was mad as fuck, as I had to get that damn pepper spray shit out of my eyes with that damn salt water. But once I could see, I couldn't have been better. I didn't know the chick running this joint was so goddamn fine. I mean, shawty was bad like a motherfucker! Had on some scrubs and tennis shoes, looking as good as one of them bitches that graced the cover of King magazine. And I was sitting in her face, looking like I just got the living shit kicked out of me.

"Okay Mr. Hall, there you go" she said, after she finished stitching me up. "You're lucky that there wasn't any real nerve damage"

"No, his dumb ass is lucky" I said, correcting her. This shit wasn't over by far. That nigga was gonna pay. "But thanks anyway, Doc. When I get outta here, I'm gonna repay you and take you out"

"Oh really, huh?"

"Yep"

"We'll see" she said. She walked out the room to go get the guard. Did she just blow me off? I couldn't believe it. I always get the women and she was no different. I guess she thought she was the shit but I beg to differ. I was gonna get her ass whether I was inside or outside of these walls. I was gonna get some of them buns.

I blew her a kiss before I was handcuffed by the CO and escorted back to my cell. We got back to where the cells were and I was getting ready to go through the door but I was stopped. "Yo what gives?" I asked.

"You ain't going in there, Hall. Your ass is going to solitary"

"What the fuck for? I ain't even do shit"

It didn't matter what I said, my words fell on deaf ears. He wasn't paying my ass not one ounce of mind. We got to one of the holding cells and he unlocked it and threw me inside. I heard the keys jingling and knew I was being locked away again. I heard the footsteps heading back down the hall and never moved from the spot I was in. I couldn't see shit in this little box. I felt around the room and it wasn't really a lot of space. Hopefully I wouldn't die in here. I wondered how long they were gonna keep me in here. I decided to do a few push-ups for a while.

After I eventually got to a hundred, I laid on the cement floor on my back. I closed my eyes and thought about my sister. About my

Gemini Betrayal

friends. Hell, I even thought about my punk ass father too. It was a miracle how far I had come over the years. The only thing that took a major toll on me was my mother, she was my best friend. When I lost her, half of my life went with her. As for my sister, it seemed as though we were becoming distant more and more these days. But her and our father seemed to be getting too close for comfort. What the fuck was that about? Tia was always our father's favorite and it was always known coming up. I know it's wrong to say, but I was glad when his ass went to jail. As for my fake ass friends, fuck all of them niggas!

I was always there when they asses needed me but when a nigga need them, that's when they ass wanna be fucking M.I.A. Depending on how long I would be in the hole, I was gonna reach out to all they asses again. You know, see where their heads were at. Because if it ain't on the money, drugs, and family, all they asses could bounce. Even my sister ass could go. Shit.

$$\ast\ast\ast\ast\ast$$

It had been a full week since I had been in the hole. I heard the jingling of keys unlocking the door. The door swung open and I stepped out. The beams of sun that shined through the windows of the prison were blinding my black ass.

"Morning sunshine" Gaines said, grinning from ear to ear.

"What you want man? Haven't I been tortured enough for a week?"

"Not in my eyes, shithead. You're coming with me"

"Where to?"

"Interrogation"

"What the fuck am I being interrogated for now?"

"Doesn't matter. Bring your ass," he said. I was cuffed and walked through the halls behind him.

We reached the interrogation room and it was another dude in there. He stood to introduce himself.

"Good morning, Mr. Hall. I'm Jeremy Morrison, your public defender"

"Cool" I said, shaking his hand while still wearing the cuffs on my wrists. We all sat down at the table. Gaines sat across from the both of us and stared deadly at me.

"Shall we get this shit started?" I asked, giving him the same look back.

"Well, you are being held accountable for more than four murders and-," Gaines began.

"And why is that?" Morrison asked, cutting him off. He wrote down on his little pad as Gaines continued.

"We found fingerprints at the crime scene that may have belonged to him"

"May have? Meaning your aren't 100% sure? Is this why my client has been here for over a month? For a damn assumption?" he asked, raising his voice a little. I think I liked this dude. Hell, I would like him even more if I can be released.

"Well, yeah. As a matter of fact, that's exactly right"

"With all due respect, I advise you to release my client on bail. And I mean immediately before I sue your ass, Gaines"

"I'm not doing shit" Gaines said, sitting upright and laughing.

"Either you do so or I will go to the commissioner's office and he will have your ass"

Gemini Betrayal

Gaines pondered the thought for a moment then caved. "He can get his ass out but his bail is set to 500,000" he said, standing up.

"500,000?! Are you a fucking mad man?" Morrison asked, jumping up as well.

Gaines laughed and walked around the table towards the door. "As a matter of fact I am. Take it or leave it, Morrison" He turned away and walked out the room.

I just sat there still quiet as a church mouse. This shit was pure fucking madness. Now that I could get out, I couldn't. Where the hell was I gonna get that kind of money? I didn't even know where the fuck anybody was!

"Antonio don't worry. I will get you out of here"

"How?" I asked.

"I don't know but I will do my best. Give me everybody you know, names and numbers, and I will make some calls to see if they can help get you out"

"They not gonna help with shit. Them motherfuckers practically left me here to fucking die"

"At least let me try" he said, pleading.

I gave him all the crew members' names and numbers like he asked and stood to leave.

"Antonio?"

"What?"

"I promise I wont let you down"

"Don't promise me a motherfucking thing, man"

The guard opened the door and led me to my regular cell instead of back to solitary.

I got back to my cell and laid back on the bottom bunk. It was so much stuff passing through my head about everybody and all their bullshit. "I swear when I get out, I'm not fucking with nobody and everybody gonna die" I said in a low enough tone that I could only hear.

I glanced over and saw the big nigga again. Guess they decided to release the both of us today. He stared me down and I returned the same look. I never broke eye contact as he walked past my cell. Now he had my attention again.

This nigga really thought he intimidated me or something. I was gonna be ready for his big dumb ass next time though. You could count on it. His ass wasn't gonna catch me slipping again. I stood up to look in the mirror on my cell wall.

The wound on the side of my face was proof that this nigga had to die. Never had anybody lived to say they beat me and I wasn't gonna let it start now. That nigga had me fucked all the way up on the real. It was cool though; he was gonna feel my wrath soon enough.

He may have won the battle but I was most definitely gonna win the war.

Chapter Eighteen

Now I was really getting pissed off! It was now going into the third month of me being locked down. This shit was fucking ridiculous! That damn public defender Morrison promised that he would have me out but he was bullshitting. Just full of shit like everybody that was supposed to have my back. And that suck ass nigga, whom I found out name was Bernard, was still trying to catch these hands again.

I was in the shower with a couple of other inmates when I noticed the guard stepping off and Bernard stepped in his place. The other inmates looked at one another and scattered. But not me. I stood there and continued to shower. He dropped his towel and exposed himself to me.

"I guess I'm finally about to get that ass" he said, slowly walking towards me.

I stood there never moving an inch. Once he got close enough to me, I quickly grabbed my soap on a rope and hit him hard as I could upside his head with it. He dropped to the floor and I used this opportunity to beat him all over his naked body with it. I showed him no mercy. His ass had been asking for this for weeks. He was the one that made it worse when he decided to scar my face for life. Now, it was my turn to return the favor.

I dropped the soap and reached into my mouth to retrieve the razor I had constantly been carrying around. I pulled out my makeshift razor and delivered slice after slice to his face and upper torso. By the time the guards came they were too late. They threw me against the shower wall and I looked upon Bernard bleeding from his face and body. He moved a little but not a lot. I looked down at his face as the

Gemini Betrayal

guards were cuffing me again. He looked like he just played a fucking game with jigsaw.

"Game over, nigga" I said, as I was being dragged away by two of the on duty correctional officers. I spat on his damn near lifeless body before they pulled me too far away. Inmates had gathered around Bernard to be speculators but nobody seemed to lend him a hand. Hmmm. Maybe I was doing everyone a favor by getting rid of his ass.

We reached the hole again. This time they practically threw me inside with nothing but my bare ass hitting the cement. That shit had hurt so fucking bad that I didn't even move for about fifteen minutes. I just laid in the middle of the floor, smiling and filling the room with laughter.

✷✷✷✷✷

Not sure how long I was in the hole for this time but I was glad to be out. I was heading to my cell and I observed my surroundings. Every inmate I passed by gave me a head nod. I didn't get it but I guess I would find out eventually. I reached my cell and it was occupied with somebody else. The guard removed my cuffs, pushed me inside and closed the cell behind me.

"Hey, what's up bro?" I said to the dude. "I'm Antonio"

"Chris" he said, extending his hand to me and I took it.

"So what you in for?" I asked, sparking a conversation.

"Armed robbery. They been looking for me for days and they finally caught me"

"Where did they catch you?"

"Home?"

"Home?" I asked puzzled.

"Yep. I wanted them to catch me there. I had already buried my money somewhere for when I get out"

"True shit. How long you got?"

"Six months. That's some slight shit. How about you?"

"I don't even know, man. I been here going on three months though"

"What you in for?"

"Alleged murder and some other bullshit charges"

"Damn, dawg"

"It's cool. I'm getting outta this motherfucker soon I hope"

"Yeah, me too. I hate going to jail"

"You ain't never lied"

We talked a little bit longer then I laid down on my bunk. The bed wasn't that comfortable but I will take that over that damn concrete floor. I closed my eyes and had eventually dozed off.

Unaware of what was going on, I jumped up out of my sleep. I heard the alarms going off and cops running all over the place. I saw Chris standing at the gate of the cell and I jumped down and joined him.

"Yo, what the fuck is going on, man?"

"Shit, man, you missed most of the action. While you was up there in goddamn lala land, some dudes jumped some of the guards and beat the shit out of them. That shit was fucking crazy. I don't know how all the commotion didn't wake you up"

Gemini Betrayal

"I don't know how either. But that shit is wild. So what they doing now?" I asked, peeping down the stairs in the open space where all the madness was taking place.

"Oh them dudes got outnumbered. It was ten of them on six guards. They beat the breaks off they ass, but the guards were fighting their asses back. They were definitely with the shits"

We stared down in the space along with the rest of the onlookers who was cheering on the inmates. Were these niggas looking at the same damn thing I was looking at? Them dudes was getting punished by them guards. I just shook my head and continued to watch until they eventually got the dudes to calm down.

After the incident got handled, the entire prison was on lockdown for three hours. That shit blew me because I wanted to try to call my sister again. I guess it would have to wait until tomorrow.

Later that day, we were finally able to come out of our cells for rec time. I decided to go to workout a little. It seemed like that's all I had been doing other than playing basketball with some of the guys. I wasn't really up for it today so I just hit the bench a little.

While I was in the middle of pumping iron, a gang of niggas approached me. I quickly put the weights on the base and sat up. It looked to be about fifteen to twenty dudes but that ain't matter to me. I have been in this situation before. I stood up to my feet as they started closing in more.

"Chill. We ain't come over here on no beef type shit, man" the ringleader said.

"Then what you want?"

"We just wanna say thanks for what you did with Bernard. That nigga fucked all of us after we we refused to willingly go along with it. But none of us could stand up to him like you. And we wanna let you know if you need us for anything, we got your back, bro. No matter if we in here or outside of here"

"No problem" I said.

"By the way I'm Carlos, this is Cruise, Max, Loco, and Danny. Everybody else you can meet later"

"Cool. I'm Antonio"

"Cool. Trynna play some ball?"

"Naw not today. I'm just gonna workout a little more before we gotta go back in"

"Got you" He dapped me up and him and his gang let me be.

They seemed cool but I couldn't judge just yet.

It was nice to be back in my cell after a long day. I had made some new acquaintances today, built up my upper body a little more, had some edible food for a change, and a nice shower without any disturbances.

I was lying on my back not knowing what the good lord had in store for my life anymore. I didn't even know what I wanted for my life anymore. I had a lot of shit to think about when I got out of here. That is if I ever get out of here. I said a little prayer for myself and my sister. Even though she was acting like she didn't give a fuck about me and my well being. It just felt good to pray and talk to god. Lord knows when the last time he and I had a decent conversation.

After my little prayer, I asked my mom to watch over me and to keep me safe as I walk this earth. I stared up at the cinder block ceiling until my eyes got heavy and I fell asleep.

$$*****$$

The next day started off as usual. Chris was doing sit-ups while I did push-ups before they woke everybody up for breakfast. We had a normal talk but nothing really interesting. He told me he had kids at home that were waiting for him to come home. He said they would be coming to visit him later today.

Kids. I always wanted them but never found the right woman to have them with. I could've had them but I was afraid that whoever their mother turned out to be would be a real bitch and do punk ass shit out of spite. Like Janae's dumbass. I still don't know if her son is really mine. I didn't have time for her bullshit though. But I was still young, I might have kids one of these days. Kids I knew for sure were mine. Who knows?

We went down to the cafeteria for breakfast. It was busy for a change and everybody seemed to be getting along. That was odd. Chris and I got our tray of crap that looked like it was supposed to be some type of potato and egg mess. Yuck! We went to our normal table that everybody knew was ours and we sat down.

"I can't wait to see my kids today, man" Chris began. "I haven't seen them in weeks, Tony, man. They are so beautiful and my son, boy. He looks just like me. I just hope he doesn't end up like me though" he said, putting his head down and playing with his food with a fork.

I swallowed my food before speaking. "How old are your kids?"

"Well, my daughter Iliana is three, my daughter Anaya is six, and my son Christopher is ten"

"That's what's up, dude. They all got the same moms?"

183   Gemini Betrayal

"Yeah. She been riding with my ass since the seventh grade. Lord knows why. I done put that girl through so much hell and pain and she still rides with me. We been married for four years. Times got tough and I started robbing people. She told me to stop but I couldn't. My pride would not let me let my wife be the bread winner for our family. I couldn't do it. I'm the man of the house but I had to do what I had to do"

"I feel you, man. But if you look back on it now, was it really worth losing your family for six months?"

He got quiet. I guess he was thinking about what I had said. I continued to eat my slop as I waited for his answer. Minutes passed before he had taken a deep breath and continued.

"Honestly, no. It wasn't worth it all. I miss waking up to my kids and their shenanigans. Seeing my son play baseball on the weekends. Seeing my girls cheer for their brother. It's hard, man. But you seem to be holding up. How many kids you have?"

"Me? I don't have any"

"None?"

"Nope. No wife. No kids. But I do have a sister. She's actually my twin"

"You have a female version of your ugly ass. Goddamn it, boy" he said, laughing.

I laughed along with him. It actually felt good to laugh. You would have thought my laughter had been buried or something since it had been so long that I had done it. Thinking on it now, I don't know when the last time I had a hearty laugh like this.

We continued to eat and talk until the guards came and released us all for rec or to go and do whatever it was that we pleased.

Gemini Betrayal

We were back in our cell shooting the breeze, playing dominos, and talking about our childhoods when a guard came in.

"Hall" he said in a voice that was too big for his little body. I looked up at him from the floor.

"Yeah?"

"Pack your shit. You're going home"

I couldn't believe it. I was going home. It seemed so unreal. I think I'm dreaming. Either that or I had died and gone to heaven.

"What the fuck you waiting on?" Chris asked me. "Get your ass up and get out of here before they change their mind" He stood up and held out his hand to pull me up from the floor.

I didn't have much in the cell with me because nobody sent me shit or nothing so I didn't have to do nothing. I gave Chris my number and told him to call me whenever he needed somebody to talk to. I also told him if he wanted a job when he got out, I was gonna hook him up.

The guard came back twenty minutes later to retrieve me from the cell. Chris dapped me up and pulled me into a tight man hug. He told me to be safe and I told him the same. As I walked past the cells, I gave fives to the people I had made friends with during my three months here. It felt kind of weird walking through the halls without handcuffs cutting into my wrists. I didn't complain though.

We reached the gates that led to the prison. Just three months ago, I walked through these same gates and was charged with a damn assumption. Now I'm about to walk through these same gates as a free man from the same allegations. I swear this justice system is some bullshit to the max.

I stepped on the other side of the gates and it seemed as though I was breathing a different air. I was feeling rays of a new sun. The day seemed so much brighter than what it seemed behind those

Gemini Betrayal

cement walls earlier this morning. I breathed in the fresh air and it felt like it was my first time in life. Never did I want to lose this feeling. By no means was I ever going back in that place. They would have to kill me first.

I pulled my cell phone out of my bag and powered it on. Surprisingly, it was still damn near fully charged. I had several text messages and a few voicemails.

I saw Leana standing there, smiling from ear to ear. I walked over to her and she humped in my arms. We held each other tight before I sat her back on her feet. We kissed deeply before getting in the car. She told me she had a stop to make and I told her it was cool. I really just wanted to go home but it ain't like I could hop in my own shit and drive off. She drove away from the jail. I didn't even think to look back. I was not gonna miss that damn place. Not one bit.

I decided to check my voicemail as we drove off. They were mostly from my father Big Tone. He was telling me that they hadn't released him yet but he would be home soon enough. I already told his ass that I didn't give a rat's ass about him or his release date. I guess I wasn't too clear because he still called to keep talking about it. The other messages I checked were from females. One from Leana, one from Christian and one from some chick named Dyana, that I had met at a gas station one day. None of the messages were important except Leana's. She was the only one that reached out to me saying she was looking for me and that she had gotten a new number. Nobody else but her mattered at this point.

I opened my text messages. There were 80 texts in the gang's group chat, one from Christian, and ten from Dyana. I decided to check Christian's first since it was only one. I opened it and it was an extremely long ass message. *Ughhh.* I didn't even bother reading it but I did skim through the summary. She was basically letting me know that I was a bitch ass nigga. That she hated my guts and wish she had never met me. I just laughed because I must have really given her the perception that I really gave a fuck. I deleted the entire thread but not before I saved all the nudes she had sent. Then I blocked her. "*Well that bitch is out*" *I thought to myself.*

I opened up the thread to Dyana's texts. She had been texting me and asking how I was doing and why I hadn't been responding to her. She even sent me some pictures of her in sexy lingerie and some without a bra on asking me to come over for a night cap. Damn!! her body was banging. I never imagined that body under the clothes I had seen her in the day we met. I saved all her photos as well, but in her own folder, and texted her back. I told her I wanted to see her tonight and I wasn't taking no for an answer. She immediately texted me back with an address and what time to be there. I texted her back to let her know that I would be there just as Leana pulled up in front a store. She got out after kissing me on the cheek and said she would be right back.

She had had to have had her radio up on fucking twenty because that bass was something serious. Shy Glizzy filled the car with his music. Her ass was definitely a DC native. She came back out the store with a bag of snacks. She drove away from the store and I watched as her ass swerved in and out the cars in traffic while eating skittles. She almost hit a damn car that was disabled on the side of the ride but sped in front of a truck just in time to cut the driver off. I put my seat belt on, said a little prayer, and just hoped I would survive this goddamn thirty minute ride with this girl. No wonder nobody ever wanted to ride with her. Right now, I didn't really have a choice. I shook my head and went back to my messages. I opened up the group text with the crew.

All they were doing was going back and forth about parties and heists. These dumbasses knew better than to do that shit over the phone like that. I thought I taught they asses right but I guess not. Out of all those eighty some fucking messages, not one soul asked about my whereabouts except Leana. Not Cam. Not Twan. Not even Sienna. Not even my motherfucking sister! It's like they just wiped my ass from existence. I guess I didn't matter to anybody anymore.

Gemini Betrayal

I was still skimming through the messages when I noticed that my sister was going back and forth with Antwan about how she wanted the crew to be. And Twan didn't agree with her decisions I guess and he chose to go his own separate way. I just shook my head at all of this shit. I couldn't believe this shit. Twan had sent a message saying that I would have never ran the team the way that my sister was trying to do. And her response was, "If you wanna be all on my brother dick, then go ahead. We don't fucking need you nor do we want you. Fuck you and fuck my brother" Twan clap backed at her and told her that he would just start a team with me and take back over. So basically these motherfuckers were going into a war. And I was shocked at my sister. *Fuck me?*

After all the shit we have been through, she would really turn her motherfucking back on me? Me out of all people? That bitch must be out of her motherfucking mind! If that little bitch wanted a war, then that's what the fuck she was gonna get. I was gonna lay low for a while and not draw attention to myself. Especially since I didn't want to end up back in that fucking jail. And I already knew Cam was gonna be up my sister's ass like always. As for everybody else, I would soon see where they heads were. I wasn't gonna let nobody have me out here looking like a bitch. Not no nigga nor a bitch. Family or not.

*****

I was relieved to make it home in one piece, riding with Lean's crazy ass. If she had been an uber driver, there was no way she was getting five stars from me. I thanked her for the ride and got out. As I walked to the door, I waved back at her and told her I would call her in a bit.

I reached my porch and looked around my neighborhood. Everything had looked to be the same except people had actually cut their grass. Somebody even cut my grass. It was probably Mr. Hopkins' grandsons that had done it. They always cut my grass for me in the summer time when they were here for break. I would call later to see if it were them and pay them accordingly. I opened my front door and was welcomed by a pile of mail on the floor. I picked it all up and closed the door. The inside of my house smelled like lemon pine sol. That must have been from the last time I had cleaned up. Maybe it was those air fresheners I kept plugged in. Either way, I was just glad to smell the fresh scent.

I made my way to my kitchen. I stood over the trash can thumbing through my mail and throwing away shit I didn't need. I threw out some sale papers, junk mail, and letters about voting for a mayor. One envelope did catch my eye. It was my DNA results. I quickly opened it to see what the results said. I smiled as I read that I was 99.9% not the father. I almost burst into tears; I was so happy. I found Janae's number and sent her the picture of the results. I told that bitch to never call me again, don't text me, no nothing. I was so damn relieved.

I raided my refrigerator and grabbed me a cold beer and headed upstairs. I got in my room and practically jumped into my bed. I didn't even bother to turn the tv on. I took a long swig of my brew, kicked off my shoes and laid back on the bed. I was beat. You would have thought I just worked a seventeen hour shift or something because of how fast I went to sleep.

I had missed my bed so damn much. I never wanted to leave this bed again in my life for anything in the world. Not even if my fucking house was on fire.

✴✴✴✴✴

I had waken up to my alarm at 7:30 that night. It was still light outside and I thought it was a little earlier but it wasn't. I reached for my phone to turn my alarm off. I looked at my phone and saw a text from Leana. She was basically saying how much she missed me and was thinking about me. She said that she wished that I would talk to her because she was worried about me.

That was kinda sweet and sincere. I was about to text her back but I stopped. I had just remembered that I was supposed to see Dyana tonight. I decided to link up with Leana tomorrow or later in the week. I didn't want anybody to know my whereabouts honestly. Not even her; especially since I wasn't sure whose team she was on. She did reach out to me and she did pick me up. But that didn't mean shit for real. Sex always complicated things and I didn't need that in my life right now. At least not with Leana. Now Dyana on the other hand, I was ready to blow her back out all night long.

I had texted Dyana to make sure we were still on for tonight and she responded 'yes'. I put my phone on the charger for a little bit while I took a shower. I got in that shower and it felt as good as it did when I had busted my very first nut when I was fourteen. The beads of water felt good covering my body and splashing against my tattoos and newly more muscled body. The best part about this shower was that it was private. I didn't have to worry about other men looking at my dick or trying to rape me or trying to shank me while I had my back turned. It gave me a peace of mind. I enjoyed the shower for all of thirty minutes before I got out.

I didn't know what to wear to Dyana's house. I doubt if we go anywhere this time of night because if we were, she would have asked me to come over earlier. Right? Not knowing for certain, I donned a pair of jeans, a pair of my 12s, some of my Hugo Boss cologne, and my black watch that coincided with my sneakers. I looked like I was about to hit the block. Thinking about it, I just might do that tomorrow to see how the corners were looking and what not.

I checked my uber app and the closest driver was only four minutes away and it was a ten minute travel time. I quickly requested

Gemini Betrayal

that rider because I waited three months for some pussy and I think I have waited long enough to bust up in somebody's guts. Shit.

I grabbed my phone off the charger and my wallet and headed downstairs. Them damn uber drivers ain't give no fucks. If you wasn't outside by the time that timer went off, they was gonna roll out on your ass and charge you a fee. They were really with the shits. And so was I. I didn't want to have to blast nobody over no dumb shit. Speaking on that, I grabbed my little .22 from my secret compartment in my kitchen then headed outside. Just as I was tucking it in my pants, my driver pulled up.

"Hey, how are you this evening?" the peppy female driver asked me as I hopped in.

"I'm cool. You?"

"I'm good. Just working"

"True. You working all night?"

"Yep. I love working the night shift. It's so peaceful"

"I hear that"

"So where are you headed?" she asked. *Damn she nosey* I thought to myself.

"Over to a friend house"

"That's what's up" That was the last thing she said before turning the radio up a little. I guess that was her song because she started bouncing around in her seat and singing the lyrics word for word. As I listened in, she was playing that song by the Migos, Cardi B, and Nicki Minaj. My sister loved that song. I rapped along to the lyrics with the driver.

We arrived at Dyana's house in record time. We actually got there in less than ten minutes. Not sure if she was driving the speed

Gemini Betrayal

limit the entire time or not, but I felt like I was in Allstate's hands the entire ride. I thanked her, gave her five stars in the app, and dropped a fifty dollar bill in her hand before getting out. She thanked me and said she hoped to see me again.

I stood on the sidewalk in front of Dyana's house. It was coincidently located a couple streets over from where I grew up. That was strange because I had never seen her before the day we had met. Oh well. I walked up the steps that led to her front door and waited for her to open the door up for me.

Chapter Nineteen

"That was amazing" Dyana said, after rolling off top of me. "You must have been as happy to see me as I was to see you"

"Yeah" I replied still panting. Truth was I would have taken any pussy right now. I was so damn backed up it was ridiculous. My balls were so damn numb until I released all my hot cum all up inside her. I got up from the bed and walked into the bathroom. I rolled the condom off my dick, pissed and flushed the toilet. This bitch wasn't about to get me caught up. Uh-uh no way. I washed my hands, went back and laid down. She laid on my chest and played with my chest hair.

"Ready to go again?" she asked.

"Again? Already?" I asked. We just went three rounds and it was only almost midnight. This chick was a damn sexual deviant for real!

"Yeah. I'm so horny. It has been a long time since I had some dick"

"What's your definition of a long time?"

"About six months"

"Damn. Let me recuperate and we can go again. Cool?"

"Cool"

She got under the cover and got on her phone and played candy crush. I grabbed my phone and checked my messages. Still nothing from my sister's ass. I had a missed call but it was from a private number. I guess they didn't want me to know who it was because anybody that knows me know that I don't answer that shit.

I wasn't sure how long it was she was playing that damn game but it was time she hopped back up on this dick. I took her phone from her hand and placed it on the night table. She sat up and I placed my hand on the back of her head; leading her to my manhood.

She got between my legs and smiled down at my dick and licked her lips. It looked like she was salivating. Like she had found her prey and was ready to capture it. She started slowly placing soft kisses on the tip and all over. My dick was starting to come to life. I guess she could tell because she smiled again. She took a hold of it with her left hand and massaged my balls gently with her right. I moaned and looked down at her as she took me into her mouth.

She sucked as it became harder with each passing second. I could feel the back of her throat as she took all nine inches in. I looked down again and this time I made eye contact with her. Neither one of us broke our stares as she started to make a mess with her saliva. She spit on my dick and jerked it a little before putting it back in her mouth. After five more minutes of my dick going down her esophagus, she got on top.

She positioned herself directly on my dick and even put it in herself. She slowly eased down until every inch was inside her vagina. She rode me slow and I grabbed her by the hips. She placed her breasts close to my face and I grabbed one of them nipple with my teeth. She had moaned out in sheer pleasure. I sucked her nipple and gently bit down on it as her speed went up a little. I took the other titty in my mouth and repeated what I had done to the other one. Her pace quickened a little bit more. She placed her hands on my chest and thrusted her hips deeper into mine. She threw her head back and I grabbed her around the neck. We both started fucking one another faster without missing a beat.

She leaned back and put her feet on each side of me. She bounced up and down on me as she played with her clit. She was losing control of herself. I seen her clit let a couple drops of cum out before she exploded. She squirted and sprayed all over my stomach and chest. I grabbed her by her hips again and slammed her up and down on my dick until I came. I held her down and got as deep as possible before I came again.

She hopped off my dick, snatched the condom off and caught the rest of my cum in her mouth. The cum that she had missed, she cleaned up and sucked the precum out of the condom. That was some new shit. This bitch was freaky freaky. I ain't never seen no chick do that before. As sexy as they was, I wasn't sure if that condom was that damn good. But hey, to each his own.

She climbed from off top of me again and this time she told me she was done for the night. I checked the clock and it was nearing two in the morning. Her ass ain't have no choice but to be done for the night. I was tapping out. My nuts were probably dry as the damn Sahara now! She laid on my chest and I threw my arm around her. We soon after fell asleep peacefully.

✳✳✳✳✳

I woke the next morning to a note from Dyana. She told me that she went for her morning jog and wouldn't be back until ten. I checked the time and it was only nine o' clock. Wasn't sure what time she left, but I decided to just take a quick shower before she came back.

I looked in her hall closet and grabbed a towel and washcloth and headed to the bathroom. I got in the shower and scrubbed the sex

195   Gemini Betrayal

from my skin with the Irish spring soap. It was funny because a lot of females I had come across mostly use dove soap. I guess she was different. After I got out the shower, I saw that she still wasn't back yet so I decided to get dressed and go do a little snooping.

I looked through her drawers first. Her top drawer had sexy panties and bras, I dug underneath of them and my hand touched something. I wrapped my hand around it and pulled it out. This nasty, freaky, bitch had a 12-inch black dildo in her damn underwear drawer! I quickly dropped it back in there and put it back to where it was. I felt a little gay holding that joint the way I did. *"No wonder she was able to take my dick and ride it the way she did" I thought to myself. She had been practicing taking big dick with that damn Godzilla penis.* I went through the rest of her drawers and didn't find anything. So I decided to raid her closet.

She had one side full of dress clothes and the other side filled with scrubs. "I take it that she's a nurse" I said aloud. I was correct. She had her nurse's badge hanging on the door knob of the closet. It had the hospital she worked at and everything. She had good taste from what I could see from her clothes and shoe collection. I thought I had heard something so I quickly sat down on the bed and started flipping through channels.

She came jogging up the steps wearing a sports bra and yoga pants. Didn't know how woman's clothes fit over asses that big but it's so marvelous to look at. Especially when they gotta struggle and jump in their jeans. Their asses just be bouncing around and dogs like me just sit there lusting over the booty.

"Got back just in time" she said, walking into the room and kissing me on the lips. I kissed her back and she headed towards the closet. "How did you sleep?" she asked as she started taking off her shoes and removing her clothes.

"Good. I slept really good"

"That's good. I'm gonna hop in the shower real quick"

"Cool"

She got in the shower. I flipped through the channels to try and find something interesting to keep on the tv. Moments later, Dyana started back talking.

"You know I thought I was never gonna hear from you" she yelled over the shower water.

"Why you say that?" I asked loud enough so she could hear me.

"Because you wasn't responding to my calls or my texts. I had lost hope that we would cross paths again" She turned off the water and dried her body off.

"Yeah sorry about that. I was super busy"

"Busy, huh? For three months straight?" she asked inquisitively.

"I was locked up"

She paused for a second from putting on deodorant and looked at me. "Locked up? What for?"

"Allegations"

"Allegations? That's all?"

"Yep"

"And what did you allegedly do for them to lock you up for three months?"

"Murder"

She froze again. Maybe I should have made up a lie. "And what kind of work do you do again?" she asked, oiling up her body.

"I never told you?" I replied.

"Well you can tell me now" she said, aggressively.

"I'm a drug dealer"

"A drug dealer?"

"Yes. A drug dealer. A king pin. I run a whole crew of people. Well, I did. I put my sister in charge"

"Um, okay"

"What?"

"Nothing" she said. She rummaged through her middle drawer and pulled out a short t-shirt and then pulled a pair of boy shorts from her top drawer. She put them on then jumped onto the bed and laid back on the pillows.

"You okay?" I asked.

"I'm cool. I'm just taken aback by your, um, occupation"

"Nothing to worry about"

"Really?"

"Really"

"Okay. If you say so. Are you hungry?" she asked, sitting up in the middle of the bed.

"Naw. I think I will just grab me something to eat in a little bit. I need to go home and change clothes and hit the block" I said, standing up. I leaned in and kissed her on the forehead. I was heading down the stairs when I heard her yell "be careful" to me. I yelled back up the stairs to her that I would and left out the door.

Gemini Betrayal

I forgot that I didn't have a damn car. I requested another uber and it pulled up within a couple of minutes. I headed to my house to do just what I said. Even though I only put this on last night just to come over here, I didn't want to take the chance that someone had seen me and think I'm dirty. I can say that I never replayed the same outfit in the same week. I never have so why in the hell would I start now?

I arrived at my house and I ran inside. I went up to my room and searched through my closet for something to wear. I found some black dickies. I decided to put those on with my Timbs and a whit tee. I was gonna keep it simple. I made sure to pack an extra white tee in case of an emergency.

I heard my doorbell ring. I ran down the stairs and looked through the peephole. It was Gaines' punk ass and some other dude. I opened the door slightly.

"What you want, man?"

"Oh, open the door you little shit" he said, barging in and knocking me back. "I'm here to install your new low jack"

"Low jack? Y'all motherfuckers putting me on house arrest?"

"Yep. And you have to see your probation officer once a week. This is Simon Carter, your new probation officer" he said, pointing to the round dude with fat ass frames for glasses.

"Nice to meet you, Mr. Hall"

"Yeah whatever" I replied.

Gaines couldn't wait to put that damn cuff on my ankle. He told me to sit down and he volunteered to do it hisself.

"You cannot go outside of the state with this on" he said, like I didn't know that already. I think Gaines just talked most of the time just to hear himself talk. *I wonder if he actually thinks about the bullshit he says before he say it? Inquiring minds would like to know.*

"No shit, Sherlock" I shot back.

He stared at me like he wanted to shoot me and I stared back at him with mutual feelings. "Look, Mr. Smartass, just do what you're supposed to do and we won't have any problems. But me, on the other hand, I hope you fuck up. I'm gonna be waiting to haul your ass back to prison"

He left out the door laughing and shit. My P.O. handed me his card and told me to call him if I needed him for anything or if I had any questions.

"Yeah, yeah, yeah" I said, lightly shoving him out the door. I closed the door behind him and went to go sit back on my couch.

This was straight bullshit. I looked down at the bracelet blinking on my ankle. How the fuck was I gonna be able to do anything on fucking house arrest? I know Gaines' ass would be watching me, just waiting for me to slip up. I laid my head back on the sofa.

"I wish Tasha was here" I thought to myself. Even though she did steal from me, she was a real ride or die bitch. Ever since I met her, she always proved that she was down for whatever no matter what. Why the fuck did she have to go so damn soon? They say the realest die young and Tasha was definitely one of the real ones. She always knew how to psych out the cops. What would she do in this situation? I thought long and hard about it. Bingo. She would get a mule. I can do that. But the question was who?

I decided to call Twan. He picked up on the fourth ring.

"Yo, what's up, Boss?" he said. At least, he knew I was still in charge in some type of way.

"Nothing much. Where you at right now?"

"Finishing up these sales around 38th. You need me?"

"Yeah, I do in a little bit. Be here in about two hours."

"No problem" he said and hung up.

I called Leana and had the same conversation and she agreed to come as well. Now that I had a meeting set up. I was still missing something. I needed a goddamn car. I requested an uber yet again to take me to the impound lot. It said that they were four minutes away. I took that time to run to my safe and pull out a couple of stacks and grabbed my wallet. As soon as I got outside, the car was pulling up. These drivers did not play about their money I swear. They were better than damn taxi cabs.

$$*****$$

I arrived at the impound lot and it was not going good. This funny looking bitch at the desk wasn't trying to give me my damn car.

"Look bitch, that's my car. I mean I got the damn key" I said, showing her the key to the car.

"Like I said, nigga, you're not getting shit without showing me your license, and insurance, or something that you have on the car. Plus you have to pay the impound fees"

I shook my head. This bitch must not have any idea who I was. I was getting fed up with this broad. "How much are the fees?"

She hit a couple of buttons as she smacked on her gum. I swear I hated that fucking gum-popping noise. She looked from the screen and looked at me. "The total fees are $1, 843.23."

"Here, man" I said, throwing two stacks of 100s on the counter. She grabbed it through the slot.

"This is more than the fees"

"I know that. The rest is for you. Now give me my car"

"For real? Shit take it" she said, letting me go through the gate. I knew that would get her attention. All these hoes were money hungry. Everybody had a price. It's nice to have money; it makes the world go 'round.

She stopped me on the way out and handed me her number. She asked me to call her so we could hang out sometimes. I told her 'okay'. As soon as I hit the freeway, I threw her number out the window. I had enough of these trifling, gold-digging bitches for a lifetime. I headed to grab me something to eat from Subway then headed back home to wait for my peeps. It would be nice to see them and catch up on everything that has been going on between everybody.

A little after thirty minutes of me being home, I had crushed my food and caught up on a little bit of tv. My doorbell rang and I looked out the peephole. Both Leana and Twan were standing on my doorstep. I opened the door and Twan dapped me up. I reached to give Leana a hug as Twan disappeared into the living room and I got nothing but a cold shoulder. She rolled her eyes at me and kept walking. *What the fuck was that?*

"Yo, where you been, man?" Twan asked when I got in the living room.

"Well, um-."

"Probably at some bitch house" Leana said, rolling her eyes again. Both me and Twan looked at her strangely but I ignored her.

"Actually I was locked up"

"What?" Twan said.

"Yep. Leana picked me up yesterday"

"What for again?" Leana asked, sounding all concerned now.

"They said I murdered somebody. Actually a few people"

"Shit. That's crazy, man" Twan said, shaking his head.

"Yeah it is. But you know what's even more crazy?" I said, waiting for both of them to give me their attention again. Once I got it, I continued, "I wasn't at none of those crime scenes but my fingerprints somehow were"

"Huh? That doesn't even sound right" Leana said.

"I know that but it's true"

"If that's so, how the fuck did you get out?"

"Not sure really. I guess my public defender came through and got me out. I got his number. I will call him and reimburse him."

"Cool" Twan replied. Shit had got quiet for a few moments and we all were just exchanging looks at one another.

"Actually I got your black ass out" Leana said.

"You paid $500,000 to get me out?" I asked.

"Yeah I did. You're welcome"

"Thanks. So, what's up with the crew?" I asked.

"What crew?" Leana asked. "Your sister don't fuck with us two anymore so she kicked us out the crew"

"What the fuck you mean? This my crew" I said.

"I know man" Twan said, "but your sister said if we want to worship a snitch, then go be with that snitch because she don't fuck with snitches"

"She surely did. Got a whole new crew and everything" Leana added.

"What about Sienna? Where is she?"

"She said if it's not a family no more, she out. She bounced about two months ago. Moved her and her family away to Cali and said she will stay in contact with us. But as far as Tia's crazy ass, that bitch done lost her fucking marbles. She got little ten year old kids taking shit to school and selling for her. And she got some hot-headed seventeen year old dude on her team. This nigga shoots on sight; no questions asked"

"Who else she got?"

"Mostly motherfuckers from the west side"

"This shit don't make no fucking sense. I'm going to talk to her. This shit is getting way out of hand"

"She's not gonna talk to you, bro" Twan said.

"You watch and see. She don't have a motherfucking choice"

"We hear you, Boss" Leana said.

We chatted and caught up a little bit longer. As it grew later into the evening, Twan parted ways with Leana and me. As soon as he left, Leana grilled my black ass.

"Really, Antonio? Were you out at a bitch's house last night? And don't fucking lie to me, nigga" she yelled at me.

"I'm not lying, Baby. I was in here sleeping all night. I wouldn't lie to you" I said, trying to hold her. She pushed me away.

"You could have at least fucking called"

"I did"

"I didn't receive no calls"

"You don't answer blocked out numbers neither. Besides I didn't have your new number, remember?" I said, smiling.

She looked at me and jumped up in my arms. "I'm so sorry, baby. If I would have known that was you, I would have answered. Then I would've been in contact with you once I changed my number" she said, kissing me.

"I know boo" I said in between kisses. I carried her up the stairs to my bedroom.

We wrestled to strip each other out of our clothes. We didn't stop until we both were completely naked and under the blanket on the cool sheets. We fucked and made love all night long. This was way more fun than it was with Dyana last night. I felt kind of bad for fucking somebody first instead of Leana. If she ever found out, she would probably fucking kill my black ass.

For my sake, I wasn't gonna say a damn thing. Some things are better left unsaid.

Chapter Twenty

My sister had agreed to come to my house to talk to me about what was going on with business. She had told me that ten o' clock this morning. I looked at my watch and it was going on four o' clock. My sister was about to blow my fucking soul. Like what the fuck kind of games was she trying to play? I ain't have time for no damn playing. Especially not when my fucking money was involved.

Time kept passing and it started to grow later and later into the evening. I checked my watch this time and it was going on five minutes to eight. I blew up my sister phone some more. Twenty minutes later, I heard a hard knock at my door. I swung open my door and it was my sister. She didn't even speak to me. She just walked right past me into the living room. I could smell the odor of weed and Hennessy oozing from her pores. Oh god.

"So what's up, bro?" she asked, sitting down and sitting with her legs gapped open like a straight dude.

"I should be asking you that. What's going on with business?"

"Oh shit, man. Business is fucking booming more than ever"

"I hear ya. What's this about you splitting up the crew and starting a new one?"

"Yeah I did. So what?"

"So what? How the fuck you gonna split up the crew? They family"

Gemini Betrayal

"They were family. Just like I thought you were family"

"What the fuck that supposed to mean?" I asked defensively as I stood to my foot.

"Just like I fucking said, big bro. Family don't turn they back on family" she said, standing up too.

"How the fuck I turn my back on you?"

"When me and Cam got locked up but you didn't. You was a motherfucking free man while we was doing time. Then we get out and then you disappear. What the fuck was that about? Explain that shit to me"

"I got knocked for murders"

"Bullshit"

"That's true shit"

"Oh that's bullshit Antonio and you fucking know it! If you got hit with murder, we all would've went, too. If we all be together, how the fuck they only get you?"

"Because I didn't snitch"

"You mean you didn't snitch this time?"

"No. I didn't snitch no time. I would never turn my back on my crew"

"Correction, you mean my crew. Remember? You stepped down now I wear the crown"

"I want my crew back"

"This ain't your fucking crew no more, Antonio. And I advise you to get that through your fucking head, big bro. I wouldn't want to see you get hurt in these streets. So keep your fucking mouth shut" she said, heading towards the door.

"Are you threatening me?" I asked drawing my gun from behind my back. She pulled hers as well and turned it on me.

"I don't make threats" she said. "And lesson one; don't ever pull your weapon unless you're gonna use it. We both know I have no problem pulling the trigger. Don't tempt me"

She turned her back on me and walked out the door. She knew I wasn't gonna pull the trigger. How could I? I had nothing against her. Well at least I didn't at first. But it seemed as though she wanted a war. I don't know what the fuck was wrong with my sister but I wasn't gonna let her get to me. No motherfucking way in hell.

I put the safety back on and locked my front door. I went upstairs and laid across my bed. I didn't even bother with the tv like I usually did. I didn't even cut any lights or anything on. The only light I saw was coming from my cell phone.

I looked at the caller id and it was Dyana calling. I silenced the call and let it continue to ring and light up the room with it's bright blinking light. Seconds later, it stopped and started again. This time it was Leana calling. I didn't feel like being bothered with anybody right now. I was stressed out to the max. It was so much shit going through my head right now. So many different scenarios playing throughout my mind. But there was one thing for certain, I needed money.

I texted the connect to set up a meeting at his earliest convenience. He texted back a few moments later to meet him at the Baltimore Harbor tomorrow at 3 on his boat. I agreed and got my money together that I was gonna need. I stuffed it all neatly in a duffel bag and put it under my bed.

I went to bed feeling a little relieved that at least we still had connections with Pablo. I wouldn't have known what the fuck to do if we lost him. He had been a part of this family forever. Family. It used to mean something to me. Not anymore though. Now it was just a word. A simple word that doesn't mean shit anymore.

$$***** $$

The next day came and went in a blur. Twan and I had met with Pablo and his Italian mafia at the scheduled time and we left with a lot of info. We found out that he was actually the only connect we had left out of everyone. He informed me that while I was locked down, my sister had a meeting with all the drug lords.

He informed us that she had cut everybody's portion and basically she got the biggest cut. I don't understand how the fuck she even thought Pablo was gonna go for that shit. Why in the hell would anybody supplying us drugs even take that deal. I guess since they were still making a profit, it didn't matter. Now me and Twan was just riding through the hood smoking a jay.

"I can't believe your sister, man" Twan said, hitting the blunt.

"I know, son. She wilding and that ain't doing nothing but bringing police our way. And we don't need that shit right now"

"True that"

I took the blunt from him and hit it twice. "Tia's ass needs to be stopped"

"Yeah she do but how?"

I sat there in thought as I continued to drive. I really wasn't sure how to deal with the situation. That was my sister and I loved her. I tried talking to her but that didn't work at all. Her head so big right now and she think that she can't be touched. She had another thing coming. And then Cam's ass was supposed to be my boy. His damn head so far up my sister's ass he can't even think straight no more. If it

Gemini Betrayal

wasn't about Tia or money, he didn't wanna hear shit nobody had to say.

We got to Twan's house and I decided to chill there for a little bit. Leana had texted me and I told her I was gonna be there. She said she would be there in about an hour. We went into Twan's house only to be greeted by his girlfriend, Ashley, and a Louisville slugger.

"What the fuck are you doing, Ash?" Twan yelled as we ducked from her swing.

"Who the fuck is Mia?"

"I don't know no damn, Mia, Babe" he said, trying to grab the bat from her.

"You're a fucking liar!" she screamed, swinging the bat again. "Move out the fucking way Tony before your ass get hit, too" She didn't have to tell me twice. I moved my black ass right out the way and made my way into the living room. Glad I still had a good view of the action though.

"Bitch, if you hit me I will fuck you up. Now I said I didn't know nobody named Mia"

"Then why the fuck did she show up here to bring back your fucking watch?"

"How the fuck you know she ain't some bitch just trying to get in your head, Baby? And how do you even know it was really my watch?"

"Because it has the fucking engraving I put on here for you" she said, throwing the watch at him. He bent down to retrieve the watch and she cracked him right on the back with the bat. The way he dropped, I know that shit had to hurt. Shit! I felt that in my damn back!

"Bitch are you fucking crazy?" he said, lying on the floor trying to get back up. She swung the bat again; this time hitting him in the leg.

"Ahhhhh" he yelled out in pain. She was about to hit him again but I stopped her. I snatched the bat from her hands and pushed her away a little.

"What the fuck are you doing, Antonio? Give me that back" she yelled at me.

"I'm not giving you shit back, Ash. You're gonna kill his ass"

"Good. At least I won't be getting cheated on anymore"

She had a point. A dumb one but a point nonetheless. I gave her the bat back and as soon as she raised the bat to hit Twan again, he shot her.

She dropped to the floor holding her thigh. "Why did you shoot me, Twan?" she asked crying. Was she serious right now? Now she wanted to act innocent like she wasn't just seconds away from killing this nigga. I laughed and walked back to where I was. This ain't have shit to do with me so I just picked up the remote and flipped through channels.

Twan got up from the floor and limped over to Ashley's aid. He extended his hand and she took it. "I need to get to a hospital, Twan" she said. Twan looked down at her leg.

"Naw, you gonna be good. It's just a flesh wound. I can fix that upstairs"

They told me they would be right back. I wasn't even paying their asses no mind. They were so damn dumb because at the end of they day, neither of them were going anywhere. He's been cheating on her ass since they were in high school and he always lied but she always knew the truth. I guess some people will put up with anything if they're in love. I would've killed that bitch if I was him. But since he not me, she gets to live.

Gemini Betrayal

Fifteen minutes had passed and I hadn't heard a peep out of the two. I crept up the stairs and peeped in the bathroom. She was giving this nigga some head! I shook my head and went back downstairs. As soon as I did, the doorbell rang. I opened the door and it was Leana.

"What the hell are you doing answering somebody else's door?" she asked laughing.

I pulled her inside and kissed her deeply. "Don't talk shit woman"

"What was that for?" she asked after I eventually let her come up for air.

"Damn, I can't kiss you like that or something?"

"I mean, yeah, but nothing. Yeah you can"

"Aight then" We made our way to the living room and watched a little tv.

"So there's something I had to tell you, Antonio" she said, during a commercial break.

"What's up?"

"Your father is out"

I looked at her strangely. "What?"

"Yep. He's been out for a couple days I heard"

"And? So what?"

"Well, word is he's gonna be riding with your sister and her crew"

I tossed the thought back and forth in my head. Again, he had proved that she was his favorite. Not that I would want his ass with me anyway. "Oh well. Hope she knows what she's getting herself into"

"That's it? That's all you're gonna say?"

"What else am I supposed to say, Lee?"

"Say about what?" Twan asked, entering the room.

"About his father being home from jail"

"Oh word? When did Big Tone get out?"

"Earlier this week. Tony doesn't seem to care though"

"Why would he? He can't fucking stand his father; he never did"

"Exactly bro"

"Whatever. But anyway I heard about this meeting that they are having in a couple of weeks to get some new territory" She looked at me. "They trying to take over and push us out the loop"

"I don't give a shit about them motherfuckers!" I yelled. "Look if they ass wanna try to run us out, they better have the manpower to do so. Ain't nobody running me outta no motherfucking where. I run this city. Let a bitch or a nigga try to stop me and they ass is done. Family or not, they ass getting bodied"

The room got silent. Everybody was looking at everybody. I didn't have time to feed into shit about my fake ass family. They asses deserved to be around each other. I didn't need their asses.

"Any word on a shipment?" I asked Leana.

"Yeah"

"When and where?"

"Tomorrow night at midnight. Lake Arbor Park"

"Who's doing the run?"

"Some newbies named Los and Kel."

"You know them?" I asked Twan.

"Yeah I do"

"Cool. We gonna rob they ass on their way there. They wanna fuck with us, do they? Well I hope they ready to play. I got a plan. Huddle up"

✳✳✳✳✳

It was nearing midnight and the plan was already in effect. We had been following Tia's runners around for the past hour so we could catch them slipping. Unfortunately we didn't, but we wasn't giving up. We had to get this lick and put our names back in the streets.

Kel and Los were unaware that we were trailing them which was good. That meant that these fools didn't watch their surroundings. That's one of the first things you learn when you start living the street life. I guess these niggas didn't get the memo. Either that or my sister just sent the two motherfuckers here, blind as fucking bats.

We parked our car a few feet away from where they had stopped. I guess whoever they were meeting was in the car on the other side of the playground. They were flashing their headlights as a signal. Twan and I watched as they got out the car carrying two medium sized duffel bags. They walked slowly across the grass without even looking around. If somebody wanted to stick them up right now, it would have been so easy. I didn't even see guns on them.

The transaction took all of ten minutes. We tried to see who they had met up with but whoever it was, never got out the truck. So once they got their product, they walked back to their car. I saw as they tossed the three large duffel bags in their trunk. Not even looking around to make sure they were not being watched by the police or anybody, they hopped in their car and drove off. Fucking rookies. This lick was gonna be a fucking piece of cake.

We were about fifteen minutes away from the park and an unmarked police car came out of nowhere and drove around us. They had stopped Los' and Kel's car on side of the street. We fell back a little and turned on a residential street. We cut the engine and crouched down in our seats.

The officer knocked on the window. Kel rolled down the driver side window and smoke escaped out. "Do you have any idea while I pulled you over?" the officer said.

"No I don't officer" Kel said.

"You were swerving back there and ran two stop signs"

"Oh shit" Kel and Los said in unison, laughing. The officer, however, didn't find it hilarious at all.

"License and registration please" she said. He handed her his information and she took it back to her car. She waited there for about ten minutes then walked back over. "Here you go" she said handing him his stuff back.

"So what's the charge officer?"

"You're being charged with being at the wrong place at the wrong time."

"What?"

He looked back at her and a double barrel shotgun was staring in his face. She shot him twice and shot Kel once in the head. Leana took the key from the ignition and opened the trunk. She grabbed all the bags and walked back to her car toting her shotgun over her

215   Gemini Betrayal

shoulder and got in. She threw the bags on the passenger seat and put the car in reverse; driving back to the street where Tony and Twan was. She pulled up beside them and rolled the window down.

"We all good, Lee?" Twan asked.

"Oh we're fucking great" Leana said, smiling. They all drove down the street away from the scene and headed to Tony's house"

Chapter Twenty-One

They arrived at Tony's house and headed straight to the basement. They all opened a duffel bag and dumped its contents on the table.

"Holy shit" Leana said. Her eyes grew wide as she looked at a pile of white powder spread across the table.

"Holy shit is right" Twan said in agreement.

Antonio just looked on. A smile spread across his face as he looked at what all came out of this hit. He was definitely proud of them. He grabbed some baggies and handed a box to both Twan and Leana. They all slipped on their gloves and went to work. They were bagging up drugs for at almost two hours before they had completely finished.

After they completed the first task, Antonio opened the secret spot behind his wall and they put all the drugs inside. He felt safe doing so because nobody could get in without his handprint. It was the best three thousand dollars he had ever spent.

They retreated back upstairs to just hang for a bit. "I can't believe how smooth that shit went" Twan said, giving both Leana and Antonio dap.

"Yeah that shit was crazy. Lee you did your thing, boo"

"Well, that's what I do" she said, laughing and flipping her hair. Antonio grabbed her and kissed her on top of the head. She in turn stole a kiss.

"Well since y'all about to gross me out, I think I'm gonna bounce" Twan said. They said their goodbyes and Twan left.

"I am exhausted" Antonio said, looking at the time. It was going on four in the morning.

"Yeah, I'm beat too boo. How about we call it a night?"

"Thought you would never ask"

The couple made their way upstairs and stripped out of their clothes. It took all of ten minutes for both of them to fall into a deep sleep.

✳✳✳✳✳

"Where the fuck are those niggas at?" Tia asked, looking at her watch. "They asses should have been back here by now. Call they ass again" she said to Cam. He quickly pulled out his cell phone and tried calling both Kel and Los. Neither one answered.

"No answer T" he said.

She pulled her gun out and walked swiftly over to Cam. She cocked her .45 and pressed it into his neck. "Them motherfuckers were here because of your ass. You said they could be trusted. So where the fuck are they?"

"I don't know" he said, trying to talk. He wasn't scared of Tia but he knew not to try and move. She was a crazy motherfucker and didn't mind shooting your ass. She didn't care who it was; she had no chill whatsoever.

"You don't know? What the fuck you mean you don't know? You better know if you know what's good for you"

Everybody in attendance just looked on and was glad that they weren't Cam right now. They looked at each other and started to worry that she would actually pull the trigger.

"I will go and try to find them"

"Ain't no motherfucking trying, Cam. You better find their asses and you better find my drugs. I'm not playing with your ass. I'm not playing with none of y'all motherfuckers" she said, pointing the gun at everybody else. They all jumped in fear except for Sienna. Other than Tia and Cam, she had also been shot before. Everyone else there were new to the crew and she didn't really know their backgrounds that well. Either way, she didn't trust they asses one bit. "All y'all get the fuck out and find them niggas. And bring they asses back here and I will handle them. Now get the fuck out"

They all scattered like roaches to get out of Tia's sight. The sun was already coming up as they sped from the spot. Tia poured her a shot of Jack Daniels and sparked a jay. She sat back in her chair and tried to calm down. "These motherfuckers gonna really try and play me? They got the game fucked up" she said, aiming her gun and shot a hole in the wall.

She tossed her drink back and puffed on her jay until she started to feel good. She sat in the chair with her gun resting in her lap. She closed her eyes and listened to the chirping of the morning birds nearby. Now that she was high, she could peacefully sleep and wait patiently for them to bring Los and Kel back to her.

✶✶✶✶✶

"Damn I slept good" Leana said, stretching next to Antonio.

"Yeah, me too. Did you know you drool in your sleep?" Antonio asked her laughing.

"No I don't you jackass" she said, punching him in the arm.

That started an early morning wrestle between the two. Antonio ended up on top and held her down by her arms. She tried to bite his arm, but he ended up biting her neck and sinking his teeth into her flesh.

"Ahhhh" she yelled. This turned Antonio on and he sucked her neck harder. He made his way down to her sweet center and made love to it with his tongue. She moaned softly and his tongue got deeper. He ate her out for a few more minutes before climbing on top. He positioned himself, placed her legs on each side of him, and got deep in her guts.

He was thrusting his manhood so deep in her pussy that it disappeared from sight. And she was taking it all like the big girl she said she would be. They were both in the middle of climax when they heard banging on the front door. They finished and rushed to get dressed. Antonio threw on his sweats and she threw on one of his big shirts. They both made their way downstairs. Antonio looked through the peephole and was surprised at who was on his doorstep.

"It's my father" he said in a hushed tone.

"Well, open it" she said, whispering back.

"Fuck no. I don't have time for his shit right now"

"Suit yourself" she said, walking towards the kitchen.

"I know your ass in there Tony" my father said from the other side of the door. As he continued to bang on the door, I contemplated on opening the door. *Fuck it.* I just opened the door. "It's about damn time" he said.

"Hi, dad" I said dryly. He just walked in uninvitingly and bumped me as he passed by. "What the hell do you want early in the morning man?" I asked, closing the door and walking over to him.

"Just checking on my favorite son"

"I'm your only son, Big Tone" I said sternly.

"At least that's what you think" he said. I disregarded his statement and walked to the kitchen and he followed.

"Oh hi, Mr. Hall" Leana said, extending her hand.

"Damn Lil Tone, you got a bad bitch here" he said, looking Leana over.

"Oh I got your bitch, motherfucker" she said, trying to lunge at my father but I grabbed her.

"And you feisty. You better watch her and she better watch her fucking mouth. You don't want none of this"

"No you don't want none of this, nigga" she said from behind me.

"Enough" I said. "Leana chill"

"Whatever. I'm going upstairs to watch the news. I will get ready when you come up"

"Cool"

She grabbed her cup of coffee and made her way back upstairs. She kept looking back at my father as she headed out the kitchen. If looks could kill, my father would have been a dead motherfucker right now.

"She got a nice ass on her man" he said.

"Cut the shit. What do you want?"

"Damn I can't come and see you? You damn sure ain't come and see me"

"I don't even wanna see your ass now, but you're here"

"Anyway I need some work. You got me?"

"Fuck no. Tia got you"

"Tia? I left you in charge"

"And I put her in charge. She got her own crew now"

"That's crazy, man. So what you gonna do?"

"I already got me a crew, too"

"I guess so. Well, since I'm not welcomed here, I guess I will see what baby girl got for her old man"

"I guess you better"

I followed him to the door. I was right on his heels as he made it to the foyer. He turned to look at me. "I want you to know that I'm sorry for everything"

"Don't be sorry about shit. Just don't come back to my fucking house anymore. Ever" I said.

He got close to my face. Our noses were practically touching. "You better watch your fucking mouth lil nigga. You forgot I'm your motherfucking father"

"Fuck you. You ain't shit to me"

We glared at each other before he turned his back on me and walked out my house. Well that was easier than I thought.

I walked upstairs to where Leana was. She was lying across the bed watching channel 5 news. I walked over and sat on the bed next to her.

"Everything okay?"

"Yeah"

"What happened?"

"His ass left. I told him to never come the fuck back here"

"Good. I was gonna kill his ass"

"I know" I said, laughing. "I could see it in your eyes"

"You know it. Lucky for him I wasn't strapped because I would have shot him right between the eyes"

"I bet you would have and I wouldn't have stopped you either"

"Good to know"

We watched the news for a few more minutes as I let the shower water run. Once it was hot, we both hopped in the shower to wash. We were in there longer than we were supposed to be because we were doing more than showering.

After we got out, I dressed in a simple outfit; wife beater, jeans, and fresh all white air force 1s. Leana wore some cargo pants, a tank top, and low top all white air force 1s.

"Why do you always wear baggy clothes?"

"Because if I wear tight clothes people will see everything. I don't want that"

"I guess you have a point"

We both tucked our guns away and went to the basement. We stuffed the baggies on us and the rest in a separate bag for Twan. I checked the time on my watch. It was 12:15 p.m. The block was just starting to get popping for the day.

We got in the car and headed to our spot. We dropped Twan his share and we all agreed to meet up at Leana's house around 9. Since

Leana rode with me, we didn't have to worry about neither one of us showing up late.

I got to my corner and it was on. Shop was now open for business and I was ready.

✶✶✶✶✶

"So ya'll mean to tell me that both of those niggas were dead when y'all found their car?" Tia asked Cam and Micky.

"Y-y-yeah, boss" Micky said, in his stuttering voice.

"They were both shot, T" Cam said.

"So where's my shit at Cam?" she asked.

"Gone"

"Gone? Are you fucking kidding me?" she asked, laughing. She began to laugh hysterically and throwing her head back. Cam and Micky exchanged looks with one another. The other crew members just sat there staring at her suspiciously.

She suddenly stopped laughing. In one motion, she back handed Cam with her gun and shot Micky in the shoulder. Cam didn't fall but Micky did. "Fuck!" he yelled, holding onto his right shoulder.

"Shut the fuck up" she yelled at him. "This is why you should not hire motherfuckers that can't be fucking trusted" she said, waving her gun at everybody else. "Next time, don't offer your fucking help" she said to Cam. "Sienna take Micky to the hospital. Tell them he got shot by a stray bullet"

"Sure thing Tia" she said. She helped Micky up from the floor and took him out to the car. After making sure he was secure, they drove over to Washington Hospital Center.

"Now the rest of y'all lazy motherfuckers get to work" They all walked out swiftly. She stopped Cam and told him to wait. "Don't ever let this happen again. Do you know how much product we just lost? And don't forget about the money. Tucker is gonna be on our asses. We need to hurry up and get this money together. All those corner boys that's been out all night, go pick up my fucking money. If we have to, we will rob all the motherfucking niggas in the hood. Got it?"

"Got it" he said. She kissed him on the lips passionately then sent him on his way.

She was once left alone again. She decided to kill time by playing a little pool. She was in the middle of her game when her cell phone rang.

"Hello?" she said.

"Hey baby girl. Where are you?"

"At the spot on 68th"

"My old spot?"

"The one and only, dad" she chuckled.

"I'll be there soon. We gotta talk"

"I'll be here"

She already knew this wasn't gonna turn out good for her. He must have found out she running the streets and in charge now. She knew that if this was the case, she wouldn't hear the end of it.

Gemini Betrayal

Chapter Twenty-Two

The block had been booming all damn day! Leana and I had already sold out of all of our product an hour ago. Now we were headed to grab something to eat. We decided to go to T.G.I. Friday's at the Boulevard. We got there during the time it wasn't so busy. I was glad because I hated when it was packed; especially with all the ghetto people that acted like they didn't have any home training whatsoever.

"I'm starving like shit" Leana said, looking over the menu. I looked at different stuff and didn't know what the hell to order. Moments later, our waiter came to take our orders.

"What can I get you, sir?" he asked me.

"Let me get a, um, motherfucking, um, t-bone steak meal. Well done with a baked potato and a long island iced tea. And I wanna get the unlimited appetizers the boneless buffalo wings."

"And for you ma'am?"

"I'll have the same thing he's having" she said.

He wrote down our orders and scurried away.

"Do you always act like an ass?" Leana asked me.

"What you talking about, man? I'm not acting like no ass"

"Whatever you say"

"You be tripping Lee"

"That's you nigga" she said, smiling.

"You love it though"

"Love? Nigga, I don't even fucking like your black ass"

"Yeah, yeah, yeah" I said, throwing a sugar packet at her. The waiter brought us our drinks and appetizer and we went in. I mean we was dogging them wings.

They brought our steaks and some more wings and we crushed that, too. We were in the middle of our meals when my sister and her crew walked in. We made eye contact and Leana saw it. She put her hand on top of mine and I looked at her.

"Chill out, Antonio"

"I'm Gucci. As long as she don't start with me"

And she did just that. They all came over and circled our booth. They stood there blocking us in.

"Can we help you?" Leana asked, rolling her neck.

"Bitch don't play with me" my sister said to Leana.

"Can you leave us alone, Tia?" I said.

"I don't think I want to"

I looked at her with evil eyes and this bitch had the biggest grin on her face. I just shook my head.

"Now I wanna know if y'all had anything to do with my people getting hit last night?"

"I don't know what you're talking about"

"Of course you do. You're the only person that I can think of that would do this"

Gemini Betrayal

"Look he said we don't know shit about it" Leana said, jumping in my sister face. My sister just stared at her with a smile on her face.

"Aww, little baby getting defensive? You got something to hide, Lee?"

"I ain't got shit to fucking hide" she said, stepping closer to my sister. My sister didn't even budge. Her goons closed in closer on Leana and that's when I stood up.

"Everybody get the fuck back" I said, pulling both of my guns out from behind my back. Tia and her crew stepped back a couple inches. Leana stood alongside of me aiming her gun as well. I saw the other patrons in the restaurant all ducked under their tables while others fled the scene. I noticed our waiter come from the back. He saw the guns out and went right back through the doors.

"You ain't gonna do shit with them guns, bro. So you and your little bitch might as well put them down"

I cocked my gun and aimed it at my sister. "Don't make me shoot you, Tia." She slowly walked towards me and stopped when the gun was poking her in the chest. "I'm warning you, sis"

"Go on. Pull the motherfucking trigger, Antonio" I contemplated but I dropped my gun to my side. "That's what I thought. You ain't nothing but a bitch ass nigga"

Pop.

Leana had slapped Antonia across the face with the gun. She flew into the table next to us. Then all hell broke loose. Leana jumped on top of Tia and Sienna jumped on her. Cam thought he was about to get in on it but I stopped him quick with a left hook. He hit me back with a right. Two of Tia's guys jumped in and started jumping me with Cam. Somehow, Leana got a hold on her gun that had fallen on the floor and opened fire.

228   Gemini Betrayal

I seen two of the guys fly back across some tables. They stopped moving before they even hit the floor. Cam pulled out his gun and shot me in the shoulder. I dropped to the floor and I shot him in the leg. He dropped too. I looked over to the girls and Leana was still fighting my sister even though Sienna was on her ass. I could tell my sister was giving up because she wasn't fighting back anymore. Leana stopped hitting my sister and jumped on Sienna's ass. She banged her head on the table as she tackled her to the ground. Sienna caught Leana with a right hook and Leana hit her with the same one back.

I struggled to get up from the floor when I heard sirens in the distance. I managed to get to my feet and I grabbed my guns and grabbed Leana off of Sienna. I saw our waiter and handed him $500 for the bill and his pockets. We ran out the restaurant and jumped in the car. We drove away slowly so we wouldn't look suspicious. Once we got to the light, we saw the cops running inside the place. We headed to Leana's house and then my house to grab some clothes and money. We had to lay low because I knew the cops were gonna be looking for us. We took my car to the chop shop and gave it an entire new makeover. When we left, the car was a whole new vehicle. My car now had a Honda logo instead of a Chevy one.

We headed to a hotel at the National Harbor and told Twan where to meet us at. We decided to stay there for a few days until the police died down a little. Shit was getting crazy as fuck.

$$\ast\ast\ast\ast\ast$$

We arrived at the hotel and immediately checked in and went to our room. Lucky for us, we were able to get a suite away from others. The room was big as shit. As soon as Leana stepped in the room, she kicked off her shoes and ran to the bathroom to hop in the Jacuzzi tub. I just made some phone calls to people to see who can be the lookouts on our corners. Once that was all set up, I joined Leana in the bathroom.

229   Gemini Betrayal

She had the tub filled up with bubbles and steaming hot water. I threw my clothes on the floor and hopped in with her. Neither one of us spoke a word of the day's events. We just spoke around it, changing the subject. We washed and dried our wet bodies with the full body towels that the bed hotel provided. I bandaged my shoulder up then threw on a pair of boxers after I lotioned my body, and then put on one of the complimentary robes. Lee did the same except she just threw on a bra and panty set. I stole a glance at her before she closed her robe and I wanted her. But I couldn't get her right now because somebody was at the door. It must have been Twan's ass. I looked at the time and it was almost ten.

I dropped my gun in my robe pocket and walked over to the door. Leana sat back on the bed with her gun under the pillow beside her for quick access. I peeped through the peephole and it was Twan. I unlocked the door and let him in.

"Damn, what happened to you Boss?" he asked, seeing the swelling on my face.

"Long story"

He walked in and repeated the same thing to Leana.

"Something that's never gonna happen again" she said, with an evil glare.

"Shit, who did this?"

"Tia and her crew"

"So what we gonna do Boss?"

"Well this is what I had in mind" I started.

✳✳✳✳✳

Tia was pacing the floor in her living room with the remainder of the crew with her. Sienna was in attendance along with a new dude named Cash and another newbie named Krissy. Micky and this other new guy named Bone had gotten shot at the restaurant and was dead before the paramedics arrived. Cam was at the hospital getting x-rays and stitches for his gunshot wound.

"I am so fucking pissed off!" Tia yelled. She continued to pace and look at everybody. "There was no way we should have lost two soldiers today. No motherfucking way!"

"We couldn't help it Boss. They shot at us" Cash said.

She looked at him. "Do it look like I give a fuck? Do it look like I give a fuck because I don't. Y'all motherfuckers act like y'all didn't have motherfucking guns on y'all. Sienna was the only one that fucking helped! And Bone and Micky. And Cam, too. So if y'all not riding for the team, what the fuck I need y'all for? To get in my pockets and get paid? Fuck that!"

She was fuming. She couldn't even look at them. She looked at Sienna and they never broke stares. Sienna wasn't afraid of Tia and she knew it. Out of everybody in her life, Sienna was the only person she never tried. Not that she was scared but she knew Sienna had survival training and was always ready for any attack.

"Great work today, SiSi"

"Thanks T. You need anything else?" she asked, holding an ice pack on her head.

"I need you to stitch me up before you go"

"Cool" Sienna went to go get some needle and thread and came right back. She quickly sewed Tia up and sat back down. Tia's face was so swollen it had numbed after awhile so she barely felt the needle going in and out of her skin.

Gemini Betrayal

"We need to think of a plan to get their asses back. I know they asses had something to do with my drugs missing. We need to find a way into my brother's house and get our shit back"

"I'm on it" Sienna said, jumping back up.

"No not you, Sienna" she said, looking over to Cash. "You"

"Me?"

"Yeah, you motherfucker. Did I fucking stutter?"

"No, Boss"

"You wanna prove your loyalty? Go and bring me my shit back. Sienna, I want you to put your ear to the streets. Find any and everybody that's on my brother's team"

"And what you want me to do when I find out?"

"Kill them" she said bluntly.

"Kill them?"

"Kill them"

Chapter Twenty-Three

The war had begun again between my sister and I. Between the both of our gangs, bodies had been dropping for weeks. At the most, we done killed three of her crew members in one day! Gaines and his entire department had been trying to catch up to us but we keep changing locations. My sister and Cam have been getting arrested but let back out because they didn't have any hard evidence. This fucking city was wild and everybody and they mama was caught in the crossfire.

Just last week, we had a shootout at the damn neighborhood park. Micky's ass had opened fire on me and Twan and ended up shooting and killing two kids. I felt like shit when that happened. So, I sent my condolences to their families and helped pay for both funerals. They had the funerals for the six and ten year old kids yesterday and me and my whole crew were in attendance.

Now it was another night on the block. We were finally wrapping up for the night and headed home. Twan hopped in his car and Leana and I hopped in separate cars as well. I drove down to the gas station at the end of the block. I needed a roll-up and some snacks for when I get the munchies. I go inside and the attendant doesn't even pay me any mind as I spoke to him. I grabbed a couple bags of chips, some candy and some soda. I headed to the counter to pay for my junk and grab me some paraphernalia. I didn't even notice that somebody was behind me until I turned to leave out.

"Damn, nigga. Give me some fucking space" I said. They didn't even respond to me. They just stood there with their hood over their head looking down. I eased my way out and headed back to the

Gemini Betrayal

pump to pump my gas. Once it stopped at $30.00, I put the handle back on its stand and jumped in the car. I started the car and picked up my phone to dial Twan's number. I was getting ready to pull off when I heard my back door slam.

"What the fuck?" I said turning around. It was the guy from inside the gas station with the hood.

"Turn the fuck back around and drive, motherfucker" he said, pointing a small handgun at me.

I did what he said because I had to try and retrieve my gun from under the seat without him knowing.

He had me take all types of backroads and turns until I ended up driving through Waldorf.

"Man, what you want?" I asked.

"I want everything you got"

I drove down the street and removed my watch from my wrist and my chain from around my neck. I pulled a little bit of money out that I had in one of my pockets and threw in the backseat to him.

"This can't be all you have, big baller"

"I don't know what you talking about, man"

"Bullshit. I know who you are and I know what you do. Don't bullshit me"

I listened closely as I continued to drive. That voice sounded so familiar. Why did it sound like my father? I knew his ass was fucking crazy but robbing your own son? I guess this family didn't have any standards. As long as they got paid, that's all that mattered in life. I continued to listen intently.

"Run me the rest of that shit, nigga" he said, pressing the gun to the back of my head. I sped up a little bit on the highway. "Slow the fuck down, motherfucker" he yelled.

"Fuck you" I said, driving like a bat outta hell. Once the speedometer got to 110, I slammed on brakes, and slammed into a light post; hoping his ass would go flying through the windshield. Unfortunately, it didn't work out that way but I did manage to grab my gun when it flew from under my seat.

I shot the gun towards the back but it missed him and went through the back window. He punched me and my head spun and hit the steering wheel. I tried to open the car door so I could get out but the door was jammed. His ass managed to get out as the car started to smoke. He limped all the way around the car in pain from the impact of the crash.

The smoke was starting to cloud the air more and I was coughing profusely. I was getting dizzy from the smoke inhalation. I was able to roll my window down a little but it stopped midway. The car had a small fire starting. I looked over to the hooded figure that I knew for sure was my father and offered him pleading eyes.

"Dad, help me" I said, through short breaths. He snatched off his hood so I could see his face. And I be damned if it wasn't this nigga.

"Fuck you, Antonio. You didn't want to help me when I needed you so why should I help you?"

"Please" Cough. Cough. "I'm gonna die. I don't wanna burn alive"

"Don't worry you won't " he said, pointing his gun at me. The last thing I heard was the driver side window shatter and the beeping of the car horn as my head fell on it.

✳✳✳✳✳

"Everything is taken care of, Sweetie" Big Tone said to Tia once he got back to her house.

"Damn I wish I was there" she said, smiling and laughing. "How did his face look when you pulled the trigger?"

"That little nigga was scared shitless"

"And you made sure he was dead right?"

"Are you questioning my street skills, Tia?" he asked, stepping to her.

"N-n-no, dad. I was just making sure"

He grabbed her chin tightly. "Don't you ever question me when it comes to my skills. You got that?"

She nodded her head 'yeah' and he released her from his grasp.

"Now what?" he asked.

"Now we get back out there and make more money. Since he out of the way, we shouldn't have anymore problems"

"What about Leana and Twan?"

"Those busters ain't gonna clap-back about shit. They're gonna be too busy planning a funeral and trying to figure out how to stay getting money. I don't have time to worry about their asses"

"Damn. Spoken like a true Hall. Your grandfather would have been proud. I'm proud"

"Really?"

"Really"

"You don't know how long I have been waiting to hear that, dad"

"Well now that you have, time to get back to work"

"Right. So I need you and Cam to head to Arlington this weekend" she said, pulling out a map of her plan.

They went over it for a couple hours until he got it down pact. Cam had been invited in on the planning and they all ran it down again. Once they were secure with the plan, they parted ways and agreed to speak within the next couple days to go over the plan again. Big Tone went to one of Tia's houses and Tia and Cam ended up going to Cam's house for the night. It had been a long and exhausting day for Tia and all she wanted to do was hit a blunt, drink a beer and chill with her man.

✳✳✳✳✳

"You still ain't heard from your boy?" Twan asked Leana.

"No, and I'm starting to get worried. I knew I shouldn't have left him" she said, rubbing her forehead as she paced the floor.

"Don't worry. I'm sure he probably in the house chilling"

She took a deep breath. "You might be right Twan. Maybe he just don't wanna be bothered tonight"

"Maybe. Just call me if you hear anything"

"Yeah sure" she said, quickly hanging up the phone. She dialed Antonio's cell number for the twentieth time in an hour. The phone still rang and went to voicemail. She continued to call for another thirty minutes straight and still nothing.

Gemini Betrayal

She went down to the kitchen to pour herself some shots of Hennessy. By the third shot, she had an idea. She called in a favor to her friend Lucas.

"Hello" he said, answering the phone.

"Hey Lucas, it's Leana. I need a big favor"

"Anything honey" he said, in his gay voice.

"I need you to track an iPhone for me"

"What's the number?"

"2409760125"

"Okay, give me a sec" Leana heard him tapping his keyboard hard as hell. "Okay, I'm back" he said.

"What you got?"

"The phone belongs to one Antonio Hall and his phone is located at 60607 Palimar Road in Waldorf"

"Waldorf?!" she yelled through the phone. "Are you sure, Lucas?"

"Yes ma'am"

"Okay, thanks, hun. Can you text me the address please?"

"Just sent it"

"Thanks. I owe you"

"Girl, I know you gonna look out for me" he said, smacking his lips before hanging up.

She immediately called Twan back on his phone.

"Yo?" he said, answering the phone.

"I found Antonio"

"Where the fuck that nigga at?"

"Waldorf"

"Waldorf? What the fuck he doing out there?"

"I don't know but we gonna find out. Come scoop me and we gonna go get him"

"Be there in fifteen"

✳✳✳✳✳

They arrived at the location and it ended up being an old looking ass house.

"Where the fuck are we?" Twan asked. "Who the fuck he know that live out here?"

"I don't know but let's see"

Leana and Twan parked the car a few feet up the street from the house and crept back down the street. They were dressed in all black so they would be barely noticeable through the darkness. They quietly stepped through the bushes and peeped through the open window.

They could see Tia and Tony's father, Big Tone, and like five other niggas sitting around. They went over a quick plan to bumrush the house and shoot everything in sight. Leana went around to the back door and Twan went around the front. Twan threw a brick in the bush to signal for Leana to kick the doors in.

Boom. Boom. The doors both came crashing in simultaneously. The dudes jumped up and reached for their guns.

Gemini Betrayal

"Put y'all fucking hands up" Leana yelled at them. They froze and threw their arms up in the air.

"Don't fucking move either" Twan yelled. "Get against the motherfucking wall. Now!" The thugs did as they were told and stood there like they were about to be frisked.

"What the fuck you can't hear, nigga?" Leana said, aiming her gun at Big Tone. He just sat there sipping on his beer.

"I can hear perfectly fine. I don't take orders from no bitch or no bitch ass niggas" he said, looking over at Twan.

"What you say to me, nigga?" Twan said, pressing the gun to the side of Big Tone's head.

"You ain't gonna do shit, lil nigga" he said, sipping his beer again. Twan put a bullet in the chamber so he could show Big Tone he wasn't playing games. "What's that supposed to do?"

"I will blow your motherfucking brains out, nigga"

"Twan chill!" Leana yelled. I redirected my eyes back to Big Tone. "Where the fuck is Antonio?"

"Not sure"

"You're fucking lying"

"Nope"

"His fucking phone is right here" she said, snatching the phone from the side table. "Now where the fuck is he?"

Leana and Twan saw one of the dudes move a little and Twan shot him in the back of the head. Blood splattered all over the wall and the other dudes watched as his body slumped to the floor.

"If you don't want that to be you, I advise you to tell us what we wanna know"

"I ain't telling you shit" Big Tone said.

"Oh you think it's a game, huh? Well let me show you how much of a game this is" Twan cocked his gun and shot two more of the dudes in the back of the head. They fell into the wall and slid down to the floor as well. Only two dudes remained.

"I don't give a fuck about that"

Twan cocked his gun again. This time he shot Big Tone in his foot.

"Ahhh, fuck. Shit!" he yelled out in pain.

"Now, tell me where he is"

"I ain't telling you shit"

Boom. He shot him in the leg this time.

"Give up yet?"

"Okay, okay. I will tell you where he is"

"That's more like it" Leana said.

"No, show us" Twan interrupted.

"Get up" Leana said to Big Tone. "We going for a ride"

Big Tone got up and walked slowly through the living room. Leana followed closely behind, with her gun aimed to his skull.

"What about these two?" Twan asked.

"Get rid of them"

Pop. Pop. They left the house almost as quickly as they had come. They all walked down the street together towards the car. Twan got in the driver seat and Leana sat in the back with Big Tone.

He directed them towards where he had left Antonio. They arrived there in about ten minutes tops. They parked the car behind Antonio's car and got out. Twan crept up to the driver's side and saw Tony still slumped over the steering wheel. The car was burned up in the front from the fire. He was surprised it hadn't escalated from the looks of the car's impact.

"Lee, you need to see this" he said. Leana walked over to where Twan was and immediately got hysterical.

"Oh my god. Antonio? What the fuck?" she said, trying to pull the door open. With Twan's help, they both managed to get the door open. She checked his pulse and it was very faint. She stood up and looked over at Big Tone who just stood there smiling. "Kill him, Twan"

"Got it"

"Better yet? Let me do it. Call an ambulance. Tell them to get out here fast"

"Got it Lee" he said, pulling out his cell phone.

Leana walked over to Big Tone. "Walk" she said. She led him deep into the woods where nobody would hear anything. She shot him until her clip was empty. She didn't even have any remorse for what she had just done. It felt great.

By the time the paramedics and police had arrived, they were able to wipe their guns clean, ditch them and take all the incriminating stuff out of Antonio's car so they wouldn't have anything on him.

"What happened here?" the police officer asked.

Gemini Betrayal

"Not sure, Officer. I was looking for my boyfriend and I tracked his phone to this location. He was like that when we got here"

"And who are you?" he asked Twan.

"I'm her brother"

The officer wrote down everything they told him. "You two will have to come down to the station for questioning"

"What about Antonio?"

"He'll be fine" the officer said.

Leana and Twan got back into Twan's car and headed down to the precinct. While they drove to the police station, Leana couldn't help but think about Antonio. *Was he gonna live? Why would his father do this? At least, he got what the fuck he had coming to him.*

Gemini Betrayal

Chapter Twenty-Four

It had been three months since Antonio had been in a coma and everyday Leana was there by his side. She wanted to make sure she was the first one that he saw when he opened his eyes.

She was sitting, talking to him as usual and there was still no response. She got up to go to the bathroom. When she came back, she noticed his eyes flutter a little. *Am I tripping?* she thought to herself. She stared at him without blinking. *There it is again!* He's trying to open his eyes. She ran to his bedside and grabbed his hand. She gave him a gentle squeeze and he gave her one back.

"Nurse?" she yelled out to the hallway.

"Yes?"

"I think he's awake now"

"Let me see" She pulled out a small flashlight and shined it in his eyes. He blinked rapidly and she turned the light out. "Well, welcome back, Mr. Hall" she said.

"Where am I?" he asked in a low voice.

"You're in the hospital. You've been here for three months?"

"Three months?"

"Yes. You were in a coma. But your girlfriend has been here every single day taking care of you" she said, gesturing towards Leana. "I'll leave you two alone for a while. I'm gonna bring him some water"

"Thanks" Leana said. She looked down at Antonio and a tear fell on his pillow.

"What you crying for, boo?"

"I thought I lost you"

"You ain't gonna lose me, shorty. How the fuck did I end up in here?"

"You don't remember what happened?"

"No"

"Well, long story short your father tried to kill you"

"What?"

"Yep. He left you in your car to die. Twan and I found him and he brought us to you. Luckily, we got to you when we did. You were almost a goner" she said with a slight chuckle.

"Where is he now?"

"Who? Twan?"

"No, my father"

"I took care of it"

"Thanks"

"No problem"

The nurse had brought back some water and a straw. He sat up and drunk the water to the middle of the small pitcher. "That really quenched my thirst" he said. He grabbed Leana and kissed her.

"I missed that" she said.

"So did I" he replied.

Gemini Betrayal

"But I do have bad news though" she began.

"What's wrong?"

"Twan got hit in a drive-by"

"Oh shit. Is he dead?"

"No, but he paralyzed. He in a wheelchair but that ain't stopping shit. You know him" she said, laughing.

"Yeah I do" I said, joining in the laughter. "Has he been up here?"

"Yeah. He should be coming back shortly. He and Ashley came yesterday but he had to go and re-up and change clothes and shit"

"True. How's the block looking?"

"Well. Your sister took over eighty-five percent of the city. We getting enough money just to get by"

"Don't worry. I'm gonna be back at it before you know it"

"There is something else I have to tell you though" Leana said.

"What's up?"

"I'm, uh-"

Knock. Knock.

They both looked towards the door and saw Twan rolling into the room.

"What's up, bro?" I said, dapping him up when he got to the side of the bed.

"What's up? How you feeling?"

"Will be much better once I get the fuck up outta here, my nigga"

"I hear that"

"What y'all in here talking about?" he asked, looking towards Leana.

"Well Lee was about to tell me something. Go ahead, boo"

"Naw, it's okay. I think I'm gonna wait until we're alone"

"Okay"

They all sat and talked about the good old days when the crew was still a crew. They talked about what's been going on since Antonio was in his coma and what they were planning to do as soon as he got released.

Three hours later, Twan left and said he would come see him in a couple days. Leana stayed there for the night like she had been doing for months now.

She was lying in the hospital bed with Antonio as he stroked her head and they watched tv. As soon as a commercial came on, he started back their previous conversation.

"So what did you wanna tell me earlier, boo?"

"I went to the doctors two months ago and I, um, I'm pregnant"

"Pregnant?" he repeated sitting up on the bed. She sat up beside me.

"Yeah pregnant" she said, with a slight smile.

"Oh my god" he said, wrapping my arms around her and squeezing her.

247   Gemini Betrayal

"So you're not mad?"

"Mad? Fuck no! I'm fucking excited. I love you"

She paused and looked at me. "You love me, Antonio?"

"Yes. I love you"

"I love you, too"

They kissed again and ended up missing some parts of the show after the commercial break. Antonio didn't give a fuck. He was gonna be a father.

Me. Antonio Hall was gonna be a motherfucking dad.

✱✱✱✱✱

Everybody had gathered at Tia's house to celebrate her father's birthday today. There was liquor and drugs being passed all around the room amongst the crew members.

"Can I get everybody's attention?" Tia said, standing in front of everybody.

The entire room fell silent and all eyes were on her.

"I like to thank all y'all for coming here today to celebrate for my dad. May his soul rest in peace. He was a good man and a good father. And the most thuggish motherfucker that had ever lived. Well, other than me" she said, laughing. "But on the real I'm glad to say that I was his daughter. I know some of y'all are newbies so you don't know but it still means a lot y'all are here with your bosses" she said, looking at Cam who stood proudly next to her.

They passed around bottles of Hennessy and Bacardi until everybody's glass was full. They made a toast and said a silent prayer for Big Tone.

"Next on the agenda" she began, "it seems like there's a new gang called the Sopranos trying to take over our spots. You will definitely know them if you see them because for one, they're Mexican and for two, they're the darkest Mexicans you may have ever seen in your life. They are dangerous, but we can handle them. Everybody on the east coast knows our name and fear it. That's not gonna change not now, not ever. Cam the floor is yours" she said, taking a seat on the arm of the chair.

"So the leader of the Sopranos name is Chico. He a little dude but he an ex-cop. He may be kind of hard to take out without anyone noticing because he still in contact with the district attorney and shit. Then, he got his brother named Paco. He's more of an easy target. He's all about money and beautiful women" he said, looking at Sienna.

"Me?"

"Yeah. You're in charge of taking him out"

"Okay Boss. I got it"

"We know you won't let us down. Now, we have everybody's pay right here" he said, picking up a stack of envelopes. He passed them around to everyone in attendance. They all opened the envelopes and smiled. Tia knew she did good by throwing in a little extra for their hard work.

"Now that everything is said, we can continue to party" She signaled for the DJ to start the music back up. They all stood back up and started having conversations while others danced a little. Tia and Cam had snuck off to her bedroom after they informed Sienna to watch the crowd downstairs.

Gemini Betrayal

Once in the room, they kissed one another like they hadn't seen in months. They knew they couldn't be missing for too long so they opted for a quickie until later on. Cam bent Tia over the bed and put his already rock hard manhood up in her wet vagina.

He gave her long deep strokes; making sure she felt every inch. His paced quickened as her moans got louder. Before they knew it, they were both starting to sweat a little and Tia's juices were beginning to run down her inner thigh.

"Oh, baby" she moaned loudly as Cam banged her insides out.

"You love this dick?"

"Yes"

"Yes what?"

"Yes daddy"

"You better"

He continued to pound her insides. When he was ready to explode, he held her by the waist tight and came all inside of her walls. His cum had been released in waves inside her. They didn't move for moments after they both came.

"Damn that was a good quickie" Cam said, walking to the bathroom.

"Yeah it was" Tia said in agreement as she followed behind him.

They both went into the bathroom to do a quick wipe down of their bodies. They put on fresh deodorant and sprayed perfume and cologne on. They did a once over in the full length mirror before heading back downstairs to the party.

When they had come back, they noticed that a couple of the crew members had vacated.

"Where did they go?" Tia asked Sienna.

"Micky had to go check on his mom in the hospital. Marcus took his girlfriend home because his wife was blowing him up to come home. And as far as Jason, he got a call from some bitch and rolled out. Said he would catch up with y'all tomorrow"

"Oh aight. So what you got to do tonight?"

"Oh the usual. It's Thursday so you know I'm going to the gun shop to check out their supply."

"It amazes me how you have been doing that since I have known you" Tia said laughing.

"Hell, if I wanna keep my job I gotta make sure I stay prepared, right?"

"You got that right"

She gave Tia a quick hug and left too.

A couple of hours had passed and Cam and Tia had kicked everybody else out. They relaxed for a bit then Cam left Tia to herself.

She showered and watched tv. She couldn't stop thinking about her father though. "I'm gonna make you so proud of me" she said aloud. Then she just continued to watch rerun episodes of The Fresh Prince of Bel-Air.

✳✳✳✳✳

"It's always nice to see you, Marcus" his mother said to him.

Gemini Betrayal

"You know I gotta see my favorite girl" he said, kissing her on the forehead. "I'll be back tomorrow, ma. I love you"

"I love you, too, son. Be careful out there"

"Always, ma"

He was a little exhausted after sitting in the hospital for the past three hours, but he loved spending time with his mother. She was diagnosed with cancer and they didn't know for sure how long she would be here. So he made sure to spend as much time with her as possible.

He was walking down the hall when he had bumped into Leana by accident.

"Oh, my bad" he said.

"It's okay" she replied.

He looked at her. "Damn you're beautiful" he said.

"Thanks" she said and started to walk away.

"Hold on. What's the rush?"

"I gotta get back to my boyfriend"

"Oh, okay. My bad. I was just about to ask if you were single. Do your man allow you to have friends?"

"I already have two male friends"

"You can't make room for one more?"

"I don't think my man and my brother would like that" she said, referring to Antonio and Twan. Just then Twan rolled up beside Leana in his wheelchair.

"You okay over here, Lee?" he said, looking up at Marcus.

"This your nigga?"

"No, I'm her brother" Twan replied.

"I'm her nigga" Tony said, stepping in front of Marcus' face.

Marcus looked at Antonio strangely. "Aye, don't I know you?"

"Naw, you don't know me, fam" Antonio replied.

"You sure? You look real familiar. It seems like I've seen you somewhere before"

"You gonna know my motherfucking nine if you don't step away from my girl, dawg"

"We cool. Ain't no problems" Marcus said, stepping back and walking down the hall. He looked back at Antonio and them. Twan made a gun gesture towards him and he turned his head around.

All along while staring at them, he was taking a mental photo of them. He wouldn't forget their faces, that's for sure.

*****

"What you doing back here?" Tia asked Marcus.

"I think I forgot my phone here earlier. I been lost without that motherfucker" he said laughing.

"Nigga, you forever losing that damn phone. What if we had a job or something?" Tia said.

"If that was the case, y'all know where I live"

"That's besides the point"

She helped him look down in between the couch cushions and under the chairs. They didn't see it there. They looked all over the downstairs.

Tia looked on top of the mantle over top of the fireplace. "Is this it?" she asked.

Marcus looked over to her. "Yep. You're a fucking lifesaver, Boss" he said, kissing her on the cheek."

"Aye, aye, aye. Cut that shit out"

"My bad" He looked at the pictures in the frames on the mantle. "Aye, this dude in the pictures look familiar. How do you know him?"

"That's my brother. How do you know him?" she asked, looking at him quizzically.

"I don't know him, know him. I seen him before. As a matter of fact that's the same dude I seen earlier today."

"Ain't no motherfucking way you seen him today" Tia said, picking one of the frames up off the mantle and handing it to him.

Marcus took the frame and looked at it closer. "Nope that's him"

"That's impossible. My brother got killed almost four months ago"

"Do he have a twin?"

"Yeah, me"

"Well, that would explain why he looked so familiar to me when I seen him. Is it another one of y'all?"

"You mean am I a part of triplets?"

"Yeah"

"No. It's just me and him. We're fraternal twins"

"Well you might wanna check into it because I just seen this nigga at the hospital today with another nigga and a female"

"How did the dude and the girl look?"

"The girl was pretty as shit. Long hair, nice body, full lips, and hazel brown eyes. And all that ass. I think the dude called her Lee. And the dude, he was a brown skinned dude in a wheelchair"

"That was definitely Leana and Twan" Tia thought. *He described Lee perfectly and Twan, too. She remembered Twan was in a chair now after they got him in a drive-by when they shot up their corner two months ago. "But how the fuck was Antonio still alive?" Big Tone said he killed him.* Tia had to see for herself.

She got the info from Marcus on what hospital he had seen them at. After she got everything, she put him out and ran upstairs to her room. She called Cam as she quickly threw on some sweatpants, tennis shoes and a t-shirt. She tucked her gun in a holster under her shirt.

"What's up, boo?" Cam said when he answered his phone.

"Get your ass dressed and get over here. I think we have a problem"

Chapter Twenty-Five

It was 7 o'clock in the evening when Tia and Cam arrived at the hospital. They approached the nurse's desk and asked for Antonio's room.

"I'm sorry but Mr. Hall has already been discharged, ma'am" the nurse sitting behind the counter informed her.

"How long ago?" Tia asked

The nurse tapped a couple of keys on the keyboard. "He just left about twenty minutes ago.

Tia walked away without even saying thank you. She and Cam walked steadfastly back to the bank of elevators. Just as they stepped on the elevator, and their doors closed, Leana and Antonio stepped off a different elevator.

They walked over to the nurse's desk and he informed the nurse that he had left something in the room.

"Did you say your name was Antonio Hall?"

"Yes, ma'am I did. Why what's wrong?"

"Oh, nothing. A young lady just left here looking for you"

"Who was it?"

"Not sure. When I told her you were already discharged, she just walked away with a guy."

"How did she look?"

"Just like you except a female"

Cam and Tia I thought to himself. "Okay thanks" Antonio said. They rushed to the room to get the couple things they had accidentally forgotten and hurried back over to the elevators, got on the middle elevator and headed down to the parking garage.

"What do we do now?" Cam asked Tia as they sat in the car in the parking garage.

"Simple. We go to his house" she said, starting the car and putting it in gear.

Just as they were driving up to the gate to get out, Antonio and Leana were stepping off of the elevator. They checked their surroundings before fully stepping out the elevator. When they saw that the coast was clear, they headed to Leana's rental car. They hopped in the car and drove out of the garage.

"I think that dude might know something" Leana said.

"What dude?" Antonio asked.

"The one that was trying to hit on me"

"Naw I don't think so. I never seen that dude before. But he swore he knew me though" Antonio said recalling the dude had been looking at him.

"There just may be a possibility. How ironic is it that your sister comes here looking for you but she hasn't this entire time? It's because she thought you were dead. I'm telling you he told her you were here and that you were alive"

"Say that is true and whatnot. Why would she come here?"

"To kill you" she said bluntly.

Antonio got quiet. That was a good point though. They were in a war against each other.

They decided that it wasn't a good idea to go to either one of their houses. Antonio called up one of his homies and got the address to one of his rental properties. Once he got the directions, they hopped on the highway.

"Where we headed?" Leana asked, lying her head against the seat.

"Jersey"

Leana said nothing else. She grabbed a hold of Tony's hand and they held hands the entire ride to Camden.

✳✳✳✳✳

"That motherfucker not here" Cam said when they pulled up in front of Tony's crib.

"How you know?" she asked in a smart tone.

"Do it look like anybody here, T?" he asked, looking at the dark house from the passenger seat.

"Nope it don't but that don't mean shit. We gonna go in there and wait for him"

"That's all fine and dandy but a nigga hungry, boo. Can we get something to eat real quick?"

Tia rolled her eyes and started the car back up. "Your fat ass getting a meal from Popeyes and that's it"

"That'll work" he said, rubbing his hands together vigorously and smiling.

They headed three blocks down to Popeyes and they both ordered a two piece meal special. They ate it right in the parking lot instead of taking it back with them.

Once they finished devouring their food, they gulped down the rest of their drinks and cleaned up their hands and mouths. It was time to get their ass to work.

$$*****$$

They managed to get in from picking the lock. "I can't believe his punk ass changed the locks on me" Tia said.

"You think he wouldn't? I, mean, damn you are trying to kill the nigga" Cam said, with a slight giggle.

"You're a fucking idiot" Tia said, checking the time on her phone. It was 11:30 and he still hadn't shown up. Tia started to do her usual pace that she did when she was distracted by her thoughts.

"What's wrong, T?" Cam asked her.

"Like where the fuck is this nigga? I'm trying to get this shit over with"

"I feel you, Boo. We have been here for a brick" he said, looking at his watch. "Can I ask a personal question, T?"

"No. I don't answer personal questions"

"Why do you want to kill your brother so bad?"

She cut her eyes at him in the dimly lit room. "Didn't I say I don't answer personal questions?"

"Oh well. I asked and I want an answer"

"Well you're not getting one"

"Why not?"

"Because it's none of your fucking business, the fuck" she said, walking away.

She headed upstairs to his room and Cam followed in tow.

"What are you looking for?" he asked.

"Money, drugs, guns, anything. Help me" she said.

Cam joined her as she rummaged through the drawers. They heard a car pull up and they looked out the window. The car was put in park and four figures dressed in all black exited the vehicle. Two went around back and two walked to the front door.

Tia and Cam slowly walked out to the hallway and stood by the railing listening for any noises. They heard when the glass had broken from the back door and hit the kitchen floor. They eased backwards into the darkness once they saw the two intruders unlock the front door.

Cam and Tia were trying to listen to what they were saying but they were speaking to one another in a whispered tone. Tia peeped over the railing and saw three of the perpetrators go in different directions while the fourth came up the stairs. Tia silently pulled back the cylinder on her pistol and placed a bullet in the chamber. She nodded her head at Cam and he did the same.

Gemini Betrayal

They saw the small figure walking into the guest room at the end of the hall and they followed quietly behind. Once the trespasser was distracted and checking through drawers and whatnot, Tia closed the door and it startled him. It didn't help the fact that Cam had flicked the bright light on in the room.

The person stood upright with a gun aiming at Tia. They just stared each other down and didn't neither of them moved a muscle.

"Cam, go take they mask off" she said, using her gun to motion him towards the stranger. Cam walked towards the perp and they both aimed their guns at one another. "I wouldn't try shit if I were you" Tia said. "If you so much as blink, I'm gonna blow your whole motherfucking face off"

The person behind the mask wasn't afraid. He kept the gun on Cam. When he reached for the mask, the gun became closer to his face. They didn't give a fuck. Cam had his gun up in their face as well and Tia never moved hers.

While trying to pull the mask off, the person was making things difficult for Cam. They were squirming and ducking and dodging him. Cam had had enough now. Whoever was behind the mask just ordered an ass whooping courtesy of Cam. He balled up his fist as tight as possible and landed a right hook into the stranger's jaw. The person hit the floor with a loud thud. Tia rushed over and pulled the mask off the person's face.

Her eyes grew big and her mouth went dry. For once in her life, she was completely quiet. She stood over top of the trespasser again and pointed her gun to their temple.

"What the fuck are you doing here?"

Chapter Twenty-Six

Leana rolled over to my side of the bed. She jumped up out of her sleep when she felt the empty spot. She hopped out the bed and grabbed her gun. Wearing nothing but a t-shirt, she walked the perimeter of the room, searching for me.

She looked in the bathroom but I wasn't there. She searched the other rooms as well, but there was still no sign. She slowly headed down the stairs towards the living room and dining room, with her gun leading the way. She still didn't see me.

Where the fuck is he? She thought to herself. She ran to the room to get her phone to call me.

She dialed my multiple times but didn't receive any answer on my end. She was so busy calling and dialing my phone, that she didn't hear the door open. When the door suddenly shut, she turned around and let off one round. Pow.

"What the fuck is wrong with you girl?" I asked her and put the bags on the floor.

"Where the fuck have you been?" she yelled at me. She walked over to help me with the bags.

"I obviously went to the store to get some groceries. You know your ass can't go too long without food" I said, laughing.

She smiled and laughed as we took the bags into the kitchen. We sat them on the table and began removing the contents and putting the items where they belong. I left out the waffle mix and eggs so that they could fix breakfast.

Gemini Betrayal

"How long were you gone, babe?" Lee asked as she mixed the batter and heated up the waffle iron.

"I wanna say probably about an hour or two. Why?"

"Why would you leave me alone?"

"It's not like you were really alone. You take that damn gun with you everywhere you go like it's your child or something"

"Whatever. Just don't do that shit again" she said.

I walked over to her and grabbed her from behind. I pushed her hair to the side and planted soft kisses on her neck. "I'm sorry, boo. How's the baby?"

"He's fine" she said.

"He?"

She turned around to face me. "Yes him. We're having a son" she said, smiling.

I grabbed her and hugged her tightly. "Oh my god. Are you fucking serious?"

"Yep"

"Yoooo. That's what's up" I said. I got on my knees and kissed her stomach. I was so damn happy right now. Nothing was gonna change his mood. *Am having a motherfucking son!*

We cooked breakfast and then went back to lay down in the bedroom.

"So what's the plan?" Leana asked.

"Well, I thought we would stay here for a while then head back once everything died down"

"You sure that's a good idea?"

"Yeah. My sister is probably pissed off right now but she will be fine"

"If you say so, Antonio. I just don't have time for your sister and her bullshit"

"I know, baby"

She gave me a kiss and turned over to the other side. Guess it was time for her to take a nap. I let her rest and went into the living room and called this dude named Jah. I had met him earlier.

Jah must have been some neighborhood drug dealer because he approached me trying to sell me coke.

"You need anything? If so I got you" he said, when I walked past him on the sidewalk.

"Naw I'm good" I told him.

Thinking that was it, I went into the store. This fool followed me through the store. By the time I had gotten to aisle four where the cereal was, I was getting annoyed. I turned around just as he was close enough.

"What the fuck are you doing, my nigga?"

"You not from these parts are you?" he asked.

"No I'm not. Why?"

"I could just tell. You dressed different and you talk different" he said, looking me over.

"Whatever" I said and walked away but he just kept coming.

"So where you from?"

"The south"

"I hear you, son"

"How long you been dealing?"

"For about four years now. I think I do pretty good"

"Well, I've done it almost the same if not longer. And I know I have made a killing. Me and my team"

"Oh shit, I need you on my team then"

"We can talk about it"

He gave me his number and I said I would text him before the day was out. I thought this was the perfect time if any.

"This Jah," he said when he picked up.

"What's up man? This Tony."

"Tony? Who the fuck is Tony?"

"Nigga, I just met you at the fucking store" I yelled.

"Oh yeah, I remember. You better calm all that noise. If you know what's good for you, you will cut that shit out"

"Man look. I don't know who the fuck you talking to but this is about business. If you ain't about business, then get the fuck off my phone"

The phone went silent for a couple minutes. "Where you at?" he asked.

"Don't worry about all that. What you need?"

"See you in action. Meet me at Jefferson and T street tonight around eleven"

Gemini Betrayal

"Aight"

I hung up the phone and looked through my text messages. I had texts from different girls that I had ran through a few or more times. It was crazy how even after I don't speak to them, they still send nasty pics.

I opened up the text from a girl named Tamia. She had the invisible ink covering her photo. I could swear that iPhones makers were fucking geniuses when they created this. I swiped the picture and nothing but a shaved pussy was there. I blew the picture up and rotated the phone. "Goddamn" I said in my head. I remember when I used to fuck her. No matter what, this damn girl squirted and that was everywhere. It's been of numerous times I had to get the car cleaned and detailed because of her cum stains all on the leather seats.

The next one I opened was from a little white chocolate girl Mariah. She was a mixed chick but looked more white than anything, but you could tell she fucked black dudes. Ain't no white girl gonna get no ass like that. Her mama didn't even have no ass so that's the theory I came up with.

I thought I heard footsteps and quickly closed out the messages and started playing weed farm. When I looked back, I could still see Leana laying on the bed sleeping. I laid back on the chair so I could see her if she came out the room, opened the messages back up and continued to look at the sex messages.

I was starting to get aroused. I looked down at my pants and my dick looked like it was about to bust out. I looked back down the hall and she only turned over on the other side. I unzipped my pants and started stroking my dick at the pictures. By the time I got through all the photo messages from all the ladies, I had busted a nut. I dropped my phone and hurried to the bathroom to clean up the mess. After finishing, I went back to the living room to check the couch. It was free of cum, so I got back in the spot. I slid the phone into my pocket and fell asleep right there.

*****

"I can't believe that bitch was at your brother's house" Cam said, brushing his teeth.

"I know right. This shit is wild but I'm glad we were able to negotiate something"

"Yeah. Do you trust her?" he asked Tia.

Tia looked him dead in his eyes. "I don't trust no goddamn body. Even motherfuckers that's your blood can't be trusted. I'm living fucking proof" she said, extending her arms outward.

Cam continued to brush his teeth and then went to get dressed. Tia didn't pay him any mind. She got up on the bed and laid down.

"What's wrong with you?" Cam asked.

"Not sure. I'm not feeling good. It must be that time of the month"

"Maybe. You wanna sit today out?"

"Yeah I think I will. You're in charge today. Don't fuck up, Cam"

"I won't boss"

"Yeah okay. I hear you. Don't make me kill your black ass Cameron"

Cam finished getting dressed by two o'clock. He grabbed his phone and kissed Tia on the forehead. He told her he would be checking in on her throughout the day. She told him to be safe and he left.

As soon as she heard the door slam, she waited a few minutes to get up. She peeped through the slits in the blinds and waited for Cam to drive off. Once he did, she ran back to the bed and grabbed her phone. She scrolled through her contacts until she landed on Sienna's name. As soon as she answered the phone, Tia let her know that Cam was gone for a few hours. Sienna told her that she would be with her in less than a half an hour.

$$***** $$

I woke up to the smell of food, sat up on the sofa and rubbed my eyes until they were no longer blurry. I walked into the kitchen to find Leana cooking pork chops. "My favorite" I said.

"It sure is" she replied.

I kissed her cheek and went to the bathroom. When I finished, I went back into the kitchen and my plate was sitting on the table. I sat down and started digging in.

"Damn, you couldn't wait for me?" Leana asked.

"Nope. I'm hungry as a hostage right now"

"I bet you are as long as you slept"

"Damn how long was I asleep?"

She checked her watch. "You have been sleeping since probably like eleven and it is now seven in the evening."

"Goddamn. I must have been tired"

"Yeah must be"

Ring. Ring.

We looked around to see whose phone was ringing. It must have been mine because Lee had hers. She got up from her seat to go and retrieve mine from the couch and I continued to eat. She came back in the kitchen with a disgusted look on her face.

"What's wrong?" I asked her, swallowing my food.

"Who the fuck is Brittany?" she asked, throwing my phone at me.

"Watch it, Lee. What the fuck is wrong with you? You could've broke my phone"

"Fuck that! I don't give a damn about your phone. Who the fuck is she?"

"I don't know a Brittany"

"So why the fuck is her name saved in your phone?"

"I don't know" my phone started ringing again. The caller id read Brittany.

"Answer it" she said.

"I don't want to" I shot back.

She reached over, snatched the phone and ran to the room. I chased behind her only to be stopped by her cocked gun.

"Hello" she said, answering the phone and putting it on speaker.

"Hello? Who is this?"

"No, who the fuck is this?" she snapped back.

"This is Brittany. I'm looking for Antonio"

Gemini Betrayal

"And why are you looking for my man?"

"First of all, Bitch, that's my nigga. He was just with me this morning"

She threw the phone at me. "You better tell that bitch about me"

I caught the phone and she still stood there with her gun aimed.

"Look, Brittany that shit is over between us!" I yelled into the speaker phone.

"Over? Nigga you got me all kinds of fucked up. You better stop fucking playing with me, Nigga"

"Bitch ain't nobody playing with your dumb ass. We done. I love my girl"

"Motherfucker fuck you and your fucking girl. I will fuck both of y'all up"

She continued to go on and on until I hung up the phone. I immediately placed her on the blocked list on my phone then looked over to Leana.

She was still standing there pointing her gun and I could see tears running down her face.

"Baby" I said, walking towards her. She raised her gun and aimed it at my head.

"Don't get no fucking closer, Antonio. I am so done with your black ass," she said through clenched teeth.

"Don't be like that, Babe. I fucked up"

"You damn right. You fucked up" she screamed at me. Just then, I saw her grab her stomach and leaned over in pain.

"What's the matter, Boo?" I asked, rushing to her side to help.

"Don't put your fucking hands on me. I gotta go" she said.

"Where are you going?" I asked as she grabbed her phone and car keys off the table.

"To the fucking hospital. This pain hurts like hell and I wanna make sure the baby is okay"

"Want me to come?"

"Fuck you" she yelled back. She slammed the front door and I watched from the window as she wobbled to the car. She put the car in reverse and backed down the driveway. I watched as she drove down the street and disappeared from sight.

"Damn I fucked up," I yelled out.

✳✳✳✳✳

Tia held Sienna down on top of her as they kissed one another and rolled around the California king bed. Tia sucked Sienna's dark nipple into her mouth and bit down gently.

"Ahh" Sienna moaned softly. "Oh, shit" she said, as she moved her hips back and forth on top of Tia.

"That's right. Ride that dick, Baby" Tia said, holding Sienna by the waist. They went long enough for Sienna to cum all over Tia's strap-on. Once she finished releasing all of her juices, she laid on the bed next to Tia.

Gemini Betrayal

"How much time we got before Cam gets home?" Sienna asked.

Tia picked up her phone and looked at it. She had a missed call and text from Cam. She opened the text and it read "on the way" She looked at the time it was received. It came through twenty minutes ago. "Oh fuck" she said, jumping up. Sienna jumped up as well.

"We gotta hurry up and get dressed. My damn phone was on vibrate and Cam said he was on his way home"

"Damn"

As they were scrambling to get their clothes and undergarments from the floor, they hadn't even noticed Cam at the door.

"Did I interrupt something?" he said, startling them.

They both froze and looked at him. They looked at one another and then back at him.

"Cam, I'm sorry Baby" Tia said, pulling her pants up and buttoning them. She threw on her shirt and walked over to him. She hugged him but didn't receive one back.

"This doesn't even amaze me, you know?" he said, looking back and forth between the two ladies. "I had a feeling something was going on between the two of you bitches, but I gave y'all the benefit of the doubt" He walked into the room and hopped up on the bed and propped his feet up. "So how long has this been going on, Sienna?" he asked.

"Um, um" she stammered looking over to Tia.

"This was the first time" Tia jumped in.

"Bullshit" he responded.

"No it's true, Cam" Sienna said in agreement.

He jumped off the bed and charged at Sienna. He grabbed her around her throat with both hands and slammed her into the mirror in the corner. "Don't fucking lie to me!" he yelled. "Y'all hoes been fucking each other. Now tell me the truth. Stop fucking lying"

His grip was getting tighter with each passing second and Sienna's oxygen was slowly slipping from her body.

"Put her down, Cam" Tia said from across the room. He turned around and looked her way. She was aiming her desert eagle right at him.

"Oh you gonna shoot me over some pussy, T? That's how it is now?" he asked still holding onto Sienna's throat. Tia looked at her and could see her face changing color. The life was literally been choked out of her. Her pupils were getting smaller.

"I will if you don't put her down"

"What if I don't?"

"Then I'm gonna put a hot one in you"

"Right" he said, laughing.

She cocked her gun. "Don't tempt me. Just put her the fuck down!" she yelled.

Without thinking, Cam dropped Sienna and ran across the room and lunged at Tia. He managed to tackle her to the floor as they wrestled for the gun. Then three shots rang out. Sienna was lying on the hardwood trying to catch all the air that she could. Once she managed to get her breathing back under control, she got onto her knees. She looked over at Tia and Cam's motionless bodies by the bedside.

"Tia?"

Gemini Betrayal

Chapter Twenty-Seven

Ihadn't heard anything from Leana's ass in a couple of days. I had been blowing up her phone for two whole fucking days! I figured she was mad the other day when she left and that's why she wasn't answering my calls. But two days? Never. I decided to call the hospital.

"Thanks for calling New Jersey Regional. How may I direct your call?"

"Yeah, uh, hi. I'm calling to see if my girlfriend is there"

"What would she have come here for, Sir?"

"Well, she's pregnant and she was having pains the other day"

"What's your girlfriend's name, Sir?"

"Leana Daniels."

"Hold one second please" *I could hear the typing of keys on the line.* *"She could have at least put me on a real hold"* I thought.

I waited impatiently on the phone as I paced back and forth across the floor. I was getting pissed off the longer I was on hold. If it wasn't Leana, I would've hung up by now. *What the fuck was taking so long?*

"Hello, Sir? Are you still there?"

Duh. What the fuck do you think? I wanted to say. "Yes I'm here"

"Well, it looks like she was here but she was discharged"

"Well when was this?"

"The same day she came in. Two days ago"

I didn't even say 'thank you' to the lady. I just hung up the phone. I thought hard as to where she could have been as I continued to call her phone back to back. I did this for about an hour. I decided to call her mother.

When I spoke to her, she informed me that she hadn't heard from her either and they talked everyday. Her sister nor her brother had not heard from her either. I was quickly running out of people and didn't have a clue as to where she and my unborn child were.

Maybe she left me for good. I don't deserve her. She's too damn good of a woman to be hurt like this. She's probably never gonna come back. She's gonna probably find a better man that will take better care of her. And what about my son? He's gonna be calling another nigga 'daddy' Oh fuck no! I was gonna find her ass. She playing games.

The ringing of my phone had brought me out of my self-doubt party. I looked at the number and it was a blocked number. I ignored it and went to get a drink. As I was opening my beer, the phone ring again. Unknown popped up on the screen again. I ignored it for the second time. I took a couple of swigs of the beer and, yet again, the unknown caller was calling again. This time I answered.

"Yo, who the fuck is this?" I yelled into the phone.

"Antonio? Baby help me" It was Leana on the other end of the phone crying hysterically.

"Leana? Baby where are you?"

"I don't know. I need you. Ahhh" I heard her scream into the phone.

"Tell him what the fuck I told you to say, Bitch" I heard a male voice say in the background.

275   Gemini Betrayal

"Who the fuck is that? Lee?" I yelled into the phone again.

"I'm here, Baby. They kidnapped me when I was getting in the car the other day. They want you to pay them one million dollars or they're gonna kill me and the baby" she said crying.

My mind was racing. Who the fuck would kidnap my girl and unborn child? Then want me to pay a ransom? What kind of Cuban shit is this? Cuban? Pablo!

"Tell Pablo I'm gonna fucking kill him!" I yelled.

"Look you motherfucker" I heard Pablo say on the other end of the phone. "I want my fucking money that you owe me"

"But I don't owe you anything. Let my fucking girl go"

"No, no, no. That is not true, Antonio" he said in his Cuban accent.

"What the fuck are you talking about?"

"When you went to jail, you still had some birds flocking around. They never flew back home to me and now I have put interest on it. So I want my fucking money or I'll kill your bitch"

"Baby, please, help me" I heard Leana crying in the background.

"You'll get your fucking money. Don't you worry"

"Me? Worry? I have no worry bone in my body" he said before hanging the phone up in my ear.

"Fuck!" I yelled. This shit was beyond fucking madness. I called Twan and told him to meet me at the house and to bring all the money he had. He told me he would be there in about three or four hours.

While I waited for Twan to get his black ass up here to Jersey, I went into my stash where I had some money put away for us. I counted out two hundred thousand. I needed more money. I just remembered about the money I had stashed at my house back home. I quickly called Twan back.

"Yeah Boss" he said, answering on the second ring.

"Go to my house"

"Your house? I thought you was in Jersey?"

"Motherfucker? Shut up and fucking listen. Go to my house and call me when you get there. I will give you instructions on what to do from there"

"Aight Boss"

We both hung up the phone. I grabbed my beer bottle and threw it across the room. It broke against the clock on the wall. I was furious now. I couldn't even think straight at the moment. I had to calm my nerves though. I didn't wanna be on edge when Twan got here because we had to find Lee and the baby.

I walked fast to the bedroom. I decided to roll me a fat ass jay to calm down.

✳✳✳✳✳

Sienna limply stood to her feet and crept her way over to where Cam and Tia were. Tia began coughing underneath of Cam.

"Oh my God, T" Sienna said, dropping to her knees at Tia's side. They both used the strength they had to push Cam off top of her. They pushed him to the side and sat on the floor next to one another.

They stared on at Cam as his eyes blankly stared at the both of them. His entire body was motionless and they could see the three holes that Tia had put in him.

"I'm so glad you're okay" Sienna said, hugging Tia.

"I'm glad you're okay, too" Tia replied. They both stood up and looked over Cam's body again. "We need some backup, SiSi"

"I'm on it" she replied, grabbing her phone. She called up her uncle Gee that worked for a cement company.

"How long before he gets here?" Tia asked.

"He said no longer than fifteen minutes"

"That's good. That gives us time to hide the gun and clean ourselves up"

"Exactly. I just need to borrow some sweats and a shirt until I can get home in a little bit"

"I got you" Tia said. She kissed Sienna on her lips like it would be her last. Sienna returned the kiss by doing the same.

They both hopped in the shower together. Sienna washed the blood off of Tia that had covered her face and parts of her upper body. By the time they had finished showering and throwing on loungewear, Sienna's phone was ringing.

"Hey Unc" she said.

"I'm pulling up around back" he said.

"Around back?"

"Yeah. Don't need these nosey ass fucking neighbors in our business"

"That's true"

Gemini Betrayal

"Just unlock the door and my crew is gonna come and get him"

"Got it"

They both went downstairs to the door in the kitchen and let the guys in. Tia showed the guys where Cam's body was while Sienna stayed downstairs talking to her uncle.

Moments later, the five guys were carrying a cardboard box outside that had Cam's body folded up like a pretzel inside. They thanked Sienna's uncle and Tia gave him two stacks of money for him and his boys. They closed and locked the door and went back upstairs.

"Well, that worked out good" Sienna said to Tia.

"Yeah it did" she responded.

"What's the matter?"

"I can't believe I just killed Cam"

"You did what you had to do. Don't feel bad" she said, stroking her face.

Tia looked at Sienna. She could see the fingerprints and bruises Cam had left behind. She held back the tears because she didn't wanna cry in front of Sienna. She was a thug and thugs didn't cry. Or at least they didn't want people to know. "You're right. I shouldn't feel bad and I don't. I'm just glad you're okay"

"Same here"

"Wanna watch some tv?"

"That's cool"

Tia and Sienna watched tv for a few hours. They got hungry and instead of going out to eat, they ordered Ubereats. They didn't want to be out in public with bruises and shit all over Sienna's neck and some nosey ass white person call the cops. They were trying to avoid the police at all costs.

As the night went on, Tia was starting to feel little to no remorse about what she had done. She loved Cam but lately she had started falling for Sienna. And in her book, whoever had her heart, she had to protect.

She looked over to Sienna who was distracted by the tv. She watched her and looked her over. From her hair to her eyes to her feet, Sienna was a beautiful person no less.

"What?" Sienna asked when she finally caught Tia staring.

"I just love you"

"I love you too" Sienna said. She kissed Tia on the cheek and continued to eat her food. Tia kissed her back on the cheek and finished scarfing down her food as well.

✱✱✱✱✱

"Yeah Boss, I'm here" Twan said to Antonio as he reached the top of the porch stairs.

"Cool. Look under the last brick on the top step and get the spare key"

"No need to. Your door is cracked open a little"

"What the fuck you mean?" I said, pressing the phone closer to my ear.

"Yep. Somebody has been here" Twan said, taking his gun out and taking off the safety. He walked throughout the downstairs looking for anything out of the ordinary.

"You still there, Twan?" I asked after the long silence.

"Yeah Boss. I was just checking out the downstairs for you. Need me to check the upstairs too, Bro?"

"Naw it's cool. I need you in the basement. If you see anything or anybody, just shoot they ass. Don't ask no questions"

"No problem" he replied. He descended down the basement stairs as instructed. "Okay I'm down here"

"Aight. Listen carefully. Go over to the wall and push on the center of it"

He did exactly what I asked him to do. "Holy fuck" he said out loud as the wall displayed a safe.

"What? What's wrong?" I asked in a panic.

"Nothing, dawg" he said. "What you want me to do now?"

"Enter the code. It's 6-8-0-2-3-1"

I could hear the beeping in the background. I heard the safe beep three times at and knew he had gotten in it.

"It's open, Tony"

"Grab all the money out of there and throw it in a hefty trash bag. I will see you in a few hours"

"You got it, Boss"

I hung up the phone and relaxed a little. Knowing that Twan would be here before nightfall was good. I was gonna kill that nigga Pablo for kidnapping Leana and the baby. He didn't know who he was fucking with.

Ring. Ring.

Gemini Betrayal

I looked at the caller id and it was the unknown number again. I answered on the second ring.

"Is this you Lee?" I asked as soon as I picked up.

"Lee? No motherfucker it's me." It was Brittany's dumb ass again.

"Man what the fuck do you want, Brittany? I told your ass the other day I was done"

"Like I told you the other day, you got me fucked up. Don't no nigga quit me, motherfucker."

"Well I did"

"Anyway, when you wanna get some more of this good pussy?"

"Good pussy? Bitch that shit smell like motherfucking catfish and sardines. Don't call me no motherfucking more, Bitch" I said, hanging up the phone in her ear.

I don't understand bitches. When you tell them you done, they wanna act all fucking crazy. Maybe I shouldn't have dicked her down the way I did. This bitch was strung out on the D now. I didn't have time to deal with her and her whiney crybaby bullshit right now. I had better things to worry about. I had to find my goddamn family.

✶✶✶✶✶

I checked the time and it was nearing 9:30 at night. I called Twan's phone to see where he was.

"Yeah what up, Boss?" he said.

"Where the fuck you at, Nigga?" I yelled.

"I'm right here on Barnaby Street"

"So you should be about to pull up soon. The house I'm in the only one without the porch lights on so you're gonna know which one I'm in. Just ring the doorbell when you get here"

"No doubt"

We hung up and I waited for him. I didn't have the number to call Pablo and get in touch with him. The number that I had listed for him was out of service. That wasn't surprising though. Most drug dealers tossed phones after a few months. Me, on the other hand, I got rid of my phone and had a new number every two weeks. I ain't play that phone tapping shit with the feds. They can miss me with that shit.

I heard a hard knock at the door. I looked through the peephole. After confirming that it was Twan, I snatched open the door and grabbed him inside by his shirt.

"Damn what's that about, Boss?"

"Nigga I said ring the motherfucking doorbell"

"Oh I forgot"

"That motherfucking fast, Nigga? Your ass need to stop fucking smoking" I said, shaking my head. He handed me the trash bag and I dumped all the money on the coffee table.

We sat there and counted all the money for about two hours.

"We got enough?" Twan asked.

"Yeah"

"Cool. So what's going on?"

"Pablo got Leana" I said short and sweet.

Gemini Betrayal

"Oh shit. How he get her, man?"

"I don't know. She said he grabbed her outside the hospital the other day"

"Oh shit, dawg. Don't worry though. We gonna get her back"

"I know" I said reassuring myself.

"So what now?" he asked as we packed all the money inside two duffel bags.

"We wait until he calls"

"That could take forever though"

"Do it look like a give a fuck right now, Twan?" I asked, jacking him up by his shirt.

"Naw, dawg" he said, staring me in the eyes. I saw the rage building behind his eyes. I released him and he straightened up his clothes.

"Now chill out. We just gotta wait"

"Aight, man"

We both sat down and waited for the phone call from Pablo. Twan had pulled out a Ziplock bag that contained five rolled up jays with different herbs inside of each one of them. He took one out and passed the bag over to me. I took one out and lit it as he lit the one he took out. For about an hour, we passed the jays back and forth until we only had one left to spark.

✳✳✳✳✳

Gemini Betrayal

I jumped up out of my sleep when I heard the ringing of a cell phone. I searched around the couch and grabbed my phone. I looked at the caller id and turned off my alarm.

I rubbed my eyes and realized it was the morning. That was my 8:00 alarm for me to get up and get my day started. I quickly checked my phone to see if I had any missed calls. I scrolled through the call list but no missed calls were listed. I looked over at Twan. He was slouched down in the chair knocked out sleep.

"Yo, Twan? Wake up, man" I said, kicking the side of his leg when I stood up.

"What? What? What's going on?" he said, pulling his gun out.

"Put that shit away Bro" I said, smacking the gun out the way. "We slept all fucking night, man"

"Did Pablo or Leana call?"

"Naw and I'm worried. What if he killed her, Bro?"

"Don't think like that. I don't think he would have done that. Especially if he wants his damn money"

"Yeah you right, I guess"

"You damn right I'm right"

I sat back down on the chair and laid my head back. I needed to calm down. I was a wreck and ain't no telling what the hell Leana was going through. We were sitting quietly in the living room, battling our own thoughts when my phone began ringing. Both Twan and I stood up and I put the phone on speaker.

"Yeah, hello?"

"I take it that you have my money, Antonio?" Pablo asked.

"Yeah. I have your money. Where is Leana?"

"One thing at a time, please. Your bitch is fine" he said.

"Don't fucking lie to me, Pablo. I wanna hear her voice"

"So demanding for somebody that owes me money" he responded. I heard him call to someone in the distance and then I heard Leana get on the phone.

"Baby? Please tell me you're coming?"

"Yeah I am, Boo" I said to her. As thuggish as I was, this shit was tearing me up inside but I had to be strong.

"Please hurry"

"I will"

Pablo got back on the phone. "We will meet you on Saturday night and I will send you the address?"

"Saturday? That's three motherfucking days away! What the fuck is wrong with you?"

"Saturday or I kill her now and then come kill you. Which do you prefer?"

I let out a deep groan. "I guess I'll see you Saturday"

"That's a good boy. Chow"

"I'm gonna kill that motherfucker" I said to Twan.

"We're gonna kill him, Tony"

"You right, dawg" I dapped him up and went to my room. I told him I needed to come up with an attack for Pablo's ass. He told me he would be back in Jersey Saturday morning and ready to ride out. He got in his car and headed back down to Maryland.

Gemini Betrayal

I did feel a little relief. At least, I knew that Leana was still alive. But what about the baby? He better not hurt my fucking son or I'm gonna kill that nigga's mama. I don't have no chill when it comes to mines. I would kill my own goddamn family to protect my child.

There it was again; family. Even though my sister was out to get me, I still loved her and had nothing against her. She thinks I went behind the crew's back when in actuality I went down on some assumptions and bullshit charges. I didn't give a fuck anymore. I did my time and I was hoping eventually my sister will realize I've had her back this entire time. And that's a strong motherfucking hope.

Gemini Betrayal

Chapter Twenty-Eight

Sienna jumped up and down with joy after she hung the phone up. She ran upstairs to the room where Tia was. She walked into the room just as the commercial break came on. She knew how much Tia hated to be interrupted when she was watching sports. But, honestly, she would love this news.

"I got some great news, Babe" Sienna said, jumping on the bed next to Tia.

"Oh yeah? What's that?"

"I can't tell you"

"And why the fuck not?"

"Because I'm gonna show you"

"Well show me then. What the fuck is waiting for, SiSi?"

"Oh my God. Just chill out. You have to wait about fifteen minutes"

"Then why the fuck you come in here distracting me from the fucking tv? You be acting so stupid sometimes" she said, getting aggravated.

The smile disappeared from Sienna's face. "You get on my fucking nerves" she said hitting Tia with a pillow. She jumped off the bed and headed out the room. "Have your black ass downstairs in fifteen minutes" she yelled back at Tia.

Gemini Betrayal

Tia shook her head as SiSi jogged back down the stairs. "Fucking dumb bitch" Tia mumbled. She focused her eyes back onto the screen. She was enjoying her basketball game. Miami was in the lead and LA wasn't too far behind.

She was so into the game she had been upstairs way past the fifteen minute mark. Since Sienna hadn't come back upstairs, she didn't think too much of it and watched the last quarter of the game uninterrupted.

After the final buzzard, Tia was ecstatic. Miami Heat had one the game and she was getting ready to go collect all her money from people that had bet on the game. She totaled $1,200 in her head and it was time for those motherfuckers to pay up.

She slid her phone into her baggy pants and put her keys in her pocket. She jogged down the steps and went to look for Sienna. She walked towards the kitchen looking for her.

"Yo, Sisi, I be back" she said, walking into the kitchen. Only SiSi wasn't alone at the breakfast bar. "What the fuck are you doing in my house?"

"Damn it's like that?" Twan asked.

Tia grabbed her gun that she hid inside the cabinet and pointed it at Twan. "Yeah, motherfucker, it is like that. Now I'm gonna ask you again. What the fuck are you doing in my house, Nigga?"

"You remember the good news I was telling you about, T?"

"Yeah" she replied, never taking her eyes off of Twan.

"Well, Twan was the good news"

"How the fuck is this trader good news?"

"Trader?" Twan said appalled.

"Yeah, Nigga, a trader. You sided with my brother and he's the enemy. And since that's your boy, you're an enemy now, too. I don't like snakes in my yard so you need to get the stepping"

"I guess so if you don't wanna know where your brother is" he said, walking out the kitchen. Tia stopped him in his tracks and aimed her gun higher to his head.

"How do you know where he is?"

"Because that's my boy. Remember?"

"Where is he?" Tia asked.

"I'll tell you for a price" he said, folding his arms across his chest.

"Or you can tell me before I kill you" she said.

He stepped closer to her and looked down into her eyes. "You know I ain't afraid to die, T. So try that shit with somebody else"

"Where is he?" she repeated through clenched teeth.

"Everything has a price"

"What's your price?"

"One million"

"A million dollars? Motherfucker, you must be on something stronger than goddamn weed if you think I'm about to pay you that"

"Guess I'm gonna go then" he said, walking out again.

"Wait" Tia said. She looked over to Sienna. "Go to the safe in the room and put a mill in a duffel for this clown ass nigga." She looked back at Twan. "You better not be trying to play me, Nigga"

"Nope. Not at all" he said.

Gemini Betrayal

Sienna came back twenty minutes later carrying the duffel bag full of money. She handed it to Twan and he sat at the kitchen table and counted it.

"Are you fucking serious?" Tia asked him.

"Hell yeah. I don't want to be cheated"

Sienna rolled her eyes at him and went over to assist him. It took them ten minutes to count every stack of hundreds. When they were finally finished, Twan put all the money back in the bag.

"Well?" Tia asked.

"Your brother is in Jersey"

"Jersey? What the fuck is he doing there?"

"Relocating I guess" Twan said sarcastically.

"Well, is he there alone?"

"Nope. Leana is there, too. Well, she was anyway"

"What you mean 'was'? Where is she then if she's not with him?"

"Not sure honestly. Pablo got her ass"

"Oh shit" Tia said, laughing. "That's what the fuck his punk ass get. If he never turned his back on the squad, he woulda been good."

"You right"

Tia paused for a second. She looked back at Twan and pointed her gun again. "How the fuck I know you ain't lying, Nigga?"

"I'm not. He is in Jersey"

"Prove it"

He pulled out his phone and showed her the text he had sent him with the address to where he was. He forwarded the text to her like she had asked. He gathered all of his money and headed out the door. He didn't even give a damn anymore about loyalty. "Fuck loyalty" he said as he backed out of Tia's driveway. He headed home to Ashley a million dollars richer.

$$*****$$

I was lying on the bed staring up at the ceiling. I have been doing this for a few hours now. I couldn't sleep. I was too worried about Leana and our son. For some reason, I knew my sister and Cam had something to do with this shit. I had to get their asses back. They turned their backs on me and then gonna retaliate against me like I did something to them. I was loyal to the game. I get locked up one little time and now these motherfuckers wanna call me an enemy. A trader. A backstabber. Them fucking words weren't even in my vocabulary.

I looked at the time on my phone and it read 3:30p.m. I decided to get myself cleaned up and try to go out the house. I had been moping around the house for an entire day. I was a goon. What the fuck was going on with me?

I turned on the shower water and stripped down to my boxers. I closed the bathroom to keep the heat inside and to put my dirty clothes into the hamper. I saw a picture of Leana and a copy of the baby's sonogram on the dresser as I passed it. I picked them up and started to feel down again. I did something I hadn't done in over ten years. I got on my knees and prayed.

"Dear Lord, our Father art thou in heaven hear me. I know I have done wrong in my life and you are not proud of it, but I need you. Please protect my girl, Leana, and our unborn son. This is my first child and I want him to make it. I want them both to make it out of this bullshit alive. Don't punish them for my mistakes. Let them live. If you have to, just let me die. If I have to die so they can live, let me die. Amen."

I went and got into the shower and thought about what I said. I really meant that shit. I didn't want Leana and the baby to be harmed because of my bad decisions. I will die for them. Take a bullet to save them without hesitation. This must be what real love was all about that my mama used to preach to me about.

I finished my shower and dried my body with a towel. I changed my mind about going out so I just threw on a pair of boxers and lounged around for a little bit. I didn't turn the tv on because I didn't feel like being bothered with all the noise. I picked up my phone and called Twan. It rang and went straight to voicemail.

That was odd. I just realized that I hadn't talked to him since he went back to Maryland. I hoped everything was okay. I heard my phone chime and I picked it up. It was a text message. I opened it and it was from Twan. What the fuck? This nigga message said some damn 'what's up, bro'?

Was this nigga serious? I dialed the number two more times and it did the same as the first time. He sent me another text back asking me the same question. I asked him what time he would be here on Saturday and he told me around six in the evening. I told him 'okay' and put my phone back on the nightstand.

I took a couple of sleeping pills and washed it down with some JD. I laid down on the bed and waited for the meds to take effect. If my body wasn't gonna go to sleep willingly, I had to force it. I had to get as much sleep as possible. I didn't know what those Cubans had in store for me on Saturday . Whatever they planned to do, I was gonna be ready. Me and my nigga, Twan.

       Gemini Betrayal

✳✳✳✳✳

"This information is pure gold" Tia said to Sienna. They were riding back from the grocery store as they usually did on Fridays. They pulled up in the driveway and got the bags out the trunk and went inside.

"Yeah it is" Sienna said, putting can goods in the cabinets. "Question is, what are you gonna do with it?"

"I guess you and I are going to Jersey"

"When?"

"Tomorrow I guess. Twan said it's a four hour drive to where my brother is"

"I guess we're gonna just stay the night there?"

"Yep. We can stake out the place then move in when he least expects it. Twan said that he was going up there on Saturday. That would be a good day to surprise him" Tia said, smiling from ear to ear.

"That would be one hell of a surprise. I can't wait to see my old compadres" Sienna said, walking out of the kitchen.

"Where you going?" Tia yelled behind her.

"Well, I do have to pack for the trip"

"We're not leaving until tomorrow though.l"

"True. But I have to check my artillery and see which of my babies are coming with me" she said heading down to the basement.

"I hear you" Tia replied.

Sienna went down to the basement. With the click of a button, an entire wall turned around. She smiled as she looked at her collection. Every week, she was adding to her gun collection and 'my oh my' has it grown over the years.

From her glock 17 to her biggest machine gun to her military grade sniper rifles, Sienna was always ready for anything. She grabbed her case that she kept her sniper rifle in. She took it down form the wall and dismembered it and placed each part in its spot. She grabbed a couple of duffel bags and packed her AF-15 rifle along with about ten more guns. She made sure she had packed enough bullets that would last an army for about a week or so. After going over her checklist of guns, she turned the wall back around and headed back upstairs.

As she walked into the living room, she could see Tia lying on the couch. She walked closer and realized she was playing candy crush like she always did.

"Do you ever have a better use for your leisure time?" she asked moving Tia's head out the way so she could sit down. Tia rested her head on Sienna's lap.

"Nope. You're just mad because I be kicking your ass in this game" Tia said, laughing.

"Not even"

"Stop being so fucking salty, you big baby" Tia grabbed the back of Sienna's head and kissed her lips. Their make out session was cut abruptly by the ringing of Sienna's phone. She reached over and grabbed it. She looked at the caller id and saw that it was Twan. She answered it and put it on speaker.

"What's up, Twan?" she said.

"Nothing much. What y'all up to?"

"Nothing much" Tia chimed in.

"So look, I'm gonna head up there Saturday like I said originally"

"We know" Tia said, rolling her eyes. "We're gonna go tomorrow"

"That's cool. I don't wanna go up there too early. Antonio said he had a plan to get Leana back"

"And what's that exactly?"

"Not sure. I won't find out until Saturday"

"Well, we gonna see you up there. Me and Sienna got stuff to do"

"Aight. Holla" Sienna hung up the phone and looked at Tia.

"What damn stuff we gotta do?" she asked.

"I'm about to stuff you with my dick" Tia exclaimed. She sat up on the chair and Sienna took off into the room. Tia chased behind her and grabbed her from behind and they both fell onto the bed.

They kissed each other passionately as they tore at each others' clothes. Five minutes had passed and they both were butterball naked. They intertwined their bodies and began their love making session.

✳✳✳✳✳

I ended up going to the 24/7 gym in Camden. It was eleven o'clock at night and it was barely anybody here except the staff. I started off with running on the treadmill for about an hour. I had this idea in my head that if I had run fast enough, I could outrun my problems. It didn't do a damn thing except make me sweaty. I took off my shirt and headed downstairs to hit the bag a little.

Gemini Betrayal

I entered the area where they had the boxing ring and punching bags at. It was empty and dimly lit in the room. I didn't sweat it though, I was strapped at all times. I ain't have no worries. I put my wireless beats headphones on and warmed up a little.

I started out tapping the bag a little bit with a left hook then a right. My pace quickened and I started doing left right combos. I was throwing blows that coincided with the music I was listening to. I was so caught up into my workout that I didn't notice that somebody else had entered the room. I felt a tap on my shoulder and I swung. Luckily for them, they had ducked. But it wasn't good for me because they uppercut me.

"Goddamn" I said grabbing my chin.

"What the hell is your problem?" she yelled at me. Her fists were still balled up and she was ready to swing again.

"What the fuck are you doing sneaking up on me?"

"I wasn't sneaking up shit. I was here the entire time" she replied.

She walked onto the other side of the ring and turned the lights on. The bright lights had burned my corneas and I had to cover them with my hands. Once they were adjusted to the light, I put my hands down to my sides. I could see a much better glimpse of the girl now.

She had on tight shorts and a sports bra with sneakers. Her spandex shorts were too damn tight to hide all that ass and her sports bra was too damn small to cover her tits.

She was hitting the bag on her side of the ring but she noticed me staring at her. She stopped and went to lock the door.

"What are you doing?" I asked her as she walked back over to me.

Gemini Betrayal

"You wanna box, Papa?" she asked, pushing her breasts up in my face.

I took a deep gulp before answering. "I can't. I have a girlfriend"

"Oh okay. I completely understand," she said turning away.

In an instant, she had turned back around and jumped on me. My legs weren't stable and I had lost my balance and we both fell onto the floor. She positioned herself on top of me and began dry humping me. I grabbed her hips to push her off top of me but in her mind, I think she thought I was doing something else.

"I told you I have a girlfriend" I said in a hushed tone.

"Shhh" she said, putting her finger to her lips. " She doesn't have to know" she replied.

She planted her lips on mine and kissed me hard. She pulled back after a couple of minutes and her lipstick was smeared.

She pulled my dick out and massaged it. Once it had gotten completely hard, she pulled her little spandex shorts to the side and forced my dick inside of her. She placed her hands on my chest and rode me fast and steady.

She must have been enjoying herself because she started throwing her head back and moaning. She dug her nails into my bare chest and made scratches across my chest.

She held onto my shoulders tight. I just laid there on the cold floor and tossed my head with each of her movements. She clenched her pussy muscles and moments later, she had came all over my dick.

She climbed off top of me and placed her mouth on my manhood. She slurped and sucked on me until I came too. She licked and cleaned up the mess that we had made. She stood up and wiped her mouth. She winked at me and left out of the boxing room.

Gemini Betrayal

What the fuck was all that about? I thought to myself. *Why deep in the back of my mind do I feel like I just been raped by a beautiful woman?*

✳✳✳✳✳

"Yeah Boo, I don't mind waiting up for you" Sienna said to Tia on the phone.

"Cool. I'm gonna be there shortly. Love you"

"Love you too"Sienna replied. She looked at the time and it was three in the morning.

She had been quickly getting fed up with Tia's ass lately. She didn't know what to do. Tia had been coming home late all week long. She hoped that Tia wasn't taking an interest in somebody else. Or even worse, a nigga.

She heard a loud knock at the door and walked into the living room. She looked through the peephole and saw Gaines on the other side of the door. She took an exhausting breath then opened the door.

"What is it, Gaines?" she asked.

He stepped into the house and three officers came in close behind him. He directed them to split up and told them which ways to go.

"Whoa, whoa, whoa. What the fuck is going on?" Sienna yelled at them.

"Calm down, Sienna" Gaines instructed her. "We're just looking for Antonia and Antonio"

"What the fuck for now?"

"You know the usual. Drugs, murder, guns. This time we have hard evidence on both of their asses to put their asses under the jail"

Gemini Betrayal

"Well, I haven't seen either of them" she replied, crossing her arms on her chest.

"Oh SiSi is it?" he asked, walking up to her. "I thought you were gonna be the one to help me nail those two motherfuckers" he said, stroking her face. He grabbed a handful of her hair and pulled her head back. "But I guess not. I thought you were a lot smarter than everyone else. I guess I was wrong"

"Fuck you, Gaines!" she yelled. "I ain't helping you with shit"

"No worries" he said, releasing his hold on her hair. " I will be staking out the house until I catch one of their asses coming or going. I don't care which of them it is. I want them both"

He walked back to the front door. He got on his walkie and told everybody to come back. Once all three came back, they informed him that all the areas were clear of Tia and Antonio. They walked out the door and didn't look back.

Sienna ran to lock the door and grabbed her phone. She called Tia's phone five times in a row but didn't get an answer and she couldn't leave a message because the mailbox was full.

She ran to the window and looked out. She looked down the block, about six houses up, and saw an unmarked police car sitting there. She could see Gaines and Wilson clear as day. She knew they had a clear view of the house as well. Since she couldn't get in contact with Tia, she sent her a text.

"Don't come home, T. Gaines is scoping the spot" she texted her. Hopefully she reads it in time.

Chapter Twenty-Nine

I was losing my sanity. Even though Saturday was tomorrow, it still seemed liked it was an entire week away. It has been so stressful wondering about Lee and the baby. I just wanted them back home safe and sound. But knowing them Cubans, I knew they weren't gonna let her go peacefully without starting a riot. So I had to be as prepared as possible.

I looked over my inventory of guns that I planted under the floorboards throughout the house. I packed fifteen hand guns and a semi-automatic. If Twan didn't have enough, I was damn sure going to. I didn't play games with people and I wasn't about to start now. Pablo and his Cuban friends were in for a motherfucking rude awakening. After I had packed all of my weapons in my trunk, I headed back in the house to try and relax.

With each day that passed by, I felt more and more like shit because of what I had done to Leana. I treated her like shit and she didn't deserve that. I should be the one being punished not her.

I grabbed my jay from the ashtray and sparked it up again. I inhaled some good shit and exhaled all the bullshit. I don't know what blend of herb this was but it was strong and the aroma filled the air. I was so caught up in my own world that I just let my phone ring off the hook. I was feeling too good right now and didn't want anything or anybody ruining this moment. After I finished facing my jay, I decided to check my phone before I rested a little.

I picked up the phone and scrolled through the missed calls. They were all blocked and unknown numbers. "Fuck" I yelled out loud. I had missed Pablo's call several times. My dumb ass was trying to *69

Gemini Betrayal

the damn number! That's how desperate I was and how pissed off I was with myself. I tossed the phone on the bed and started pacing.

I was walking fast back and forth and rubbing my head. I could've fucking slapped myself for not paying attention and ignoring my phone. My phone started ringing again and I jumped across the bed. I just happened to grab it before it bounced off the bed.

"Hello? Hello?" I said frantically.

"Did I catch you at a bad time, Antonio?" Pablo asked.

"No you didn't. I was waiting for your call" I said, calming down a little..

"Really? I see. That's why you were ignoring my calls, yes? I thought you had changed your mind and was giving me the green light to kill your little bitch and then come for you"

"Where are we meeting at tomorrow?" I asked sternly. I didn't have time for his shit.

"We will send you the address around eight. Goodbye for now" he said, hanging up on me.

I rubbed my head again. As stressful as this week has been, it was finally coming to an end. By tomorrow, I would be holding my girl in my arms and not worrying about shit. I made sure to pack up the extra money I had put it in a duffel bag with our passports. After I got Leana back, we were leaving this fucking country. We had no reason to stick around and I damn sure didn't wanna raise my son here.

It hadn't dawned on me until now that I haven't eaten all day. I ordered Ubereats like always. I ordered chicken wings, fried rice, and egg rolls. That shit came up to almost $30 with the delivery fee. I might as well had ordered from the carryout. Ubereats was highway robbery, charging all that damn money. Sheesh.

✻✻✻✻✻

Tia and Sienna had to put their trip on hold because of Gaines and Wilson. They had been secretly meeting at a restaurant. Sienna would drive there and watch in her rearview mirror as Gaines would whip in and out of traffic to follow her. Once there, they would just sit outside as she went in; guess they didn't want to cause an unnecessary scene. Luckily for Sienna, she was able to put all their bags in the trunk by parking inside the driveway for a change. Wilson and Gaines were clueless. Now all she and Tia had to do was try and shake the fuzz.

Today was no different. Sienna showered and dressed in a simple outfit that wouldn't seem too skeptical. She threw on a pair of skinny jeans, tank top and some pumas. She threw her hair in a ponytail, grabbed her phone and headed. She had passed a couple of houses down from Tia's and looked in her rearview mirror. Like clockwork, Gaines and his flunky Wilson were right on her tail.

They were smart but not too smart. When she drove slow, they fell back a little too. When she hit the gas, so did they but not as much. She hit the highway and boonkganged their asses. She was doing 85, dodging in and out of traffic. She looked back a few times to see if she had ditched them. She could still see them so she kept at it. A mile down the road, she had a call come through. She hit the button on the steering wheel to answer the device.

"Yeah, hello?"

"SiSi where you at?" Tia asked as her voice came through the car speakers.

"I'm headed to you. I just gotta shake your boy"

"You still see them?"

Sienna looked in the rearview. Surprisingly, she didn't see them. "Nope. The coast is clear"

"Good. Get your ass here and pick me up. We got a long ride to Jersey"

"Be there in five" she said, hanging up. She hit the gas until she was going over 100. She had made it to Tia in about ten minutes.

She slowed down when she was on the street to pick Tia up. She pulled up to the restaurant and Tia hopped in the passenger seat.

"What's up fast and the furious?" she said to Sienna as she sped away from the curb and got back on the highway.

"What's up to yourself" she replied.

"Did you pack everything?"

"Yep. I was just waiting for you"

"Good. How long until we get to where my brother is?"

"Well, the gps says we will be there around eleven because of traffic."

"That's cool. I changed the plan a little"

"A little?"

"Yeah. We not gonna get his ass tonight. We're gonna wait until tomorrow"

"That's cool with me"

Tia leaned over and gave Sienna a quick kiss on the cheek. She put her seatbelt on and laid her seat back. She got deep in her zone and replayed their plan over in her head a couple of times.

Gemini Betrayal

She couldn't wait to see her brother's face when he saw her. She wished she could see her own face. It was crazy how this entire time she thought her brother was dead and he was walking around damn near unnoticeable to her and her crew. The shit was unreal. The area they lived in wasn't that goddamn big that she wouldn't have seen him. "*The doctor did say he had been in a coma though*" she remembered.

She pushed her brother out of her mind. She listened along to the music that had occasionally got overshadowed by the Waze gps app. She eventually fell asleep because she had been up all night smoking and drinking and now she had to pay for it. She hoped that when she woke up, they would be in Jersey. But until then, she needed to rest and that's all.

$$\ast\ast\ast\ast\ast$$

"I was awakened by the ringer of my phone. I reached over on the nightstand and grabbed it.

"Yo?" I said, answering the phone.

"You busy?"

"Who is this?" I asked.

"Really, Antonio?" the female voice asked. Upon listening closer to the other on the other end of the phone, Antonio recognized the voice.

"I know this ain't Tia?" I said.

"Yes, it is me. I was just trying to be make sure it was really you that was alive. People had been telling me but I wanted to be sure"

"You already knew I was alive. You tried to kill me, Tia. Or did we forget?"

Gemini Betrayal

"Nope I didn't forget at all. How you been?"

"Bye Tia. Nobody has time for your games" I said and hung up the phone. Only seconds had passed and somebody was leaning on my doorbell. I ran to the door and snatched it open but nobody was there.

I stepped on the porch and looked around and checked my surroundings. Nothing looked suspicious or out of the ordinary to me. My phone chimed in my hand. It said that I received a picture message from my sister's phone. I opened the message and studied the picture carefully.

The picture looked vaguely familiar. It was a house that looked exactly like the one Leana and I were currently staying in. I took a step back and thought. Ain't no fucking way she found me up here. Either she had followed Twan up here or captured him and made him tell. There was no way Twan had given me up. Maybe it was a harmless joke. It was just very coincidental that there was an identical house like this one.

Another picture message came through and I almost dropped my phone once I had opened it. It was a picture of me standing on this very porch only a few seconds after I had stepped out the door. I looked around again and didn't see anything. I slowly walked backwards into the house and closed the door. I grabbed my gun and I called Twan.

"What's up, Boss?" he said normally.

"You a fucking snitch, man?" I asked short and sweet.

"Snitch? Me? Never. What are you talking about?"

"Tia found me"

"Oh shit" Twan said, still playing into character. He couldn't let Antonio know that he had spilled the beans for some cash.

"I don't know how she knew. She must've had a tracking device in my car or some shit.

"Maybe" Twan said in agreement. "I can't call it. When did you see her? Or did she call you?"

"She called me, man. I was in here sleeping like a motherfucker" I said.

"You must have been asleep all day because you ain't even hit me up"

"Yeah I have been"

"Better be lucky it wasn't a permanent sleep" Twan uttered under his breath.

"What you say, Twan?" I asked.

"Huh? Oh nothing"

"Fuck tomorrow. I need your ass here ASAP just in case something pops off"

"I will see you in a couple of hours"

"Cool. Make sure you have your ass here tonight, Twan"

"Aight, man" he replied back.

I hung up the phone on his ass. I could've sworn that nigga said exactly what I thought he said. This nigga was acting like I wouldn't whoop his ass like he was a random ass nigga. I ain't tripping though. One thing I knew for certain was that Twan didn't want this smoke. He didn't wanna catch this fade.

I made sure to have a gun especially for him in case he tried to be funny and hop out there with me. Friend or not, his ass will get this work. I would shoot his ass up so bad to the point where nobody would recognize him. The only way they would be able to tell it was him was from his dental records.

I grabbed my gun and looked through the blinds for my sister. Even if I didn't see her physically, I could tell she was nearby. I could feel her presence at this moment but where she was, I had no clue. If she was a snake, like the one she had grown to be, she would have tried to bite the shit out of my ass.

I sat a chair in the middle of floor. I had it facing towards the front door because whoever was brave enough to bust up in here, they were brave enough to die. I didn't give no fucks.

I sat there for a while thinking. If it really came down to it, would I really take my sister out? Could I honestly kill my own flesh and blood? I'm not sure but at the end of the day, it was either me or her. Only time would tell, you know what I mean?

✳✳✳✳✳

Tia was dying, laughing as she and Sienna watched as Antonio stood on the porch in a panic. They looked on as he held the phone and looked around for them. They were happy to know that he didn't think to look up. If he had, he would have noticed them sitting on top of a vacant house at the end of the block. They were able to see him very clearly through their binoculars.

"This is classic" Tia said as she and Sienna climbed down the ladder and headed back to their car.

"Yeah it was. Did you see how scared he was?" Sienna said in agreement.

"Yeah. That shit was too damn funny. I didn't think he was gonna freak out that bad though"

"Neither did I"

They hopped in Sienna's rental car, to discuss their plan again, as they headed back to their hotel.

"I think Twan said they would be meeting Pablo tomorrow night, right?" Sienna asked Tia.

"Yeah but he said he wasn't sure of the time. He said he was gonna send us the details as soon as Tony gave them to him"

"Aight, cool. So, are we gonna meet him there or follow him?"

"I'm still wishy washy with that. It would be nice to follow him, but knowing my brother, he would be watching his surroundings more closely"

"That's true. I think we should follow. We can always follow from a good distance. Remember, we do have the experience"

"That is true" Tia agreed.

They pulled up to the hotel and parked in the lot. They got out the car and headed to their room. They too, watched their backs as they walked up the stairs. They both were always packing their heat so it would be a dead mission to catch them slipping.

Sienna hopped in the shower as Tia flipped through the tv channels and ordered them a pizza for dinner. She put on an old gangster movie that her and Tony had watched a numerous of times growing up. Her thoughts drifted to her brother.

Even though he was only a few minutes older than she was, he always made it seem like he was much older. Nonetheless, he had always protected her and fought beside her. That is until now. Now, in Tia's eyes, he wasn't nothing more than a trader. A low down, sneaky, snitching ass, betraying ass, punk ass trader. And in the streets, there was no coming back from that.

Sienna emerged from the bathroom wearing nothing but a towel. Tia looked at her and watched as water still dripped from her body. She strutted over towards Tia.

"Is everything okay, babe?" she asked, rubbing her cheek.

"Yep. Just sitting here thinking about tomorrow"

"You sure you wanna go through with this, T?"

Tia looked at her dead in her eyes and said "yes".

Sienna snatched the towel from her body and dropped it to the floor. She got up on the bed and laid down on her back. Tia scooted up on the bed and laid next to her. She looked in her eyes again.

"You ready for the shit that may go down tomorrow?" Tia asked Sienna.

"I surely am"

"You know our motto. You either get down-."

"Or you lay down" Sienna finished.

They managed to get a quickie in before their pizza arrived. Hours later, they were both loading all their guns for tomorrow's war. They made sure that their bulletproof vests were free of holes and that they had their gloves; just in case they had to drop their guns, no fingerprints would be left.

They went to sleep around midnight that night. Tia went to sleep with a smile on her face just thinking about how good it was gonna feel to have her brother dead once and for all.

Way across town, Twan and Antonio were still up going over their plan for tomorrow.

"We don't need no fucking slip-ups and bullshit tomorrow, Twan" Antonio said. "We need to get Leana out of there safely and be ready for whatever may go down. You ready, dawg?"

"Nigga I was born ready"

Chapter Thirty

The day of reckoning had finally come for the Hall twins. Sienna and Tia were doing some last minute running around while Antonio and Twan were loading their weapons and making sure all the money and everything was counted properly and secure for Pablo.

It was already nearing three in the afternoon and Antonio was getting beyond frustrated. "Man, what the fuck is this bitch ass nigga Pablo doing?" he yelled at Twan.

"Calm down, dawg. He's gonna call so stop worrying" he said, puffing on a jay.

Antonio walked over and snatched the blunt out of his hand. "Stop worrying? Are you fucking kidding me, nigga? My motherfucking girl and unborn son is out there somewhere being held hostage. And all you can say is stop worrying? You done lost your fucking mind, motherfucker." He took a few puffs of the weed before handing it back to Twan, who snatched it from him. Antonio looked at him and was about to say something to him but he let it slide for now.

Hours passed and it was now six in the evening. Antonio's phone rang. He looked at the caller id and saw that it was an unknown number. He wasn't sure if it was his sister or Pablo. He let it ring a little longer and didn't answer until the last ring.

"Yo?" he said answering the phone.

"Ah, Antonio? How are you doing my friend?" Pablo asked. Antonio wanted to jump through the phone and choke his ass so bad. It pissed him off more because he knew he couldn't really do that.

"Yeah, what's up?"

"Just making sure you were still alive"

"Why wouldn't I be?" Antonio thought.

"I hear things in the street. Anyway, I will be sending you the details in a few minutes. You have all my money correct?"

"I already told you the other day man" Antonio responded furiously.

"I will be seeing you tonight I guess" Pablo said before hanging the phone up on Antonio. Antonio threw the phone down on the couch. He was fuming. Twan looked at Antonio and could literally see him turning red with anger.

"We gonna find her" Twan said, placing a hand on Antonio's shoulder.

"I'm gonna kill that motherfucker. I promise you, young" Antonio replied with balled fists.

Twan looked at Antonio. He was sure that there was nothing to say that would calm him down. He had his mind made up on killing Pablo and nothing was gonna stop him. Twan sat back down after Tony had eventually sat down on the other chair.

He looked at Antonio and thought about how bad he was gonna feel to shoot him. He looked up to Antonio; he always had. While his friends wanted to grow up to be doctors and lawyers, he wanted to be a drug dealer. It was a plus that he worked with Antonio and Antonia. You got street cred and mad respect from people for just walking with the Hall twins. They were the definition of being hood celebrities. Even though he was gonna feel a little bad, he wasn't gonna

313   Gemini Betrayal

fully feel any remorse for his actions. He thought about the blocks Tia had promised to give him after they killed Antonio. He was gonna be hood rich. He had only hoped that Antonio would die quick so he can just flee the scene and never look back.

Antonio's phone chimed and alerted him of his new message. He opened the message that was from an unrecognizable number. It was the directions and time from Pablo. He wanted to meet at 11. They were ready now and Antonio couldn't wait to get his hands on Pablo. He looked back at the message. *Why does it seem like I have been here before?* he asked himself. He shook it out of his head and finished up.

✻✻✻✻✻

"The day has finally come" Tia said aloud. She and Sienna were getting geared up for today's events. They had on everything black from their shirts to their bulletproof vests to big ass combat boots.

"I'm ready to get rid of this motherfucker" Sienna said.

"So am I. I can't wait to blast his ass. And wait 'til he sees me. He's not gonna know what to do" Tia said, laughing. "I'm gonna make sure his ass is dead for real this time. Just make sure I'm the one that kills him and watches as he takes his last breath"

"Gotcha"

They kissed one another before finishing up their packing. Tia knew she had to be ready because she didn't know what to expect. Her phone dinged and she checked it. It was the address from Twan. The address looked a little familiar to her. She opened up her gps app and typed in the address. The streets on the map looked similar as well. She decided to google the address. When it came up, she smiled. Bingo!

The address that Twan sent was actually up the road from one of their dump sites. That particular one was passed down through the family. It was an old acid factory that had been given to them from Big Tone whom was given it from his father and so on and so on. It was very historical to her especially because she hadn't been there in a long time.

Her smile grew as she thought about how fun it would be to toss her brother in the hot acid. She would hear his screams and cries for mercy as the liquid ate away at his flesh. *"This will make my dad proud of me for sure"* she thought to herself.

"Babe?" she called to Sienna.

Sienna came downstairs carrying her favorite gun. The one that her father had given her when she first moved out of her parents' house. "What's up?"

"What time you got?"

"A little after 8. Why what's going on?"

"We gotta head out now"

"Why?"

"I will tell you in the car. We don't have much time"

"Aight"

They grabbed all their weapons and what they needed. They headed to the car and threw everything inside. They hit I-95 and Tia guided Sienna on where to go. Tia was so excited that she couldn't contain herself.

She had filled Sienna in on the place and told her what she had planned to do. Sienna gave back a wicked smile and cheesed as hard as Tia. It was the ultimate finish. They both were so eager to get there and get the place ready that they didn't realize they were being followed.

Gemini Betrayal

✳✳✳✳✳

"Are we all ready for tonight, Boss?" Wilson asked Gaines.

"You damn skippy I'm ready, Wilson. I've been dreaming about this day for 25 years. I couldn't kill their father but I can damn sure take them out' he responded, following behind Tia and Sienna. He didn't really need to because there was already a lojack on both Sienna and Antonio's cars. He even went as far as to bug every last one of their vehicles illegally. And they still hadn't noticed them following behind.

"This is gonna be great"

"Yep"

Tia's phone had rang and so did Gaines'. He had hooked up the phones whereas though he could tap into the calls from all of the gang's cell phones. He put the phone on speaker once she answered and listened in.

"What's up, Twan?" she said when she picked up.

"Yeah y'all still up here, right?"

"Duh, Nigga. Why would we leave?"

"Just making sure, man. But, look, wait until after Pablo meeting to move in. Then I will stall him so we could kill him"

"Why the fuck would we wait?"

"We might still need Pablo after the fact. We're gonna need a distributor"

"Thanks for your concern but we got that covered"

"We? You mean me too right?"

Tia got silent for a moment. "Actually no. I mean me and Sienna"

"You backstabbing bitch" he yelled into the phone. "You have me helping y'all and y'all bitches gonna leave me out in the cold?"

"Sorry, hun, that's the streets for ya" Sienna chimed in with a little laughter.

"I can't believe you motherfuckers betrayed me"

"Nigga you ain't loyal anyway" Tia yelled into the phone.

"How the fuck I ain't loyal?"

"Nigga, you sung like a canary and told us all the moves my brother was making. We don't need weak niggas on our team. Peace out" she said, ending the call.

"All they asses be fucking snitching" Gaines replied when the phone had disconnected. "We're gonna kill them all tonight"

"Yeah, Boss. Might even walk away with a small fortune"

Gaines smiled. He hadn't even thought about that. Free money and drugs? And the killing of the Hall twins and their affiliates? This was gonna be a great day for him and he couldn't wait.

Gemini Betrayal

Chapter Thirty-One

Everything was set in motion. It was exactly 11 when Twan and I pulled up to our destination. Pablo had already arrived and was inside the deserted building awaiting our arrival. Twan and I packed our shit on us and got out the truck.

We crept up to the building, making sure to watch our surroundings. Unbeknownst, Sienna and Tia had already arrived, and were slinking around in the shadows waiting for the right moment to jump out.

"You ready for this, man?" Twan asked me.

"I'm ready for whatever, man. I just want my girl back. So let's go handle this and get her outta here safe. Got it?"

"Got it Boss"

We continued to the building until we reached the door. I pushed the door open and it let out a loud screech and slammed against the wall behind it. It was dimly lit so we stayed close to one another and made sure to watch our steps. Pablo was famous for booby traps.

We passed by several rooms but they were all empty. We ended up upstairs in search of Pablo and Leana. This shit was crazy. *"What kind of fucking games was this nigga playing"* I thought to myself. We reached the third landing and noticed shadows on the wall and voices. We crept towards the voices and came upon Pablo and his sidekicks.

"Well, well, well, you finally found us" Pablo said. Everybody looked towards us and aimed their guns at us.

Gemini Betrayal

"Yeah we did" I responded with my gun firmly aimed at him. I looked over to Twan. He was moving the gun back and forth between Pablo's henchmen. "Where's Leana?"

"You're pushy Antonio" he replied. "How about my money first?"

I grabbed the bag from Twan and walked it over to Pablo. I dropped it at his feet and his goons picked it up as they kept their guns pointed at me. They took the bag over to a table and started counting the money. Pablo and I just stood there sizing each other up. I wanted to wipe that grin off his face so bad. I just had to be patient and wait for Leana to be handed over to me and not a second later. After the flunkies finished counting all the loot, they confirmed the amount with Pablo. He motioned for them to go out the room; I guess to get Leana.

Moments later, I laid eyes on my girl. Her face was swollen and bruised. Her hands had marks all over them, which meant she didn't go without a fight. I was getting furious with each passing second at her appearance. "You good, Lee?" I asked her.

"Yeah, I'm good" she said through slightly swollen lips. They let her go and she walked over to where Twan was.

I looked back at Pablo and his boys. They were packing the money up and didn't even notice the signal I had given to Twan. He passed his gun to Leana and came up beside me. I slid my gun over to Leana as well and I jumped on Pablo.

His dumbass workers didn't know what was going on as Pablo and I tussled around the room on the floor. One of the guys pointed their gun at me and Twan two-pieced his ass. The other one was moving his gun back and forth between the two fights and didn't know who to shoot. Leana took his ass out with two shots.

Pablo managed to get out of my hold and we began to fight for real. He was fighting like he was in a damn UFC fight. Fortunately for me, I had years of boxing lessons to match his level. He punched me and I fell to the floor. Before I could recover, he had kicked me in the head and I landed on my back. I tried to get up but my back was hurting so damn bad from that damn cement floor. He leaned over me and stared.

"You thought you could kill Pablo, punta?" he said, pulling out his gun. He pressed it into my forehead and I stared right in his eyes. I was letting him know that I didn't fear death and I wasn't afraid to die. If it was my time then it would be my time. I just prepared myself for it.

Just as I felt the cold steel, I could feel his finger getting closer to the trigger. I closed my eyes and braced myself for death. I heard six shots rang out. But they weren't for me. I opened my eyes and watched as the life drained from Pablo's eyes before he fell onto the floor next to me. I got up from the floor and looked over at Leana. She was standing there with smoke coming from her gun. She walked over to Pablo and emptied the clip I had put in before we got here. She threw the gun across the room. She walked over to me and squeezed me tight.

"Thank god you made it" she said as she broke down crying.

"You knew I was coming. I love you, Lee"

"I love you too Tony" she said. She gave me a quick kiss but we couldn't stay here long.

I looked towards the other guy. He was laying there motionless. Upon closer observation, I noticed that his throat was slashed and he was lying by the door. And its only one person that I knew that could do a cut so smooth and deadly and that was Sienna. As soon as I finished my thought, my sister and Sienna were strolling into the room.

"What are you doing here, Tia?"

"Oh you know why I'm here, Bro" she said, in a mocking tone. "I'm here to take you out"

"Not a chance. It's three against two. You're outnumbered, Sis" I said with a smirk.

"Oh, really? I think you may be misunderstood, Antonio. Just look around"

I looked and saw the bodies laying around the room. Then my eyes focused in on Twan, who was aiming a desert eagle right at me. I looked back at my sister who was smiling as hard as somebody in a damn Colgate commercial.

"Are you kidding me, Twan?" I asked looking over to him. "I thought you was my boy?"

"I was but hey, money talks."

"I'm gonna kill your bitch ass, Twan"

"You can try"

"Enough of the small talk. Get him and that bitch down to the truck" Tia said.

"You got it" Sienna said. "Move it, motherfuckers" she yelled at me and Leana. We walked down the steps as Sienna and Twan pointed guns in our backs.

We hopped in the truck between Twan and Sienna as Tia drove down a couple of blocks. I could see the building go up in flames as I looked on in the rearview. This sneaky bitch must have been here the entire time. I didn't even smell gasoline when we were heading out so she might have poured it around upstairs after we left out the room.

We arrived at another abandoned building. This one looked vaguely familiar. A light bulb clicked in my head and I remembered as clear as day. Our father used to bring us here and show us how he got rid of bodies. We haven't been here in over a decade. It was actually the first dumpsite he had ever shown us. He told us it was passed down from generation to generation.

Gemini Betrayal

Tia parked the truck and we all got out simultaneously. We entered the building and it was fully lit and warm inside. If I hadn't known any better, I would have thought that my sister came out here occasionally by the way she was maneuvering around.

We all headed inside and walked until we came to an open space. I looked around and saw all types of hooks, chains, conveyor belts, and vats of acid. The acid was already hot. I could see the steam coming from the enormous container positioned in the center of the room.

"Get the fuck over there" Tia instructed me and Leana. We walked slowly over to the middle of the floor like she said.

"Tia? Why are you doing this?" I asked.

"Why? Motherfucker! after all the snitching you've done, you really got the nerve to ask me why I wanna kill you? Your ass dumber than I thought"

"I keep telling you I didn't snitch, T. You gotta believe me" I begged.

"I don't believe you, Tony"

"I'm your motherfucking brother!" I yelled at her. "Why the fuck would I snitch on you? How you know Twan or Sienna ain't snitch on us?"

Tia moved her eyes back and forth at everybody in the room. That was a good point. Anybody could have set me up she thought. Tia was standing there contemplating now.

"What the fuck?" Twan and Sienna said in unison.

"You got me fucked up" Twan yelled at me and pointed his gun my way. I stepped back a little away from him.

"He is right though" Tia said now aiming her gun at Twan.

"Come on T, man. You can trust me"

"Can I really?"

"Yeah" he replied.

"I don't think so" she whispered. She looked back at me. "Twan told me everything, man. Told me y'all little plan and everything. He a snitch, bro"

I just looked at the both of them. I couldn't stand neither of their asses right now. I just wanted to get me and Leana out of here alive.

She looked back at Twan. "Now you're dismissed" she said before shooting him four times in the chest. He fell onto the ground. His lifeless eyes were staring over at me. He was probably dead by the time the third bullet hit him. I ran over to him to retrieve his gun but Sienna stopped me.

"Get your ass back over there, nigga. We not done with you yet" she said. I halted and retreated back to where I was next to Leana. Leana was looking both scared and angry.

"Let us go" Leana screamed at Tia and Sienna. I was too busy staring my sister down that I hadn't noticed that Sienna had stepped to Leana.

"Who the fuck is you, Leana? You ain't gonna do shit to me" she said, shoving the gun in her face.

"You know I ain't scared of you SiSi. Put that motherfucking gun down and fight"

"Bitch please. I don't fight anymore. That's high school shit" She walked back over to my sister's side. "Who should we kill first, Babe?"

"I don't know who I want dead more" Tia replied.

Sienna raised her gun and moved it back and forth between me and Leana. "I guess I'll choose then. Eenie. Meanie. Miney. Moe" She got ready to pull the trigger when her gun landed on Leana. I jumped in front of Leana as three shots rang out.

Leana and I both fell to the floor. I searched my chest for bullet holes but I was good. That wasn't me that had gotten shot. I looked back at Lee and she was also free of wounds. We looked over to my sister and Sienna. Sienna had been shot from the back in her chest and the back of the head. My sister had been shot in the arm.

"Ahhh, fuck" my sister yelled out. I quickly rushed to her side.

Even after all of this shit, I was still here for her. Nothing was gonna change the fact that I was her big brother and I was supposed to protect her no matter what.

"Lee help me get her up" I said.

As we all made it to our feet, and headed towards the door, we were abruptly stopped. We were now looking into the eyes of Deputy Wilson and Lieutenant Gaines.

"Get the fuck back in there" Gaines ordered. We walked back into the room with Tia still hanging on to us. Gaines grabbed Tia from us and threw her across the room. Tia screamed out in pain as her wounded arm hit the cement floor.

"We finally got him, Boss" Wilson said. I looked over to Leana who was off to the side near where Twan's body was lying at. I also saw his gun right there. So did she but I think Gaines and Wilson were unaware.

"Yep, Wilson. We finally got this piece of shit. Both of them"

"You not taking us no motherfucking where" Tia yelled up from the floor. Gaines walked over and stepped on Tia's arm. She

Gemini Betrayal

yelled out in excruciating pain and I could see blood trickling on the floor.

I started to walk over to him but Wilson stopped me in my tracks with his gun.

"You really thought you were gonna get to me, Hall?" Gaines said smiling. I heard another click and we all looked. Leana was standing behind Wilson with a gun pressed to his head.

"You better drop that gun, Bitch" Wilson said.

"I ain't dropping shit until you let him go"

"Fuck that!"

"You better drop the gun, Leana. You don't wanna kill a cop," Gaines said to her. "You're looking at fifteen years to life. Do you really want that?"

"Fuck you, Gaines. I never liked your ass anyway"

"Do it, Leana" I yelled at her.

"If she pulls that trigger, you die too" Wilson yelled in my ear.

Everybody was busy yelling back and forth at one another. It was so confusing. I didn't want Leana to kill a cop but I know she would. I was trying to get away from Wilson but it worked to no avail. Moments had passed and another round of shots had rang out.

I looked at Leana and her gun had smoke coming from it. She had shot Wilson and Tia had shot Gaines with her gun. I dropped down to the floor again from exhaustion.

"Thanks, Tia. You saved my life" I said to her sincerely.

"Don't thank me yet" she said, getting up and slowly stepping over to me. "I wanna kill you. I'm not gonna let somebody else have the joy of killing you" She pointed her gun at me again. "You got any last words, big brother?"

I shook my head 'no' and just got prepared to die. I would have been dead when she shot that gun but she had missed. Leana had tackled her to the floor from behind.

They tussled around on the floor. I had to stop this. I picked up the gun that had been knocked out of my sister's hand. Tia hit Leana with a right hook and Leana came back with a right of her own. They rolled around the floor and Leana had landed on top of my sister. She kneed my sister in the stomach before landing two more blows to my sister's face.

My sister laid there in agonizing pain. I guess Leana wanted to put my sister out of her misery. She rolled off top of my sister and grabbed one of the guns from the floor. She jumped to her feet and shot my sister in the middle of the forehead when she tried to get up. My sister flew back onto the floor. Her eyes were still open, staring up at the ceiling. I rushed to her side and checked her pulse. She didn't have one. She was dead. My sister was dead.

"I'm sorry, Antonio. She was gonna kill us"

"It's okay. We're okay now" I reassured her. She got down on the floor and hugged me tightly.

We heard clapping from behind us. We broke free of our hug and looked back. We stood up to our feet. I couldn't believe my eyes. I must have been seeing a ghost or some shit. The devil was standing before us clear as day and was dressed in a sexy dress with high heels on.

"Hello Antonio" she said, in her seductive voice.

I was still stunned I couldn't even speak. Destiny made her way over to where we were and stood face to face with me.

"Destiny?" I said, more as a question than anything.

"Yeah it's me"

"But how? You're supposed to be dead. I saw it with my own eyes"

"That's what my dad and everybody wanted you to think"

"Your dad?"

"Yeah" she said, looking over at Gaines. "Y'all really did a number on him" she said, laughing. "Oh well. Glad I'm an only child. Now I can get his insurance check since I'm his beneficiary"

"Is that why you're here, Destiny? Money?"

"Nope" she said, pulling a gun out from under her dress. "I'm actually here to kill you. I told you not to play with me, Antonio Hall"

"You know I don't fight women" I said, looking at her angrily.

"Good. Then this will be easy" She aimed the gun at me and pulled the trigger but the bullet ricocheted and hit the wall as Leana punched her in the face.

Destiny was definitely giving Leana a run for her money. I guess all those years of self-defense and boxing between the two were well worth it. Destiny managed to get away from Leana and lunged at the gun. She didn't hesitate to pull the trigger as Leana lunged at her.

It was just me and her now. She got up from the floor and walked over to me. She pointed the gun at me again.

"Walk, nigga" she said. She led me over to a vat of hot acid. "You can either die in there or take a bullet and still end up in there"

"Can't we talk about this, Destiny?"

"Now you wanna talk? Fuck you, Antonio. I'm done dealing with you and all y'all motherfucking niggas. All I need is my money"

"What about us?"

"Us? There is no motherfucking us. There never was"

"That's not true and you know it"

"Whatever, Antonio. Bottom line, you gotta die" she said, aiming the gun at me.

Somehow Leana made it back to her feet and grabbed another gun from the floor. Destiny heard her and turned around. She pointed the gun at Leana and I tried to wrestle the gun from her and protect Leana.

We were tugging back and forth for a while. I heard shots ring out and everything froze. Everything had went still. Everything had gone silent.

Gemini Betrayal

Epilogue

Months had gone by since the murders went down. I was missing my sister but I was loving being a dad to my son. When we left the scene, Leana and I walked away with a duffel bag full of cash, several guns, and a truck. That was one hell of a come up if you ask me.

We were living the life now. We had moved down to Atlanta and bought a house. Leana opened up a hair salon and I opened up a gun range. To the unknown eye, these were legitimate businesses. To us, they were cover-ups for our drug operation. We had found a new connect before we had relocated from Jersey.

We had just pulled up to the cemetery and got out. Leana had grabbed the baby from the car seat and we headed over to the gravesites. I walked over to my mother's grave and placed her favorite flowers next to her headstone. I did the same for my grandmother and my sister. I came up on my father's grave and I just stared at it.

I opened up a bottle of liquor and poured it over his grave. He lucky he had gotten that after all the shit he had put me through. Put all of us through for that matter. We moved along until we came up on Destiny, Twan, and Sienna's graves. I had requested this section just for them. I placed flowers on all of their graves as well.

I couldn't believe how rough my life had been this past year. So much pain and death. It never broke me though. It didn't do shit but make me stronger. Now I can say that I'm strong and made it out the streets successfully. I have been to jail. I've been shot. And I lost a lot of friends along the way. I guess it's true what people say; 'only the strong survive'.

We headed back to the car and I just stared back at my lost ones through the rearview as I drove away. One thing I can say that I certainly learned being in these streets is loyalty. Even the ones closest to you will ride on you. And if you find somebody that match your loyalty, you better hold on to them. And I'm doing just that. From here on out, it ain't nobody in this world but me, my girl and my son. I'm done with fake motherfuckers that don't do shit but betray me.

Lesson learned.

About The Author

American author Rachelle Jarred was born in Washington, D.C. and currently works full-time as the CEO of BluGem Publishing, where her books are published. She has been entranced by the magic of written words and had an unflinching love for writing since she was seven, and now lives her dream of being a published author and a poet. Writing is more than just her career; it's her way of life.

Rachelle prides herself on exploring multiple fiction genres. With sizzling hot erotica, blood-cuddling horror, and scintillating suspense, she has enticing packages for every book lover. She is looking forward to diving into children's stories in the near future.

Between her writing career and her life as a mother of two, Rachelle enjoys spending time with her loved ones and always makes time to help new authors find their way in the writing industry. She currently resides in Prince George's County, Maryland.

www.ingramcontent.com/pod-product-compliance
Lightning Source LLC
Chambersburg PA
CBHW061001280326
41935CB00009B/787